DISHING IT OUT

Dishing it Out

In Search of the Restaurant Experience

Robert Appelbaum

REAKTION BOOKS

For all the restaurant workers of the world

Published by
Reaktion Books Ltd
33 Great Sutton Street
London EC1V ODX, UK

www.reaktionbooks.co.uk

First published 2011

Printed and bound in Great Britain
by the MPG Books Group

British Library Cataloguing in Publication Data
Appelbaum, Robert, 1952–
Dishing it out : in search of the restaurant experience.
1. Restaurants – History.
2. Restaurants – Social aspects.
3. Dinners and dining – Social aspects.
I. Title
394.1'2-DC22

ISBN: 978 1 86189 807 4

Contents

Introduction

So a man walks into a restaurant with a giant, three-foot fly. It's a fine French restaurant with lace curtains, wood panelling and chandeliers, and the maître d' greets them with the usual courtesies.

You are wondering about that fly. You are wondering about how the maître d' is going to handle the situation: he pretends not to notice that there is anything unusual going on. You are wondering where the man and the fly are going to sit: it's a small table for two by the window with the lace curtains. You are curious as to how the other diners are going to respond: they pretend not to notice. You imagine that the waiter will do his job with the customary decorum. He'll say good evening, he'll take out his pad, and ask them what they would like to have. But you wonder what the man and his fly are going to order. I can tell you what the man requests. He'll have the *asperge à l'oeuf poché* for a starter. Then he'll have the *bisque de crevette à la crème*. He'll follow that with the *ris de veau à la finan-cière*, and after that he'll have the *salade de mesclun* and then the *sélection de fromages de Bourgogne*, followed by a *tarte maison aux fruits de bois*. He'll wash it all down with a bottle of the '98 Pernand-Vergelesses Premier Cru. As for what the fly orders, I will leave it to your imagination for now, but it was not the *cassolette de quenelles de brochet*.

And what next? There wouldn't seem to be much more to say, unless we were to have a punch line that would make a mockery of the whole scene. In most cases, restaurants do not seem to have stories. There is a beginning, a middle and an end to a restaurant meal, but the structure is ceremonial rather than dramatic. If anything is going on dramatically, it would be something, as we say, behind the scenes, or else it would be something going on within the scene without being *about* it. In his great novel *Lost Illusions* (1843), Honoré de Balzac has his main character, the feckless provincial Lucien de Rubempré, visit a number of prominent restaurants in Paris: the swank Véry, the fashionable seafood house Le Rocher de Cancale, the cheap bohemian eatery Flicoteaux. The restaurants are a part of the fabric of life in nineteenth-century Paris, and when Lucien visits them we find him trying to fit himself into that fabric. It is very important to the story that while Véry – a restaurant much like the establishment in our anecdote with the fly – costs far more than Lucien can really afford or even knows how to enjoy, Flicoteaux is a last resort for him. But what is there to say about the restaurants except to describe them? 'This restaurant', says the narrator about Flicoteaux, 'is a workshop suitably equipped, and not an elegant banqueting-hall with pleasant amenities: customers are quickly served.' And so on: 'Behind the scenes there is rapid activity. Waiters come and go without wasting time: they are all busy and very much in demand. The food is not very varied, and always includes potatoes.' Restaurants are part of the scene; they are part of the material of daily life. In Balzac too they even have histories. 'Flicoteaux is a name inscribed in many memories.'[1] But even in Balzac's *Scènes de la vie parisienne* not a whole lot actually happens in restaurants in their capacity as restaurants. They are places in which characters like Rubempré stop and eat and meet with people along the way to more important things, like love, wealth and fame or ignominy, crime and death.

Perhaps our man and his fly are in a similar situation. They are in a strange town for a business meeting, and they need to feed themselves and discuss the marketing strategy they have been developing back home. It just so happens that the man likes French food, or that this particular restaurant is near the hotel where they are staying. Or perhaps they are on a first date. They got to know one another over the Internet, and decided they'd meet in front of that great restaurant with the lace curtains on Second Avenue they both know so well. They are going to eat what they like to eat and drink in familiar and comfortable surroundings, but the main business is to discover whether they find each other attractive. Of course, a man and a fly make an odd couple, but perhaps they made a date without the man knowing that his counterpart was a fly, or without the fly knowing that his counterpart was a man. The restaurant is important, but it is not the real *story*.

Or is it? Perhaps there is another way of looking at the matter.

The first restaurant properly so-called opened in Paris in the 1760s. There had been public eateries in Paris and elsewhere in Europe before, but the *restaurant* – French for a 'thing that restores' – with its individualized service and its decorous ambience, was something new. The restaurant took off very quickly. By the time of the French Revolution there were about a hundred of them in the capital. Before long they spread all about the Western world, and the non-Western world was opening their fair share as well. In fact, the Chinese had their own restaurants (by another name) at least as early as the thirteenth century. Marco Polo dined in one of them. When Chinese restaurants first opened in California at the time of the Gold Rush, the restaurateurs were bringing an ancient tradition to the New World, as well as nodding toward the popularity of European-style eateries in the territory. As restaurants spread throughout Asia in the modern era, they did so in their own way, cross-breeding with Western-style restaurants at certain points where European trade and colonialism was common, and teaching Western restaurants a thing or two as well.

A restaurant is a public, commercial eating house offering individualized service. How public and commercial it is and how individualized the service should be are matters for the restaurateur to decide. But in a restaurant customers are both part of a crowd and personally singled out. They probably sit at a separate table with choice companions, like our man and his fly. Disastrous experiences apart, customers probably take a good deal of enjoyment while there. Or rather, they take more than 'a good deal' of it: for the restaurant is an occasion for what social theorists, following Slavoj Žižek, call *surplus enjoyment*.[2] The restaurant is of course a convenience. It fulfils a need. But its success has to do with a lot more than mere need. It has to do with a kind of surplus enjoyment: a big IT, as the theorist would say, as in the expression 'Coke is IT'. Our man and fly could have met elsewhere, talked business or romance elsewhere, satisfied their need for sustenance elsewhere. But they didn't. And why not? It was because the restaurant provided a quotient of surplus enjoyment: the lace curtains, the respectful waiter, the *ris de veau*, the '98 Pernand-Vergelesses Premier Cru, or whatever else you like, the chandeliers, the combination of licence and propriety – this is a place for diners to hold hands, or not to hold hands. Even perhaps if you are a fly, and you do not have any hands, if the restaurant lets you in and seats you, this surplus enjoyment is available for you to delight in.

The enjoyment is freely chosen, from a certain point of view, and merely a bonus added to other enjoyments in this life of worldly pleasures. According to classic economic theory, rational individuals, trying to maximize utility and pleasure, will freely select to patronize the desirable restaurants available to them. The *ris de veau*, the lace curtains, the tolerance of giant flies – why not? Moreover, these same rational individuals will select one restaurant rather than another based on a calculation where what is always sought is a kind of profit, a surplus of one sort or another. I need to eat, but what I desire is a lot more than that; what I desire is *ris de veau* and lace curtains. Or leave aside the fancy French place for a moment. Even fast food restaurants provide surplus enjoyment. Both Subway and McDonald's offer me food at about the same price, with the same convenience. Which shall I choose? The one, I decide, that I will probably *like more*, this extra 'liking' being a kind of bonus that motivates my choice and determines my behaviour. My 'liking' is my surplus pleasure. As for the choice between two restaurants of different quality, of different price ranges or of different kinds of cuisine, the same calculation of a bonus is at stake, for the nice, expensive French restaurant will perhaps provide me with a little bit more of what is my liking; or, conversely, perhaps the humbler, cheaper, American-style diner will provide with more, since it will be more comfortable for me there, kinder to my wallet (I get a bonus of economy) and more amenable to my simple, greasy tastes.

In so far as we make choices about restaurants, walk in, sit down, eat and pay, we are all in the position of *consumers*. And perhaps we enjoy not only the surplus enjoyments that consumption allows us today, but also the condition of being consumers, of going through life making the kinds of selections of services and goods that being a consumer offers. But how did we get to be that way? How did we start out as human beings (or giant flies), and end up as consumers? This is an important and perennial question for social theory, and it turns out that studying the origins, history and culture of the restaurant can help us understand the way the consumer came into existence. And the point is two-fold: in the first place, restaurants are places that encourage, facilitate and even demand that we approach them as consumers, seeking surplus enjoyment; in the second, seeking surplus pleasure in places like restaurants is what we *do* in view of *who we have become*, and though we can make choices among a range of surplus pleasures, we cannot but choose to choose. Whatever classic economic theory may have to say about it, from a historical and materialist point of view, making choices as consumers from items designed to attract consumers and provide them with surplus enjoyment is never really an expression of freedom; it is rather an expression of historical determinations. We have had no choice but to become consumers, doing things like eating in restaurants. And that leads to a third and more general point: we are completely limited in the choices which we must make in our capacity as consumers, with regard both to *what* we can choose and to *who* we must be, or must *not* be, in order to purchase our pleasures. In the very choice of surplus enjoyment, though we are aiming toward something we *like* and even something we think to be *good*, we are also renouncing something inside us. When I enter the room with the chandeliers and announce myself to the waiter, I am never entirely *myself*. The same is true when I walk through the doorway of the Golden Arches, and ponder whether to order a 'value meal' or rather just a large order of fries. I am not myself; I am a role that I have to play in order to achieve my surplus enjoyment. In becoming a restaurant-frequenting consumer, I become what I *am not* in order to get what I think I desire.

All kinds of questions therefore arise. What is the real nature of the surplus value of the restaurant and the roles we play in it? What are we really *doing* there? What kinds of *satisfactions* are we actually getting hold of in the restaurant? What kinds of satisfactions are derived from getting one thing at the cost of renouncing another, and of being what we are not in order to get a hold of something of which we think we are wanting? It may be that we are getting nothing out of our new enjoyments but more need for enjoyment, and therefore more restlessness and renunciation. After all, isn't *dissatisfaction* what our modern economy actually requires of us? Isn't it the case that if people were actually *satisfied* with what they had, and stopped making such an effort to consume, the whole system would collapse?

There is a song by folk singer Arlo Guthrie from the 1960s called 'Alice's Restaurant' which seems to provide a different picture. It has a famous refrain: 'You can get anything you want at Alice's Restaurant'. I've always loved the song, but I haven't always understood what it means. You can get *anything* you want? Obviously, as everybody knows, you cannot get just anything; for example, you cannot get eternal life while there. But the song expresses something that listeners are supposed to understand, and even to sing along with: a logic of aspiration toward surplus enjoyment, and a powerful fantasy about its satisfaction, a fantasy altogether bound up – even in this song of anti-establishment hippies – with a commercial institution, prescribed by the rules of modern capitalist sociality. I am sure illicit drugs are bound up in Guthrie's concept of Alice and her restaurant, and so is free love. (The movie version of the song makes some of this explicit.) But at the end of the talking blues part of the song, it turns out that the refrain is supposed to be an anthem of the counterculture, an assertion of *this is who we are,* and a proof to the official establishment world that *we are too insane to participate in your insane war* – the one in Vietnam, run by a war machine for the sake of running a war machine and keeping capitalism on the march. Knowing that you can get anything you want at Alice's Restaurant means knowing, insanely, that you can have it all, the big IT of it all, which also means that you don't have to belong to the war machine of the American military-industrial complex and put yourself in the way of killing or being killed. But this fantasy of liberation from the war-machine is also a hedonistic fantasy of unbridled and unending surplus enjoyment – the motor force of the very system, war-mongering and capitalistic, which the song is trying to reject. The song says, I don't need to join the system and do its bidding, because I am already satisfied; I can get anything I want at Alice's Restaurant. But the song is also saying, inadvertently, that at Alice's Restaurant I can get precisely that 'everything' that the capitalist system requires me to desire.

So on the one hand we have the absolute fantasy, the fantasy of having *anything*. 'Have it *your way*', said the old jingle for Burger King. 'I'm lovin' it', says the jingle for McDonald's today. (Notice how 'it' keeps appearing.) At Alice's or just about anywhere else in the restaurant world today, you can have it, one way or another, and you can be loving it. 'Dishes come willy-nilly', says the *New York Times* review of a new restaurant called Fatty Cue, in the trendy Williamsburg section of Brooklyn. '[The restaurant] can be uncomfortable. But a simple bowl of noodles that is not so simple at all, dressed in juices taken from resting hunks of slow-barbecued pork and lamb and beef, will start to turn your mood, and a small dish of coriander-rubbed house-made bacon with a curry custard in which to dip it may bring wide smiles.' 'Five stars! Everyone should go make the trip to Williamsburg', adds a reader of the *Times* online. 'I can't wait to go back!'[3] Loving it, filling ourselves with 'wide smiles', getting just what we want eventually (in spite of the service but also because of it), finding that the pleasure is a kind of *imperative*, and at the same time that one has to have it *again and again* – this is the absolute fantasy that, as it turns out, governs much of our lives today. 'Infinite reward', I call it later in this book. And who is to complain about it? Why shouldn't we sing along with Arlo Guthrie, the McDonald's advert and the reviewers, professional and unprofessional, of the *New York Times*? We don't have to kill or be killed, we allow ourselves to think. We can – we *should* – be lovin' it. And we can always go back for more.

So there we are. We like to enjoy ourselves, and why not? What else are we to do? The birds in the sky enjoy themselves being birds in the sky, scanning the trees for seeds and insects to nibble, and we humans must enjoy ourselves too. But on the other hand, the questions that may be raised about the restaurant may lead to the suspicion that there is something vain, fruitless, unfulfilling, self-manipulating, self-deluding, wasteful and unsatisfactory about the surplus enjoyment we are seeking there. What is all this fuss about, the table by the window with the lace curtains, the courteous waiter, the elaborate menu, the muscular expense, and finally the dishes themselves, the *ris de veau*, the *tarte maison aux fruits des bois*; or alternatively, under the arches and beside the chrome counter, the bun-encased burger and the salty fries and the tub of cold Coca-Cola, received from an order-taker in a paper hat instead of a waiter in a suit; or down in 'fat' bohemian Williamsburg, where the seats are uncomfortable but the coriander-rubbed house-made bacon makes you smile, and widely; or even Alice's Restaurant, where turkey and mash, free love and cannabis are the order of the day . . . what is all the fuss about but so much *ordure*? When the man in the restaurant orders his rarities of dishes, a six-course meal of costly items with complicated preparations, washed down by an impressively obscure wine of northern Burgundy, he finishes up by saying to the waiter, 'And bring some shit for my fly.'

And why not?

There is a persuasive point of view according to which all surplus pleasures, and all tastes, are relative, even though it is impossible to experience a pleasure as being merely relative. This I *like!* I like IT! The maxim *de gustibus non est disputandum* is irrelevant to a consumer in the throes of consumption. But even so, all tastes are relative. And there is a related point of view – espoused by some of the greatest thinkers in history, from Seneca to Rousseau, from Plato to Wittgenstein – that all pleasures are, at bottom, shit. The only difference between the man and the fly is that their pleasures have different names and smells. So let us have anything we want. I know a good place for it down the road.

'Restaurants for the rest of us' is the title of the first chapter in the body of this book, and it expresses a theme that I will be exploring throughout. Two things are involved, *restaurants* and *us*. On the one hand, I want to explore the nature of the restaurant in history and the kinds of surplus pleasures it has on offer – ceremonial, culinary, existential. On the other, I want to think about this 'us', critically, philosophically and politically. Who *are* we, after all, we restaurant-goers?

There are restaurants, as I will put it, for *them*: creatures of majestic consumerism, driven by the imperatives of hunger, taste, wealth, class, narcissistic self-regard and the glamorization of consumption by the media and by a large part of the food industry itself. You don't have to be rich to be one of them and inhabit their ideal world of consumption, but it helps, and good luck to you. But what about the rest of us? We may like what the restaurants dedicated to those others have to offer; we may take considerable surplus enjoyment on those occasions when we may take advantage of them. But we do not inhabit an ideal world of consumption. We can't afford to. Ours is a situated and resource-limited world, where we cannot get anything we want and wouldn't even know what 'anything' actually was, if we could wish for it, since there is so much that we are unable to try and be acquainted with. Ours is a world, moreover, all but overcome with 'McDonaldization', as George Ritzer has put it – dominated by a well-financed and globally enforced emphasis on efficiency, calculability and predictability at the expense of creativity, spontaneity and delight. The systematic homogeneity of everyday life that McDonaldization has foisted upon us all – just look down the street and you will find it, and not only at McDonald's – may be punctuated periodically by something that makes us smile: the 'fat' at Fatty Cue, or wherever your haven of culinary originality may be.[4] But in our situated, resource-limited and McDonaldized lives, the glamorous surplus values of the restaurants for *them* are a dream rather than a reality, an ideological diversion rather than a common practice. The rest of us have to *make do*. And the question is, can we be lovin' it too? Or are we only fooling ourselves? Are we only telling ourselves what we have been taught, or even forced to tell ourselves, lest we examine the situation with a much more critical eye?

Let us ask the question this way. In our own ideal world, an ideal world of our own choosing, wouldn't restaurants be abolished? Wouldn't there no longer be a need for them? Wouldn't they actually seem to be a hindrance to the good life rather than a medium for it? Utopianism, it is said, is dead; but utopias may still help regulate our ideas, still help us extract from that which we take for granted that which we can really believe in and admire. So imagine a utopia of cultural and economic democracy, a world we can really believe in. In such a world nothing that is essentially human would be missing, but nothing that is superfluous to humanity, nothing that is false or falsely needed, would be included. All enjoyments would also be satisfactions, and the enjoyment that one person experienced would never impinge upon the enjoyment of another. We would always be *ourselves* in acquiring what we desire. *All of us* would. And it may be asked whether, in such an ideal world of universal material satisfaction, one that fully realizes our deepest values about prosperity, justice and happiness, restaurants would be unnecessary, or even pointless.

Yes, we're lovin' it, now, in the real world, more or less. But do we believe in it? *Can* we believe in it? What must *we* be, and what must *restaurants* be, for the rest of us to go on lovin' it, and take our surplus pleasures?

Let's not forget what the ethic of modern-day consumerism is constantly trying to make us forget: that *my consumption* isn't only a part of *my world* but also a part of *everybody's world*.

In 1825 a food enthusiast issued a mock manifesto, relating to the promotion of a *Constitution d'une société gastronomique*. Given that a 'troubled mind' had taken possession of gourmands for the past few years, many of the 'true principles of the art of cookery' were being forgotten, and anarchy was coming to reign, both in what was cooked and in how people went about eating it. The 'rights' of hosts and guests were getting so muddled that no one knew how to cooperate any more. It was therefore 'urgent to forestall the consequences of such a regimen', he went on to say, which included the following disturbances: 'disorder and confusion in service; anarchy and trouble in sauces; dangerous and fatal mixtures in the liquids; dryness and tearing in throats; emptiness or indigestion in stomachs; and as a result a spirit of insurrection in the kitchen and among the guests'.

So, the gastronome proposed the constitution of a society which would operate democratically, but with very clear rules, rights and obligations, and an unmistakable protocol of formalities. Here are the first four articles of the constitution:

ARTICLE I. The form of the government adopted by our eating society will be a pure democracy, to be directed each day by a new leader.

II. The leader of the day is he who will provide the dinner; that is to say, he is what is otherwise called the host. His authority will last just as long as the meal over which he presides.

III. The society is divided into free men and slaves.

IV. The free men are those who dine. The slaves are those who prepare the dinner.[5]

This eating society does not necessarily dine at restaurants. Dinners could also be provided at private homes – always a major part of French hospitality – though by 1825 the *repas de commande*, served in a private banquet room set apart from the rest of the restaurant, was a well-established custom, even for gastronomic societies. In any case, the gourmet doesn't really care where the dinner of the day is served; he just wants it done right. But doing it right demands a stunning contradiction. A proper eating society has to be democratic. Everyone is equal, with the same rights and obligations, except for the president of the day, who is in power to the extent that he is obligated to his fellows as their host. All in all, the rule of law will prevail, along with a spirit of egalitarian conviviality. But in order for equality to prevail, some people will have to be slaves.

Of course the writer is joking, but he is being serious as well. When one dines in a formal situation one participates in a system of equalities and inequalities. There are brothers and sisters in blubber, knives and forks in hand, and there are people who are something along the line of slaves – *employees*, if you prefer – who cannot be one of the brothers and sisters in blubber, for they are the ones who have to *cater* and *serve*. And the aesthetic excellence of the meal apparently depends on a codification and legitimation of the inequality, where the slavery of one group of people serves to guarantee the freedom, equality and fellowship of another. Indeed, the alternative to the institutionalism of a system which ties republicanism and slavery, so far as the gastronome is concerned – and in this he is more perspicacious than may initially be apparent – is 'anarchy and trouble', 'emptiness or indigestion' and perhaps even violence.

So several problems of social justice and cultural democracy inevitably arise when the nature of the restaurant is considered in depth. The first is the problem of the inequality of the institution, divided between the equals at the table and the non-equals in the kitchen and among the waiting staff. The second, which the nineteenth-century gastronome only indirectly hints at, but which he certainly understands in his own way, is the problem of the inequality of the distribution of the goods and services of the institution. Today we can see this problem of distribution most clearly when we consider the gulf between the haute cuisine of the very few in our world and the junk food of the very many. 'Dryness and tearing in throats' and 'emptiness or indigestion in stomachs' has become the fate of the poor in the United States today, and to some extent in other highly developed countries – to be relieved by tubs of Coke and bags of fries, and to be expressed in an epidemic of obesity, diabetes and gastric disorders. Meanwhile, individuals with sufficient cultural and economic capital are faring quite well, and foodie-ism thrives. So there is a second problem. It is one thing to focus on the Véry's, the Rochers de Cancales, the Fatty Cues and even the Flicoteaux of the world; it is another to consider restaurant culture as a whole, with its enormous divisions in the quality of the provisions it distributes to different parts of the population, down to McDonald's and KFC. And so there is a third problem as well, which the nineteenth-century gastronome also hints at: the problem of the alienation of people from themselves and others which the culture of the restaurant institutionalizes. *Everybody* is enjoined to cooperate in a system that really pulls people apart, even if the official aim of dining together in a restaurant is 'pure democracy'.

The question, again, is whether we need this. Or rather, let us say, the question is, do we need to need it? That is not a common sort of question. It is a philosophic question; it is also a political and social question. Do we need to need what we seem to need? The question certainly seems odd in the context of a study of the culture of the restaurant. A man walks in . . . and as soon as he enters certain kinds of customs are observed, rules are followed, objects arranged, rituals obeyed. The whole space of the place articulates a structure where objects, uses and values are set in geometrical and chronological order. We can see that, and we can see the point of trying to understand it better. But to ask whether we need to need the whole experience seems to exceed the remit of cultural analysis and curiosity that motivates it. It seems to undermine the kinds of questions that seem more appropriate to the subject, even questions appropriate to the problem of social justice, like those concerning equality of opportunity, or the distribution of wealth, or sustainability. We need to be more equal, in a more equally equipped and sustainably organized world, but that has to do with what we need, not with what we need to need, does it not? Perhaps. But the discourse of the restaurant, to which this book is dedicated, is really about this need to need. It is about our essential commitment to something that is entirely artificial. It is about our need to need something that we do not need, and yet must need for one reason or another.

I talk about a number of restaurants in this book, and the reader will soon see what kind of restaurants I enjoy and respect. Yes, I have always been a lover of eating out, although I have never been wealthy. My stepfather's family was in the restaurant business (a sit-down kosher deli with sandwiches named after comedians and singers); I worked in a few restaurants myself while young (beginning at an IHOP in Niles, Illinois), though not for very long; and I have always been a devotee of certain surplus enjoyments. The reader will get an idea in what follows of what I think about the economy of the modern restaurant, whether an elite restaurant with Michelin stars, a humble bistro in a half-forgotten town or a fast food chain listed on the New York Stock Exchange. I have given a lot of thought to something that little critical attention has been paid to so far, the chain restaurants that crowd the landscape of the USA, the UK and other parts of the world: IHOP, for example, formerly the International House of Pancakes, now a wholly owned subsidiary of DineEquity, Inc., with over 1,400 locations worldwide ('Come hungry, leave happy'), where I landed my first job at the age of fifteen. We served pancakes and burgers, lovingly prepared. On one of my first days at work I was led into the walk-in cooler by the head cook and beaten up. The cook wanted to show me who was boss; that is, he wanted to show me that I was going to be the slave of a slave, with the job of giving other people love.

I try to explain in this book what sort of cultural artefact the restaurant has turned out to be, and how people respond to the restaurant as a social institution, and I draw upon sociologists and ethnologists. But I am by trade and training a literary historian. And so I go about my business by looking above all at what people have *written* about restaurants over the years since restaurants first appeared in Western society. Or to put it another way, I go about looking at how the experience of the restaurant has been put into language, and circulated among us as a literary phenomenon. Restaurant reviews, novels, memoirs – they all get treated here. They all show themselves to be examples of how, through writing, we are able to make intelligible the pleasures of the restaurant, and fit or fail to fit those pleasures into our other values. They show themselves, too, to be examples of good faith and bad faith, of earnest address toward the general welfare and self-deluding justifications of private gluttony and greed. And at the very least they show us, I hope, what the problem is. If I may make a statement that may seem a bit nonsensical now but that should become sensible by the end of this book, we will not succeed in enjoying and promoting restaurants for the rest of us, and our need to need them, until we have learned to *write* about restaurants for the rest of us. The restaurant needs to be adequately *expressed*.

I go at this book as I usually go about these things, a little helter-skelter, and from a variety of angles. After I explain more amply what a restaurant is, whether for *them* or for *us*, and the 'axes of meaning' with regard to which it operates (chapter One), I discuss nineteenth-century food writer Grimod de la Reynière, the first person ever to publish a series of restaurant reviews (chapter Two); then I write about no less a figure than the philosopher and novelist Jean-Paul Sartre (chapter Three), who throws a huge challenge at the idea of appreci-ating the modern restaurant, by introducing to modern ethics and politics the concept of 'bad faith'. The reader will find that I end up relying a good deal on Sartre's incomplete but demanding existentialist ethics. I wish I could say, all the same, following the poet Robert Herrick,

I sing of brooks, of blossoms, birds, and bowers,
Of April, May, of June, and July-flowers,
I sing of maypoles, hock carts, wassails, wakes,
Of bridegrooms, brides, and of their bridal-cakes . . .

But actually I go on to write, without singing, of consumerism (chap-ter Four), of the restaurant geography of modern London and Paris (chapter Five), of novels and chefs (chapter Six) and of 'culture, civi-lization and resistance' (chapter Seven). A certain chronological arc will sweep through the helter-skelter, and so will the outline of an argu-ment and a parade of recurring themes: the nature of critical judgement and the function of restaurant reviews; the relation between culture and civility and the arts of the table; the possibility of gastronomic pleasure in the face of ethical and social demands; the difference between narcissistic consumption and the practice, as I will call it, of consumption without consumerism; and finally the 'production of production', the expressive artistry and hospitality of restaurants in defiance of the consumer society's 'production of consumption'. I draw upon philosophers like Sartre and theorists of consumption like Jean Baudrillard in this study, but I end up getting a lot of my ideas from a reading of the English socialist novelist William Morris and the Danish storyteller Isak Dinesen.

And the answer is that yes, restaurants *do* have a story, and so do we restaurant-goers, and the workers inside as well. But so far it is a story without an ending, or even a punch line. There is a challenge awaiting us. A challenge we may even need to need. And that is probably how it ought to be.

one

Restaurants for the Rest of Us

The best restaurant in the world is not, in spite of what the immortal Calvin Trillin once wrote on the subject, in Kansas City.[1] And it is not a rib joint where you can order either the burnt end pieces or the juicy middle pieces of a slab of pork ribs or a brisket of beef. The best restaurant in the world does not exist. Not even in Paris, or Spanish Catalonia, or Toledo, Ohio, can such a thing be found. It does not exist because the idea of its existence is wrong; that is, the *idea* of a best restaurant in the world is wrong.

And it is wrong not only in the small and obvious ways in which such ideas are often wrong, but in a big way as well. You can say, *de gustibus* etc., or that the criteria of taste are always arbitrary. Or you can say that the kind of establishments that get involved in nominating things like 'the best restaurant in the world' come to their jobs with arbitrary rules, and that they go about this business with a presumptuous claim to cultural hegemony: to world domination in matters of taste. To claim that such and such a place, like El Bulli on the Costa Brava in Catalonia or the Fat Duck in Bray, Berkshire, England, or Alain Ducasse at the Plaza Athenée in Paris or the Casa de la Maison House in Toledo, Ohio is the best in the world[2] is to determine not only what the 'best' is but also *what the world shall be*. The 'world' will be what the media say it shall be, and it shall therefore be where the news writers and their readers are most willing to dine: London (say) rather than Lagos, New York rather than Newark.

But you already knew that. Taste is relative, the criteria by which matters of taste are decided are arbitrary and the arbiters of taste impose not just their sense of taste on the public but the *power of imposing taste*; and that implies, among other things, a power of determining what 'the world' shall be. This *power*, we know, comes along with a certain amount of expertise. The arbiters of taste are neither amateurs nor idiots; they have credentials; they have experience in both dining rooms and kitchens; they spend a lot of time around restaurants in a lot of different places and they know what they are talking about. But what the power of imposing taste comes *with* is not the same thing as what it comes *from*, and what the power of imposing taste comes *from* is not expertise and experience but power itself. It comes, let us call it, from capitalism.

Yet you already knew all that, and it is gratuitous to suggest it anew. The big story is what the idea of the best restaurant in the world says about the restaurant as an institution. For to begin with, it says that the restaurant is an institution *in competition*. Indeed, competition is the very soul of the restaurant as far as these lists and the arbiters of taste are concerned. The Casa de la Maison House is in competition with Alain Ducasse, and that is what warrants its fame and glory or else, more likely, its ignominious absurdity. There is a competition for something like artfulness and for prestige and custom among these establishments. And so, according to the idea of the best restaurant in the world, restaurants compete, in a world that is something like a hall of mirrors, where art is a matter of prestige and prestige is a matter of custom and custom is a matter of art, and also a matter of prestige, and so forth . . . And the critics are supposed to *arbitrate* this triple-faceted aporia of endless reflections with a ranking of 'the best', in keeping with the fiction that it is just to a ranking of this kind that restaurants are fundamentally competing. And that is not the only problem. The idea of the best restaurant in the world implies this other idea as well: it implies that the quality toward which the restaurant properly aspires – the thing that makes the restaurant a restaurant (like the quiddity that makes a bird a bird, a table a table, or a criminal a criminal) – is, along with its artfulness, prestige and custom, its own *institutionalism*. The restaurant as an institution competes with itself in a struggle to be an institution.

An 'institution' is an established and self-regulating organization; it is an orderly arrangement of practices and beliefs, of time and space, of people and objects; it is a fixture of behaviour whose function in the first place is to perpetuate itself. All restaurants, despite their notorious instability (they change hands or go out of business all the time), are institutions in this sense. But there is a certain kind of fetishism of institutionalism when the idea of 'the best' is at stake. Let me call attention for now to just one of the many fetishes involved: the idol of *consistency*. In order to rank as 'one of the best', the restaurant has to be consistent. Going there on Tuesday should be the same as going there on Friday. The *quenelles de brochet* should always have the same dewy chewiness. They have to stick together, but they must not be hard, gloppy, floury, eggy or greasy. The sauce should always have the same depth of flavour, slightly saline, iodine and crustacean, the same silkiness in the mouth, the same thickness, the same colour, the same warmth, the same lingering pepperiness, the same fishy, creamy savour to the nose, and it should always be served in the exact same amount. The dumplings should never be swimming in their sauce, and they should never sit on the plate like atolls, overlooking a receding tide of muddy waters. There should always be just the right amount of sauce, and the right amount should always be the same amount . . . All right, you can see where I am headed. It all sounds not a little delicious, if you like quenelles, and nicely served, if properly served. But the requirement of consistency at all costs, which is what the restaurant must satisfy if it is to be admired by the arbiters of taste, the requirement, in a word, of *reliability*, is hollow. How is this, but for the content and standard of that which is being made so reliable, any different from what we know to be required of each and every McDonald's in the world, where the Big Mac is always the same Big Mac, and the fries are always the same fries? So far as the best restaurant in the world has to be an institution of 'the best', it has to be an establishment which always, apart from seasonal variations and the slight expected unexpected of the daily special or what is called the 'evolution' of its kitchen, *the same as itself*. And why? For whose benefit is this?

The problem is that the best restaurant in the world has to be not just dependable but regimental. And it has to be regimental not because consistency is good in itself – one can imagine situations where inconsistency might be preferable – but because it is required for the estimations made about whether it is good. The main critics make a point of always returning and returning again to confirm the sameness of the restaurant for themselves. And from their point of view they are absolutely correct to do so. The best restaurants in the world are always the same as themselves, and have to be. The category of 'the best' requires it; it must *always* be 'the best'. Yet the category of 'the best' is itself a product of the system of restaurant criticism that allocates it. Fail the test of reliability – give us faultless quenelles on one day, and runny quenelles or, for lack of quenelles, or for the sake of variety, an unremarkable scallop tartare on another – and you cannot be one of the 'the best'; you have lost the competition. Don't even *think* of serving a fish taco, Baja-style, as a starter one day, however tempting it could be; that would be a disaster.

But is that what even a *good* restaurant is all about? From one point of view, it must be so. If I am someone who goes to restaurants a lot, who goes to 'the best' restaurants a lot, or tries to do so, whose own pathology of wealth and privilege demands that he or she try to do so, I am absolutely dependent on a restaurant's competitive consistency. I know that if I go to X on a Wednesday in February, or a Saturday in March, I will get the kind of meal I expect to get, and indeed the kind I have come to require, as if to satisfy the demands of a second nature. I will get 'one of the best'. I will have dined at an *institution of 'the best'*. And fish tacos simply don't rate.

But what about the rest of us? What about those of us who are not in the habit of spending £255 sterling per person on a meal, or returning to the best and the nearly best restaurants in the world on Wednesdays and Saturdays, in February and March, and so on for the remainder of the year? What about those of us who eat out but who do not, or cannot, or will not, eat often or ever at one of 'the best'?

The 'rest of us' are the hydra-headed many. We no more belong to the world of 'the best' than we belong to the high-end art world of New York and Berlin where *tchotchkes* go for millions, or the high-end entertainment industry of Hollywood and Cannes where a single day in front of the cameras is worth a few hundred thou'. We have a complex, mediatized relation to these high-end worlds: voyeurism, envy and resentment are all a part of our relation to them, as well as the fantasy that we are somehow *inside* the very world of high-end insiders that of necessity excludes us. But no, we do not belong to this world of 'the best', even if we fantasize about belonging to it and believe we are thrilling to its thrills. And what about *us*, then?

I do not know of any social thinker or political theorist who has ever thought of 'the people' as 'the people who eat out'. We will see by and by how that works. But it is possible today to think about *homo civis* as *homo gastronomicus* and even as *homo restauranticus*. Obviously, the subject in question would not be 'man in general' (or humanity in general); for the restaurant is a *modern* institution, and indeed a *characteristically* modern one: that is, if you want to think about that which is characteristically 'modern', the existence of restaurants has to be included in your assessment. There is no ancient Latin word for 'restaurant'; there are no medieval codices with margins illustrating St Anthony tipping a waitress, or the Duc de Berry finishing off his port and waving his hand to ask for the bill. On a wall of the Sistine Chapel Michelangelo portrayed a drunken Noah, passed out naked on the floor with his wine bowl empty, but nary a sommelier. In fact, the restaurant today, the restaurant our *homo restauranticus* is likely to patronize, is also mainly a *postmodern* and even a *hypermodern* institution. Modernity included restaurants among its institutions, particularly in sophisticated urban centres. Postmodernity since the Second World War and especially since the 1970s and '80s has proliferated the restaurant culture, spread it across the planet, out of the urban centres and into the suburbs and the 'non-places' of airport lounges and motorway stops, of amusement parks, tourist spots and shopping malls surrounded by car parks. Postmodernity has made the restaurant into a fixture of post-urbanity. Out of modernity, and such legendary establishments such as Beauvilliers or Maxim's in Paris or Delmonico's in New York, comes the teaming, hydra-headed, hybrid world of the restaurant today, the postmodern restaurant, where *homo restauranticus* takes his or her pleasure. And then, out of postmodernity has come the hypermodern restaurant, which is everywhere and nowhere, bombarded with online blogs, where *homo restauranticus* may delight in advertising his or her virtual delight.

And what about the rest of us then, we restaurant-goers?

Of course, we too require certain forms of regularity and reliability. *Formularity*, as I call it, is essential to the restaurant experience, at any level. No restaurant can go without a certain structure, in keeping

with a certain ceremonial form, not even the rattiest diner in ___.
And some of us happy eaters may well aspire to be one of *them*, those
majestic consumers over there. We may wish to make the fantasy a
reality, the voyeurism a participation, the exclusion an inclusion.
And why not? I will myself confess to having tried on several occasions
to secure a reservation at El Bulli, which gets booked up a year in
advance. I confess to feeling a little desperate now that the head of El
Bulli, Ferran Adrià, will soon be closing it for a couple years to
recoup his energies and do something about his financial losses. (His
restaurant has been one of the very 'best' in the world, but it has not
been the most expensive and it has never been very profitable.) I may
never get to eat there, ever. I have gone so far as to fantasize about
my actual trip to El Bulli, which is not an easy place to get to. I would
fly with my wife and maybe another couple on EasyJet from Liverpool
Airport to Girona, in northeast Spain, a hundred kilometres north
of Barcelona. We would rent a car from the airport – maybe from
EasyCar. Then we'd take the long drive north and east through hill
and mountain to the coast, and wend our way toward the seaside town
of Roses. We would stop somewhere nearby for the night, perhaps in
a neighbouring town on the coast, with better value hotels (booked
from EasyHotels). The next day we'd kill time by the sea, watching
the waves come in, and then kill some more time, and then some
more, sitting in a cafe, waiting, until finally we'd change into our best
restaurant clothes and get into the car and drive and get lost and
finally . . . well I don't actually know what it would be like when I got
there. I've seen the pictures but the pictures tell me nothing. What
would it be like to taste those crazy futurist dishes El Bulli is famous
for, the 'squid with smoked milk skin and crispy Venere rice', the
'rabbit sweetbreads with electric Chinese lanterns and liquorice air',
the 'frozen chocolate powder with lime and wasabi'? I do not know
how much I would have enjoyed it; and it would be highly unlikely
that I would ever repeat the experience. I shall always be one of the
rest of us. But I also wanted to be in touch with being one of them. I
wanted to enter the sanctuary, light the candles, kiss the relics, get the
blessing from the priest . . .

As I am *homo restauranticus* I am also, first of all, a *consumer*.
And to consume is not only to consume. It is also to participate in the

cultural fantasy of consumption, which involves a grasping toward not only more and more but higher and higher and rarer and rarer until one becomes . . . well that is unclear. As I once told an overweight (but better than me) racquetball player in San Diego when he was extolling a cruise along the Mexican coast where every night there was a banquet where you could eat all you could eat, 'If you could eat all you could eat, why would you do so?' The racquetball player did not understand me; he enjoyed, or thought he enjoyed, stuffing himself into a stupour. But you, dear readers, will get the point. If you could all eat all you could eat, why would you do so? And if you could eat whatever you wanted, wherever you wanted, whenever you wanted, what would you do? I really don't know what it would mean to be *one of them*, who could do whatever, wherever, and whenever (if any such *ideal consumers* exist outside of the myth of ideal consumption that *they* have invented), and make multiple trips to El Bulli and Alain Ducasse at the Plaza Athénée and the Maison de la Casa House as a matter of course. And as for the professional restaurant-goers, who earn a living by rating restaurants, and dine out night after night, and at all the best places and the places that want to be the best as well as at many places that have no idea what it takes to be the best – if you read about professional critics, on their own account you find that though it seems like nice work if you can get it, it is really a rather dreary business. It is like waking up every morning of the year and it is Christmas again. And you have already seen all the toys. It would be nice just for once to put on your boots and parka and go out and muck about in the mud. It would be nice just to put on a business suit, catch a bus, and *go to work* in a dreary office block and do any kind of dreary shit, anything so long as it wasn't playing with your toys, or sitting down with a waiter looking over your shoulder to yet another plate of *quenelles de brochet*.

So the rest of us may also require reliability out of the experience of a restaurant meal. And the rest of us may sometimes aspire to being one of those ideal consumers, and aspiring to being one of *them* or believing that we are also already one of *them* may well be what constitutes us as being among the rest of us. Who of us would not want to do more, eat more, know more? Who does not fantasize that 'the world' of 'the best' is ours? But what do we, as we are, actually want out of our world of restaurant-going? What do we really desire from it? And what have we the *right* to want and desire? In other words, what do we really need to need?

I do not believe that the restaurant is really an object of judgement for the rest of us, or even quite the matter of a free choice that it seems to be. The cows in the field go after the finest shoots and leaves. They love those mallows and vetches. But they have been led out to the field, and they will be led back out of it, over to the barn house to yield their milk, or to the slaughterhouse to yield their flesh. And *homo restaur-anticus* is out in the fields, making choices, yielding profit to his herders. Few of us have any clue as to what 'the world' to which the field and barn are supposed to belong to really is, and even fewer have enough experience, expertise, wherewithal or moral authority to be able to say what 'the best' in it is. We might *care* (or imagine that we care) about these things. We read the magazines and watch the television shows. We discuss them among our friends. We submit a review to an obscure online blog. We *think* we have the restaurant before us as an object of judgement, since after all the exercize of taste is an exercise of judgement, and we think we have *chosen* this object of judgement, chosen it to be our little object, our little exam paper at exam time, waiting to be graded. But we don't belong to 'the world' of the best restaurants in the world, and we don't have a say in the contest in which these restaurants seem to be competing. To us, the restaurant is less an object of assessment than a medium of experience. A restaurant is something we pass through, pause in and take sustenance, joy, social distinction and aggravation from: our experience. Or, more precisely, the restaurant is something for which we are the media: we are the vehicles through which the restaurant conducts its business of giving sustenance, joy, distinction and aggravation. It is a lot like language in Heidegger, or the genetic intelligence of the grass in the pasture. We are the organs through which the restaurant passes, processing what it has to say. The restaurant proceeds through us, pauses with us, and finds a stage in us for its performances and pronouncements and formularities, its initiation of behaviours, ingestions, metabolic reactions, waste processes and death.

And for the rest of us, then, the idea of a 'best restaurant in the world' is a bit of an absurdity. We know all about 'the best' – but so what? It is a dream. What matters is where we are, what we are doing, what we have been made the vehicles of, and what we are being made to do. For us, in the here and now, though with the past ever pressing against us and the future still in the puzzled offing, the right restaurant experience, with the right meal and the right ambience and so forth, is all about the occasion. The occasion that we pass through, and passes through us, is what counts. For us it was the sunset before us and Armin the sarcastic Austrian maître d' with a moustache, and it was the twinkle of the cheap etched glassware filled with cold Kenwood Sonoma Sauvignon Blanc on the thick white cloth in a dimly lighted room, and it was 1979 and we were 27 years old and Maggie was with us, or Liz or Joe, and the poached fillet of salmon came to the table warm, with a hollandaise sauceboat and boiled potatoes in parsley butter on the side, and it was San Francisco and the fog was coming in and . . . All right, that 'us' was me. But that is my point. The rest of us are billions of me's. And no 'best restaurant in the world' will ever mean a thing compared to that evening in San Francisco and we were 27 and the twilight was falling.

Which is not to say that all that matters is the singularity of experience and pleasure. I am not arguing that the rest of us have nothing to do but go our separate ways, and that public policy, social values, political action or community advocacy are not matters that should concern us, or that *homo restauranticus* is merely a self-indulgent, self-regarding twat. On the contrary, *homo restauranticus* is public, social, political and communal all the way through. And so is the restaurant that passes through the *homo restauranticus*, from the best to the worst – and maybe even, too, the 'best' and the 'worst': what capitalism insists on offering us in lieu of the public, the social, the political and the communal.

In any case, Armin's restaurant – it may even have been called 'Armin's', but I don't remember – is long gone. It was situated on a block of rickety old buildings opposite a small park next to Fisherman's Wharf, the park overlooking a tiny beach on San Francisco Bay, from which you could descry the Golden Gate Bridge to the left and in front of you, across the deep grey water, the green and slouching Angel Island. I was working in an art gallery next door to Armin's; there were other galleries on the block and at an end of it was the Buena Vista, a famous pub where (according to legend) the first Irish coffees were introduced to America in the 1950s, and where you could nowadays get a decent breakfast, eggs Benedict with hash browns, or for lunch or early dinner a fat homemade burger, as well as at any hour a hot, sweet, cream-topped and alcoholic goblet of coffee. Armin – and Armin's, that Austrian joint in the middle of the block – taught me a lot about restaurants and food, and it was a favourite hangout for art dealers after work, where we could sit around the tiny horseshoe bar and drink vodka. But the owner of two of the art galleries on the block was the restaurant's landlord, and he decided that it would be better for the art business, since it would generate more 'foot traffic', and hence more business for the art galleries, if the restaurant closed down when its lease expired and he rented the space out instead . . . to a tee-shirt and postcard shop. So there it went. Fisherman's Wharf lost another of its few remaining real restaurants – as opposed to its many touristy theme restaurants, serving 'Mexican' food, or 'Ribs and Bibs' or even 'Authentic Fisherman's Wharf Seafood', usually owned by distant corporations – and it gained, in return, its 25th tee-shirt shop, where you could get a cute little thing in green saying 'My grandfather went to San Francisco and all I got was a crummy tee-shirt'.

Gone. And yet for me and some of my colleagues it was for a while among the best – or rather, among the most *essential* – restaurants that there were. I hosted a pre-wedding dinner there. It was not in competition to be 'the best', and no guidebooks or even the local newspapers had written it up, but for me, in the 1970s, it was essential. Along with Vanessi's on Broadway (Italian chop house, out of business since about 1984, but one of the origins of the 'open kitchen' restaurant), the Caffé Sport (garlicky Sicilian seafood, still in business), the Hunan Restaurant (garlicky, peppery, oniony Hunan, at one time world famous) and Little Joe's (one of the many Italian-American homes of the Joe's Special, a concoction of spinach, onions, Italian herbs, minced beef and eggs that was good for the twenty-something-year-old day after) – for me and the rest of us, Armin's was essential. But its importance to me had nothing to do with any category of 'the best'. That category did not apply. Armin's and Vanessi's and the rest were restaurants for the rest of us; that other category of 'the best', the best for *them*, was only a dream; it wasn't even on our minds.

So instead, to shift forward to the twenty-first century, consider a small restaurant on an unassuming side street in the seaside town of Collioure, in the southwest of France, up the road from the Spanish border, and indeed not very far north of El Bulli. It is called Le Zouave (I don't know why: a *zouave* is a French foreign soldier in a funny hat) and the times when I visited it it was run by a married couple, who hailed from nearby.[3] There was an outdoor seating area with about fifteen tables – a narrow bricked-in courtyard with grapevines climbing the walls – and an indoor dining room with about twenty candlelit wooden tables. I always sat outside. I came to it first after an irritating drive in a rental car from Perpignan. I was taking my first real holiday in many years, touring through southwest France, and I was on a pretty strict budget. My friend Terri and I had been driving for far too long, through winding hills and vineyards and small stony villages, on roads disturbed every mile or so (it seemed) by a confusing roundabout, in order to negotiate the short distance from Perpignan to Collioure, and when we got to Collioure we were at once astonished by how quaint the town was – antique pastel *hôtels* and *cafés* perched about a small round bay and a string of coves on the Mediterranean Sea, its town centre crowned with an ancient sandy coloured chateau and a seventeenth-century fortress – and dejected by the fact that on a bright summer afternoon it was impossible to park there. We drove and drove. Coming up to two in the afternoon we still hadn't parked. Eventually we found a spot on a hilltop outside of the town, so that we walked downhill on the road into town, hungry and thirsty and angry – angry as only a frustrated tourist can be, a tourist who can scent the sea air of *happiness* all around him, but who isn't having any himself – determined, well, to *get himself some of it goddamn it*. Let me correct that. I was in a mood beyond hunger, and beyond thirst. I was at the edge of a tantrum. And as we reached the edge of town, anxious to get ourselves some happiness, I looked through a gate, into a courtyard, and saw some tables and a handful of diners and I saw a handwritten sign, on a blackboard, advertising a special menu. *Formule Tapas. 25 Euros. 2 Personnes. Vin compris.*

I stopped in my tracks and, with all the self-assurance of a child mistaking himself for a heroic soldier on a mission in a Second World War movie, took Terri by the arm and announced, in a whisper, 'We're going in.'

Inside was a vibrant young woman in jeans with dark eyes and long dark hair, tied back in a ponytail, tending the tables. We ordered the *formule*, choosing for our half-litre of wine the house-made sangria. The sangria tasted of minerals and twigs and grapes and oranges and apples and cloves and it was only very barely sweet. I wished there were more, but €25 was my limit. The tapas came French-style, in a series of courses. We began with *pan Catalan*, a kind of garlic bread with tomatoes, fresh grilled sardines, a few slices from a small wheel of hot Catalan sausage and a serving of *crudités*. A second course came, with big sweet prawns grilled in oil and garlic, steamed mussels in a spicy tomato sauce and green beans stewed in red wine with thin slices of peppery chorizo. I was not used to eating lunch like this, with so much hearty food; I wasn't even eating meat in those days. But I could not help myself. Everything was sharply and brilliantly flavoured. Everything made me smile. I felt regret when dishes for the course were empty and the waitress took them away, but also sated. I had had, in almost every sense of the word, and mainly in all the good senses . . . *enough*. It was like the Bach cantata. *Ich habe genug, mein Gott!* And then a third course came, with beans and grilled meat and salad. And after that, I think, was a dessert.

Le Zouave served us nothing that was unusual or complicated, and I had long since tasted samples of most of the dishes before. I had lived just behind a good tapas restaurant in San Francisco in the 1990s, and a day or two before my friend and I had eaten much the same food in a restaurant in Perpignan. But this time everything was fresh and exquisite (with the exception, unfortunately, of the mussels, which were a bit exhausted). You could taste the sea in the sardines and the earth in the beans and the poor young hog in the chorizo. Nothing was overcooked (which is too often the case in tapas restaurants outside Spain) and nothing undercooked. Spices and aromatics exploded from the dishes – hot smoked paprika, thyme, garlic and parsley – but the explosions were contained; they never overcame you. All the meats, apart from the dry chorizo, were juicy; all the vegetables were just a few passes beyond *al dente*, enough to soak up the sauce; and all the sauces were at once light, piquant and deep. That the whole meal for two came to just €25, tip included, was not only my good fortune; it was of the very essence of the experience.

You could eat better, somewhere else, some other day. But Le Zouave was a restaurant for the rest of us. And whether it was one of 'the best' or not for *them* was completely beside the point.

There has got to be joy in it. There has got to be an affirmation of life in it. There has got to be a freedom of art and hospitality originating from the people who cook and serve, at whatever level they cook and serve, a freedom that reaches to the freedom of the diners who get served and eat. But that is a lesson lost on too many of *them*. A lot of the people I have met since moving to the UK – even those with good taste, who take pleasure in good food – don't quite get it. They think that to enjoy food, food fine enough to pay attention to, you have to be one of *them*, and you have to go to one of *their* places, the more Michelin stars the better. But if nothing else, I hope by this book to recruit a few more individuals to be one of *us*.

Not that there are not reasons to be suspicious of the whole business. For what can we possibly mean by pleasure, in food or in anything else, in the world of global capitalism and its mangled, managed consumerism? And how can we presume to find joy – much less a public joy, a social, political and communal joy – in the private institution of the restaurant? Again, when we think about what we do in restaurants and what we try to get out of them we are faced with the quandary of surplus enjoyment, 'the mysterious and elusive X we are all after in our compulsive consumption',[4] the thing that we cannot get but are always trying to get as a condition of our willing submission to the capitalist system. We keeping thinking we can get more than we can get – the infinite reward of the best dinner ever! – even when we know we are not going to get it, because that is the nature of our bargain with the system: we proceed on the understanding that the system will allow us and even require us to want more.

Let me begin with the last question. I won't be able to address the first question until later in this book. And let me begin by asking, what is a restaurant?

That the restaurant is in the first place a *private* institution, run for profit, almost goes without saying. There are restaurants owned by the state, or subsidized by the state, and there are restaurants owned by community organizations and run as non-profits. There are even

34

dining establishments run without regard for profit and loss – subsidized canteens at the workplace, for example. But let us restrict ourselves to establishments where it is necessary that they generate at least as much income as they pay in expenses, whoever owns them, and hopefully more. A restaurant is a restaurant when it is run, or *as if* it were run, for profit. And as it is run for profit the restaurant has this peculiar identity – I say 'peculiar' because I have never seen a sociologist of food practices come to terms with it, although historians Richard Pillsbury and Rebecca Spang make a good effort – of being a *private* establishment open to the *public*.[5] Of course, it is possible for a restaurant to be closed to the public, and open only to its owners or 'members' or 'guests', who pay a fee to belong to the club. But in the modern world such establishments are exceptions, and even the exceptions are managed on the model of the private-public restaurant, open to the many. (You are served by a waiter, you get a bill, and so on.) Open to the many, the private-public restaurant serves both a private function (it generates income for its owners and workers) and a public one (it *provides food*). But restaurants are private, paradoxically, only so far as they meet the custom of the consuming public, and they are public only so far as the public takes advantage of them on the restaurants' private profit-generating terms. You cannot do anything you want in a restaurant. You cannot even do many things that would be permitted outside, on the street. The restaurant requires that every party *pays*; and it requires that every individual in it *behaves*, and behaves in keeping with protocol established and managed by the institution for the sake of its profit.

Public and private both, then, is the restaurant; and it is this doubleness that marks it out both structurally and historically. The restaurant as we know it came into existence in Paris in the late eighteenth century, and took off as a popular institution during the early nineteenth century, eventually spreading around the globe. The reasons for this, historians and sociologists and urbanologists assure us, are many. But again, the restaurant *as such* is a modern institution, and then eventually a postmodern and a hypermodern one. So far as its structure is concerned, this modern institution, apart from the myths about it generated by such media inventions as the idea of the best restaurant in the world, has a number of common characteristics.

The restaurant is a place where the customer eats. I do not mean to disparage takeaways and caterers, but a restaurant, so far as this book is concerned, is a place where the customer ordinarily eats on the premises. The restaurant can be indoors or outdoors or both; it can be attached to or merged with a bar or a cafe – institutions where patrons predominantly *drink* – and it can serve from all kinds of menus, set and not-set, with or without much individual choice (though there must be some individualization of service, I think), and even with or without servers. A restaurant can offer a buffet; a restaurant can have young immigrants and high school students in humiliating uniforms and paper caps, standing behind a brushed metal counter, in front of a thunder of crackling cooking oil and a cloud of chemically enhanced steam, saying to one and all, 'Can I take your order?' But a restaurant is a private space where the customer, a member of the public, eventually sits down and eats.

And there is more. The restaurant today is always a space with an identity that can be located along several different axes of meaning. *High* and *low* is the most obvious, though not necessarily the most important: high in the hierarchy of restaurants and class distinctions, or low in it. *Dear* and *cheap* is another axis of meaning; and it is always a consideration, whether the restaurant is *high* or *low*, and whether the diner is prosperous or indigent. A high-ranking cheap place to eat is rare, but not impossible to imagine. A low-ranking expensive place to eat – well, I have been to many of those, usually in hotels. In any case, whenever *we* go into a restaurant, we need to know how much it will cost us, and knowing that determines not only whether we will enter, but what kind of experience we think we are having, how we feel about it and how we *identify* it. And of course it is important to restaurateurs and their workers and suppliers as well.

But there is still more. *In* and *out* is yet another axis of meaning. An establishment that is high and dear may nevertheless be *out*, and one that is cheap and low may nevertheless be *in*. This is partly a consequence of fashion; a restaurant can always be identified by its relation to fashion, and it can therefore also be not only *in* or *out* but also *now* or *then*. Restaurant *x* is unfashionable *now*, but used to be fashionable *then*, even if in most essentials (including highness or lowness and dearness or cheapness) nothing has changed about it. No one eats grilled lamb chops marinated in pomegranate juice any more; or no one goes *there* to eat grilled marinated lamb chops; or, *no one in the know* eats *that* or goes *there* any more, only people not in the know. Yet the crowds a restaurant attracts or fails to attract may have little to do with the restaurant itself; the success or failure of a restaurant can be the result of simple dumb luck, and the fashion sense of diners is often unpredictable. Success itself can make a restaurant unfashionable for some diners, and more fashionable for others. A restaurant, in relation to its success, can even be both *fashionable* and *out*; or *unfashionable* and *in*.

Fashion, a big subject, a function of such ins and outs and nows and thens, is possibly best understood along the lines originally suggested by Max Weber and George Simmel.[6] Fashion, according to both, is that which changes for the sake of change itself – even in the case of lamb chops and pomegranate juice. Though the wording of the definition itself suggests that fashion must therefore be something superficial or even absurd, the fact is that change for the sake of change is a constituent aspect of human experience, even before the time when modernity accelerated things. Although we may want our best restaurants always to be the same as themselves, *we* cannot always be the same as ourselves. The mutual demands, as Simmel puts it, of adaptation and individuation, of uniformity and differentiation, require the endless parade in life of those changes in goods and habits that can be attributed to fashion. And though there must be some things that we always do (coffee in the morning, tea in the afternoon), there must be things that we stop doing and things we start anew; and there must be things we stop or start doing for the sake of stopping and starting; and things we stop and start doing for the sake of doing so not as isolated individuals but as subjects identified and operating in concert with a group, a community, a society of subjects. Of course, Karl Marx resented this, in so far as he thought that such behaviour was characteristic of advanced and merciless capitalist society. So did Max Weber and George Simmel: this mere novelty for the sake of mere novelty separated us from the blissful slumber of traditional life, according to Weber; and it served as a condition of class distinction and hence of inequality, according to Simmel. But many fashion mavens resent it too: the best fashionistas (the press often misses this, because the press believes – mistakenly – that it transacts its business under the sign of truth) are always *ironic*. Fashion is never *serious*, it is always *play*, however seriously we may find ourselves actually responding to it, and however vital it is to capitalist economy, or our sense of ourselves as economic beings. It is always something to be both resented as coercion and embraced as play: in other words, accepted ironically, with all the aggression and complacency that irony entails. ('You're a fashion victim', says the well-dressed hostess of the Australian version of the TV show *Project Catwalk*, as another earnest young contestant is first humiliated and then eliminated from the competition.)

But I digress. What I am saying is that restaurants are obviously a part of the fashion system of modern life, and inevitably so, but that the fashion for and of restaurants can operate in complex ways. *Multiplication* can make a difference. It is because there are so many Hard Rock Cafes that many people go to them, wherever they go, thinking that they are *in* precisely because there are so many of them. And it is for this very same reason that many people will *not* go to them, or only go to them because *the kids* are with them, and *the kids* don't know any better.

So, again, the restaurant can be high or low, dear or cheap, in or out, and now or then, not to mention any number of other axes, such as *formal* or *casual*, and *themed* and *unthemed*. For the users and the used of the restaurant (owners, workers, customers, suppliers) the restaurant will inevitably be located somewhere along these axes, from the highest of the high and the nowest of the now to the lowest of the low and the most out-of-date of the dated. *Cool* and *hot* are also important for some establishments, as opposed to *not cool* and *not so hot*. And these axes of meaning are not then accidental to the restaurant; they are of its very essence. It is not the case, that restaurants are private places for public dining which are *also* distinguishable by whether they are high or low, dear or cheap, and so forth; these distinctions are inherent to the functioning of the restaurant, and intrinsic to its economic viability.

There are still more axes of value to consider. The restaurant is distinctive, as we have begun to see, on the basis of whether it is *unique* or *common*. In the USA, Ruth's Chris Steak House is high and dear and even for a certain crowd in; but it is common, and therefore

38

for another crowd very much out. What could be more unfashionable than Ruth's Chris, unless you either do not know that it is unfashionable, or else you patronize it under the ironic sign of reverse snobbery? (We go to Ruth's Chris because we know that it is hokey and cheesy and they are all over the place – and yet it is expensive and classy too.[7]) But there are other kinds of examples. In provincial France, the small-town, independently run bistro is relatively low and relatively cheap but common and in; in Italy the trattoria is the same; in Britain (sometimes) the gastropub. Uniqueness and commonness is a complex phenomenon, relevant not just to McDonald's but, obviously, to Ruth's Chris and even to El Bulli. Whether a restaurant is one of a kind, one of many of the same kind, or one of many of the same restaurant of the same kind, and what the kind in either case is, is absolutely essential, though it can be essential in a lot of different ways. If all restaurants have identities, it is in part because they are treated by operators and customers alike in view of their typicality. One restaurant serves 'Beijing and Sichuan' cuisine, as we are informed at its front window and on the menu; another serves 'Cantonese' food; a third serves merely 'Chinese'. I run to the first, worry about the second and avoid the third, even though I might discover, if I go there, that the third has the best food. I have a friend in San Diego who always goes to P. F. Chang's, even when he is not in San Diego.[8] P. F. Chang's has more outlets than Ruth's Chris – 197 and counting – and every one of them, their website says, 'features an original hand-painted mural depicting scenes of life in twelfth century China'. The *uniqueness* of the 'hand-painted', presumably one-of-a-kind mural, is what is *typical* of a P. F. Chang's, and infinitely reproducible.

The typicality of a restaurant, in any case, is partly intrinsic to how it is run and what kind of food it serves. That almost goes without saying. Is there any McDonald's that is not, typically, a McDonald's, or a P. F. Chang's that is not typically a P. F. Chang's, with its own original hand-painted mural? If so, the customer may have something to shout about. Is there any independently owned and operated Beijing restaurant that is not typically 'Beijing' – either featuring too many generically 'Chinese' dishes, or actually being a lot more idiosyncratic, possibly even more 'authentic' than the typical 'Beijing' establishment? The customer may have something to shout about in that case too.

Restaurants are not only *exemplary*, they are also *expressive*. Both producing the restaurant experience and enjoying it entails an expressive activity, where general culinary and service traditions are put into practice, in view of an axis of typicality and non-typicality.

But part of how the axis of the typical, the unique and the common works is how it operates not only intrinsically in its service and food but also extrinsically in view of still another axis of meaning, the *here* and the *there*. The uniqueness of a *there* can be important to the symbolic identity of a restaurant. The McDonald's at the foot of the Spanish Steps in Rome is unlike any other McDonald's in the world: look where it is![9] I once felt charmed by the aura of uniqueness of the Subway at the intersection of Rush and State in Chicago because it was at Rush and State, a traditional high-end night life area, and another time by the aura of the 'Sbarro 'Italian' buffet at Times Square because it was at Times Square. The famous Mystic Pizza in Mystic, Connecticut is typical of its kind, a sit-down 'special sauce' pizza and sandwich joint in northeast America. But it is uniquely in Mystic. It is *there*. It is there where the movie was made about a sit-down pizza joint in Mystic, Connecticut. And by the way, it is a bit of a schlep to get there: Mystic may well be on the northern coast of Long Island Sound, and along a route that takes you from New York to Providence and Boston, but it is basically in the middle of nowhere, a seaside town that is almost too nondescript (though it is not unpleasant) even to be called a typical New England seaside town. You go *there* even though there is very little that is there worth going to, apart from its very *thereness*.[10]

But the convenience of a *here* can be equally important to the identity of a restaurant. *My* restaurant is my *neighbourhood* restaurant (the Sun Café, they call it, though it is not a cafe, and it is rarely sunny overhead in Lancaster, England). And it is where I go, and the head waiter knows me. And then there are the multiple 'here's' of multiplicity and repetition, which both draw and repel consumers with regard to their localizations. There are people who travel a lot who always go to the same *corporate* restaurant – the same Ruth's Chris Steak House, say, whether in Houston or Boston – or who always go the same *kind* of place – the same kind of independent sushi bar, whether in Boston, Paris or Lima, Peru. And there are people, by contrast, who will deliberately *avoid* going to the same kind of place everywhere they go, or who avoid going to some kinds of places all the time while seeking out other kinds of places all the time. The guidebooks for budget travel almost always tell the budget traveller where to find the 'ethnic' restaurants of a city. Outside of Asia that usually means the Asian restaurants (Chinese, Indian, Thai, etc.); outside of Italy that often means 'Italian' restaurants; and so forth. I have seen a sadly typical British tourist explain on television why this is. The British television personality Stephen Fry, visiting San Francisco's Chinatown, looked into the side streets of the district, where the fortune cookies and the dim sum are made, and assured his viewers on national television that 'the Chinese stick together'.[11] Of course, that is because outside of Asia they are 'ethnic', and to the unethnic British traveller they are all alike, in the same place. That is, they are unlike *us*, and they are assembled in a different place. They stick together, like grains of rice. But we British – it is one of the themes of Fry's show about 'America' – are all over the place, probably for lack of excess starch. (Fry doesn't seem to know that San Francisco's Chinatown was originally a ghetto where Chinese people were forced to live by law.)

Ethnicity is in any case one of the main interests of many sociologists of food: and in fact, for sociologists of food ethnicity is almost always prima facie a good thing. Non-ethnicity is suspicious, since it appears to denote the hegemony of one ethnic group (the one that is *not* ethnic but simply unsticky 'us') over others. But Stephen Fry apart, and maybe even Stephen Fry included, the complexity of ethnicity with regard to the restaurant is not a function of a simple binary opposition. It entails, again, an axis of meaning. The identity of any restaurant, let us say, will be in part a function of where it lies on the axis of the *familiar* and the *exotic*. And this works in many mysterious ways. After all, the generic Chinese restaurant is fairly familiar to people who live in Britain, as is what Brits like to call 'the Indian' as in 'my Indian', that is my favourite local Indian restaurant – which is usually in fact Bangladeshi or Pakistani. But the Mexican restaurant, a genuine Mexican restaurant rather than a *themed* one, serving *pollo en mole* and *ceviche de barracuda* rather than a selection of stuffed tortillas – that in Britain would be exotic indeed, though in Cabo San Lucas it would be the same old same old. And one has to think about this subject from the other end as well: a Mexican restaurateur opening a Mexican restaurant in Cabo San Lucas is doing something very different from a similar restaurateur opening a similar restaurant in London. An Indian restaurant in Mumbai will never be the same thing for the restaurateur as an Indian restaurant in Yorkshire.

Let me give you another kind of example of the complexity of the axis of the familiar and the exotic. For me, though I am not Italian, a casual Italian restaurant is never *exotic*. It is part of my sphere of cultural familiarity, and has been so since I was a child, growing up in neighbourhoods with a high proportion of Italian-Americans, although by the time I was an adolescent I could distinguish between a 'Sicilian' restaurant that served everything in tomato sauce and a 'Northern' restaurant where you could get a veal piccata and risotto. But eating at Sardo in London, a more formal Sardinian restaurant tucked away in a side street of Fitzrovia, was a little bit exotic, as was eating at the Osteria di Giovanni in Florence, and this was the case even though both Sardo and Osteria di Giovanni were *common* examples of restaurants of their type. I have never been to Sardinia, but I found myself a year later eating in a place nearly identical to Sardo, with much the same menu and decor, in the Upper East Side of Manhattan. It even had the same kind of customers, though in New York they had darker hair and higher cheekbones. In point of fact, though I have never eaten in a genuine Florentine-style restaurant outside of Florence, in Florence itself all the osterias and ristorantes have pretty much the same menu, featuring the same dishes – *ribbolita*, *bistecca fiorentina* and for dessert *cantuccini* biscuits served with a glass of sweet *vin santo*. Exotic to the visitor, familiar to the native, the Florentine osteria can be high or low, dear or cheap, in or out, here or there, formal or casual (ours was moderately high, moderately dear, in, here, and formally informal). But it is still almost always *the same*, and not because of what it is in competition against or for, but because of the where-when-how of what it belongs to.

The exotic and the familiar: we are always, in the public-private spaces of the restaurant, both home and away, both stimulated by a certain strangeness and reassured by a certain predictability. And we always experience this joining of the exoticism and familiarity in our own ways, in view of our own life worlds and personal histories. I will never forget that evening in Florence when my wife-to-be Marion and I visited the posh Osteria di Giovanni near the northern bank of the Arne and were treated to fried bread and cold dry spumante at the bar as we waited for our table, and were defeated when we were seated by the huge *bistecca* – a whole foot-and-a-half-wide three-inch-thick cut of the local beef on the bone, weighing at least three pounds – which kept challenging us to take on more of it, and more, and was still left standing after we had done our best with it, and in the end, after ordering grappa and vin santo for digestifs, we found ourselves treated by the hospitable maître d' (was it Giovanni himself?) with bland ingenuousness ('May I offer this? Please?,' he said in Italian) to half a bottle of grappa more. What a night. We were in love, and the whole restaurant seemed to know that, to be there for it, intoxicated with it. The very exoticism and newness and unexpected liveliness of the experience seemed to attest to the newness and uniqueness and vitality of the foot-and-a-half-wide meat of our love. When had I ever been offered so much free liquor before? And yet the restaurant, though very good for its type, was only a type, among many others of its kind in the city centre of Florence. The rest of the restaurant was filled with smartly dressed Italian-speaking diners, some in large groups, families and very likely (it seemed to us) locals. They were all having a very good time – the Italians also struggling through their *bistecca* and *cantuccini* and their complimentary grappa, and getting louder and louder and sloppier and sloppier as the evening went on, spilling their drinks, dropping plates on the floor, shouting greetings across the room – and it made me wonder: how could they be enjoying themselves so much, as if revelling on a special occasion? Don't they do this *all the time*? Isn't all this T-bone and cookies and brandy – yes, translate the words into English and they don't seem so alluring – only *more of the same*?

What is a restaurant, and of what does our pleasure in it consist? The restaurant is, obviously, a symbolic system. And it is a system in a dialectic. The users of the system, from diners to restaurateurs, are engaged in a dialogue – with one another, with the system and even with themselves. The rest of us, we specimens of *homo restauranticus*, are speaking and being spoken to, are consuming and being consumed, are taking pleasure and being profited from: finding ourselves in a matrix of highs and lows, dears and cheaps, heres and theres, nows and thens, familiars and exotics, one-of-a-kinds and all-of-a-kinds. And never mind 'the best'. At a moment in your life, for better or worse, the gastronomical you will find yourself turning to your mate, or just speaking to yourself, standing at the doorway of the matrix, and say the word: 'We're going in'.

You've got no business going there, some canny intellectuals will say. Or rather, all you've got there is *business*, this business of being at once a capitalist and a consumer, a thoughtless exploiter and an avaricious belly: Her Majesty the Consumer, as I will be calling her (and him) later. Yes, of course. But I am speaking for the rest of us. I am speaking above all for the *language* of the rest of us. For this is a book about language. It is about the language *of* the restaurant and it is about language *about* and *for* (or *against*) the restaurant. I am speaking for the rest of us who are always and ever required to do two things, to *eat* and to *speak*, and to do so, most of the time, in places that are never entirely private and never entirely public. I am speaking for the people who have to *go in*. Le Zouave in Collioure was the most essential of all places one day in my life, never mind the rest of the restaurants of the world, even that better known place down the coast. And I went back, several times, a couple of years later. And I observed. How, after all, can a restaurant for the rest of us do it?

Observing, rather than simply eating and enjoying, I saw on a warm September evening, with the outdoor terrace nearly full of diners, some thirty-strong, that there was still only one waitress, the same waitress, although now her hair was cut short and she looked (sad to say) a little bit older. And she was doing everything: clearing tables, seating guests, taking orders, bringing out the drinks, bringing out the plates, clearing the plates, taking more requests, bringing the bill, taking the money. She was always cheerful and gregarious, always proud of what she was bringing to the table, and always busy, but never hectic and never overwhelmed with all the things she had to do. Sometimes she made you wait a little longer than you might wish to wait, but only in the way that southern French restaurants make you wait: within the context of a kind of compact between yourself and the server. According to the terms of the compact, the server will never rush you, never forget you and never do less than his or her best for you. Nothing in the meal will ever go wrong. In return, the diner will never complain, never ask for something that the restaurant does not ordinarily provide and never express impatience. In fact, according to the terms of the compact, the slow pace of a meal is to be desired; it is an extra benefit. Why spend less than a couple of hours at dinner when you are eating at a place like Le Zouave, and everything is worth pausing over? So the two of you, you and the server, together satisfy the terms of a contract, performing its conditions in a spirit of good faith.

Meanwhile, on that September evening, as the wine came, and then the parade of dishes, and as the wine came for my fellow diners in the courtyard, and the food came for them too, and the moonlight tripped over our heads, and a soft music snuggled in from somewhere, Catalan folk music, and the waitress danced about from table to table, I could see into the kitchen. (I hadn't been seated at a table where I could see it before.) The kitchen was tiny, not much more than a stove, a *plancha* and a pantry. And there was only one person inside, one cook, the dark-haired, moustachioed husband of the waitress. Off to another area of the restaurant, behind the bar in the inside dining room, the third worker of the restaurant, an older man, plied his trade: pouring the drinks, washing dishes and sweeping up. Three workers, a cook, a waitress and a bartending dishwasher, provided dinner for thirty diners from a menu which featured (it was written out on the wall, and I counted) 28 items, from fresh-grilled sardines to *crème catalane* (the local version of *crème brûlée*.) These were not three socially isolated individuals, it is important to note. They were not employees who had accidentally come together on behalf of an absent employer, Catalan Bistro Inc., with its own hand-painted murals; they obviously bore a familial relationship to one another, and were working cooperatively. Nor were they labouring in isolation from the community at large. On the contrary, they were supported by their community in all sorts of ways, from laws and government programmes encouraging local agricultural and aquacultural development (where do you think all those good ingredients and wine came from?) to traditional community structures, which were also focused on food and wine production and a standard of excellence for both. It was not a *struggle* to get a good sardine to serve to your patrons in Collioure, or to make a proper sangria.

The fishing boats and the wineries were just down the road and a certain tradition, institutionalized in formal and informal community associations, already provided a key – a code, value and pathway – to culinary production. (For those unaware of this, the wines of Collioure, especially the reds, are terrific, rich with plums, violets, chocolate and minerals and very smooth.) So there were only three people working in the restaurant and all of them were remarkable in their own way, better at it than many others I have encountered, yet all of them were unremarkable too, for they were part of a community, and participants in an officialized culture, which had made a separate (if possibly only temporary) peace with global capitalism, and encouraged just the kind of local independent hospitality and artistry that the three workers seemed so eager to provide.

So I went on observing Le Zouave in action, not knowing much about the people who ran it or the financial condition of the business, but seeing that, in mid-September, when the weather was good, the restaurant was really *working*. And it had a lot to offer to keep it working. Though the *formule* was the main attraction, you could order à la carte and select a lot of different dishes and spend a nice pile of money there. Marion and I tried it one night, to test the kitchen and ourselves, and were happy, and made the chef happy too, I could see (like all real French chefs in modest establishments he poked his head into the room now and then to see how his dishes were being received, and when he saw what he wanted wrinkled his nose). We saw some others ordering à la carte, but most people stuck to a few plates of tapas, or else ordered the €25 meal for two. One night we saw the waitress refuse to serve the *formule* for two to a group of three individuals sitting together. She insisted on having the third person order something of his own. A contract is a contract, a *formule* a *formule*. And one night, while a group of young Frenchmen kept it up at a table behind us, twenty-year-olds ordering more and more dishes, à la carte to be sure, setting to the work of consumption with quiet diligence, an older English couple tried to make trouble. They were sitting quietly off to my right, with a table against the garden wall. What were they talking about? I don't remember. But they seemed out of place. The man was wearing a green polyester sports jacket and tartan trousers, I believe; but maybe my memory is making that up. It was probably tweed and khaki he had on, or linen and silk. One way or another he was over-dressed for a warm late summer night in casual and arty Collioure, and his voice, a deep, posh, proud English, which he insisted on using when speaking to the waitress, whose own English was minimal and embarrassed, seemed to disturb the atmosphere. He and his wife had apparently ordered the €25 meal, and he was getting a bit miffed. Other people around him were getting other things to eat. And those boys in the back kept piling it on. By the time it came time for dessert he and his wife had made up their minds. Instead of the *crème catalane* that came with the meal, though he would take the *crème catalane*, his wife would have the *tarte maison aux fruits des bois*. The waitress told him no. The man demanded why not. The waitress struggled to explain that there were no substitutions allowed. 'Weeth ze *formule* only *crème catalane*', she insisted. But why, he asked again. 'Only *crème catalane*,' she repeated, holding her ground. There was a standoff for a few beats. You could hear the pounding in the veins on the Englishman's forehead. He gave in, eventually, and two *crèmes catalanes* were brought to the table, and he and his wife did them justice. But all the while, as he ate his dessert, he was complaining, and his wife was complaining as well: complaining to each other, of course, for the waitress had long since abandoned them to their pudding and couldn't be bothered. They were not used to being treated this way, they each agreed. And it seemed so silly. There was no extra cooking involved. And their request was reasonable. They would readily have accepted one *tarte maison aux fruits des bois* instead of two *crèmes catalanes*. And anyway, whoever heard of a restaurant not giving you a choice of dessert? Whoever heard of a restaurant not simply honouring a request from a paying customer? In England – no, in England, this simply wouldn't, couldn't, not ever, not once happen. In England . . . and for that matter in any restaurant, anywhere, not just at home, this wouldn't, couldn't . . .

Now you may take what I am saying as a standard kind of put-down of a tourist, for acting like a tourist. There was a cultural disconnection here, you may say. And let's not rush to judgement. We have all been there in our travels. The only problem was that *I* got the code, and the waitress got the code, but the Englishman did not. He did not know, in every sense of the word, *the language*. He was unaware of the southern French *compact*. But that is not my point. My point is that, whatever else the indignant English tourist was in his capacity as a disgruntled customer, rightly or wrongly, he was in the first place operating under an illusion. He was committing a categorical error. He supposed that he was eating in one of the restaurants for *them*, the ideal consumers who are always right and otherwise detached from the community where consumption thrives. But Le Zouave was nothing like that. Le Zouave was a restaurant for the rest of us.

two

Grimod de la Reynière: Eating and Writing

If the first restaurant opened its doors in Paris in the 1760s, it would be a few decades before restaurants were flourishing throughout the city.[1] A revolution intervened, or rather a Revolution: a convocation of the Estates General, an assault on the Bastille and a Declaration of the Rights of Man in 1789; the proclamation of the Republic in 1792; the execution of the king in 1793; a Reign of Terror in 1793–4; a government by Directorate from 1795 to 1799; Napoleon, the revolutionary general, named First Consul for a new (republican) Consulate, and eventually (in 1804) declared the Emperor of the Empire of France. Through all of this innovation and turmoil, though not of course without momentary ups and downs, the Parisian restaurant *thrived*. Instead of disrupting what it was that the restaurant did, the Revolution encouraged it. One of the most famous ideas about the cause of this rise of the restaurant was that by unsettling aristocratic households, the Revolution threw a lot of master chefs out of work, who opened commercial establishments out of necessity. But that is only one of the many aspects of the revolution that encouraged the development of a restaurant culture in the capital. Many restaurants were in fact opened by restaurateurs who had never worked in an aristocratic household, and many of the best French chefs were still attached to wealthy patrons. The famous Carême (1784–1833) made his reputation as 'The King of Chefs, and the Chef of Kings'.

So something else was involved. And it was something deeper, something which speaks to the nature of the Revolution itself – the Bourgeois Revolution, as Marxist historians have long since characterized it, a revolution that put one *class* in power over others, and a

49

revolution that also put a certain *way of life* in power over others. A 'bourgeois' is an owner of capital with a share in a means of production; and a 'bourgeois' is literally an inhabitant of a city. I am not going to get into all the technicalities here of the economic interpretation of modern history, nor go into detail over its theoretical and empirical limitations, but I do want to call attention to how the development of the restaurant in revolutionary France entailed the advent of both a certain kind of class structure and a certain way of life, both of which can be summed up as 'bourgeois'.[2]

Nor were the people of the time unaware of the new development in their midst. By 1803, in the last days of the Republic, the restaurant had become not only a common institution in Paris but a cultural idea. It had become a subject of discourse. People talked *about* restaurants, just as they also talked *in* them. And the writing began. The restaurant would show up in plays and stories. Travellers to Paris commented on them for their readers back home, fondly recalling the elegance of the dishes, the alacrity of the waiters, the exhilaration of the rooms. Moreover, the restaurant would now become not only a subject *of* writing, something *written about*, but also a subject *to* writing. Like novels and plays, restaurants would now be the subject of reviews. It began with the first volume of a book called *Almanach des gourmands*, written by the witty, wily, eccentric and troubled Alexandre-Balthazar-Laurent Grimod de la Reynière. Seven additional volumes would appear over the next ten years. All of them sold well and soon there would be imitators, but Grimod was the inventor of the form, and well aware that there was something revolutionary about what he was doing, as well as something, well, *funny* about it.

There has been an 'upheaval in men's fortunes', the Preface to the first volume of the *Almanach* begins, 'which has come about as a natural result of the Revolution'. The Revolution has 'put wealth into new hands', Grimod writes. And the minds of the newly rich 'have turned above all toward purely animal pleasures'.

Grimod kicks off with a familiar dichotomy: the mind is posed against the body, the rational faculty that humanity shares with the divine against the animality that it shares with beasts. The revolution has caused the lower half of the dichotomy to have the ascendance, Grimod is saying; and he seems to be critical, even sarcastic, about it.

But Grimod was himself a man whose fortunes underwent an upheaval during the Revolution, and he is not therefore going to follow through with the critique. Instead, he is going to assert a transvaluation. He is going to accommodate himself to the new order of things. Since men are now bent toward the sensual pleasures – in fact, *les jouissances purement animales* – 'I have thought fit to render them a service by providing them with a guide . . .'

The *Almanach* would not be purely a guide, in the sense which we now attribute to the word, and would not be purely a work about places to eat. Grimod has a larger vision. His work would be about everything that would appeal to a gourmand in his gourmandism. His readers would find in his book a 'sure guide' for the satisfaction of the 'most substantial part of their dearest feelings'. The *Almanach* would be more like what we call a manual, but this time with a dedication toward nothing but the arts of the table of a Parisian man of means. And if the reader may still feel as if a kind of criticism, a mockery, is being levelled against the new bourgeois of Paris, he will find all the same that through humour and irony the author is sincerely writing on his or her behalf, celebrating what they may now become, and showing them how they may become it – even if a shadow of mockery hovers over everything he says.

> The hearts of most wealthy Parisians have suddenly metamorphosed into gizzards. Their sentiments are no longer anything but sensations, and their desires no longer anything but appetites. It is for that reason that one conveniently renders them a service by giving them, in several pages, the means of accomplishing, within the domain of good eating (*la bonne chère*), the best match possible between their inclinations and their money.[3]

Once upon a time, we had *heart*; once upon a time we had *sentiments*; once upon a time we had *desires*. All that is gone now; all we are left with are gizzards, sensations and appetites, and 'for many people a well-tended stomach is the first principle of happiness'.[4] The *man of sentiment* of the eighteenth century has in effect been replaced by the new creature of the nineteenth century, *man the consumer*.

And it is to this man's happiness that Grimod will address himself, this happiness that is now folded into that which can be consumed, and that which must be paid for out of limited resources, in a spirit of joviality, self-irony and self-criticism.

Grimod does not, I think, ever use the word 'consumer' when describing the *gourmand*, and he could not have known all the uses that later sociologists would put it to, but this is what he understands: man is a consumer, now. He is a consumer of a certain kind, to be sure. He is first of all male: although Grimod is very fond and supportive of women, he always addresses himself to the male sex. And this male consumer is secondly an *amateur*, dedicated to refined consumption: he is a pursuer of *la bonne chère*. He is in addition a man of learning, a *gourmand* (a traditional word for a glutton, here transvalued into something better and higher) who is also *savant* (learned, sophisticated), consecrated intelligently and pragmatically (since expense is always a consideration) to an art of *jouissance*. He is a man of means as well, with a certain social function: he is a giver as well as a receiver, a host of dinner parties and a patron of culinary artists. He is a dispenser of *jouissance* as well as a beneficiary thereof.

So a world that was once ruled by a system of sentiments – the high-flown ideals of the *ancien régime* – is now ruled by a system of pleasures. Whatever people believed they were up to in the old days, now, if they have the financial wherewithal, they have become something new; they have become the key subjects of this newfangled system of pleasures; they have become consumers. And this is revolution.[5]

The *ancien régime*, to be sure, was hardly devoid of *jouissance*, and it would not be the case that the post-Revolutionary world would lack feelings.[6] From a revolutionary point of view that preceded the Revolution, which Grimod shared when he was young, a standard complaint was that a frivolous ruling class went about enjoying its pleasures at the expense of earnest, virtuous, hard-working under-classes. And even as the post-Revolutionary Grimod renders his service to people for whom a well-tended stomach is the first principle of happiness, the European-wide worship of feeling and spirituality known as Romanticism will have been well under way. But Grimod points out the arrival of a new structure. A system was now in place that catered to the ethic and whims of man the consumer. The system included that newfangled institution, the restaurant, which had with great rapidity proliferated throughout the whole of Paris, becoming an integral feature of the cityscape. And it included a certain kind of text. It included, as Grimod points out, a *demand* for a certain kind of text, of which Grimod will be the first but by no means the last supplier: the critical guide. In the post-Revolutionary world, there will be restaurants, and there will also be writing about restaurants. And the writing will be ironic, up to a point. The happiness of the bourgeoisie, so far it is mainly a matter of *la bonne chère*, can never be taken seriously; it can only be envied, emulated, catered to, resented or enjoyed. And so it can never be written about seriously either – not in Grimod's hands, at least . . . up to a point.

Eating and writing is the theme of this chapter, along with several subsidiary themes: the origins of the restaurant at the time of the French Revolution; the origins of man the consumer at about the same time; the role of writing in serving, modifying and mediating consumption; the role of joviality and irony in the proliferation of writing about restaurants; the role of what I call *formularity* – ceremonial invention – in this new form of consumption and writing; and finally the limits of Grimod's project, the unsustainability of his marriage of *les mets* and *les mots*. In the end he was scarcely able to write about restaurants or food any more – not restaurants *for them*, the elite he presumably represented as a man of taste, nor even for the rest of us, the other consumers his guidebook was supposed to enlighten.

When you get the restaurant as a modern institution, you get the whole package: a site of consumption which can be high or low, cheap or dear, in or out, familiar or strange, and so forth, and so either for *them* or for *us*. You get this private place for public enjoyment, and all the inclusions and exclusions that public enjoyment entails. Grimod begins with this institutionalization. The Revolution, says Grimod, has put an end to the dominance of the great house of the aristocrat as the home of good eating, which used to employ the best 'artists' of food, hosted the best dinners and spread its largesse under the guise of the ancient code of hospitality. If the transition was already under way a few years before, still it is now that the new order has been established. 'The Revolution put all those old landlords on a diet', Grimod adds, buying into the not entirely untrue myth, 'and threw the best cooks out on the street. From then on, in order to exercise their talents, the cooks had to make themselves into merchants of *la bonne chére* under the title of restaurateurs.' The numbers which Grimod puts forward, which no historian has ever seriously challenged, are astonishing. 'There were not a hundred of them before 1789 . . . There are now at least five or six times as many.' (In a city of 550,000, that's one restaurant per one thousand inhabitants.) Other causes may have been involved as well: Grimod even mentions a desire to imitate the fashion of the English, who in his mind were already eating out in public houses a good deal more than the French. And academic historians of today are always quick to warn us against making too much of revolutionary transformation. Name the social or political phenomenon of any period in history, however apparently new or unique or revolutionary, and you will always find precedents. Taverns, inns, cafes, cook houses, caterers, pensions with *tables d'hôtes* and itinerant food stalls had long since provided food outside the home, well before the first 'restaurateur' put a sign outside his door in the 1760s, saying he was serving a restorative broth as well as other dainty comestibles for a select clientele, at private tables, with personalized service.[7] Maybe the restaurant was not so new, then. Maybe we shouldn't let that damn exaggerator Grimod mislead us. But Grimod is onto something all the same. At some point, as Marx once urged, quantity turns into quality; and by 1803 the quantity of restaurants in Paris was such that a new quality of experience had come into being: the experience of *restaurant-going*. And this was not just an accidental feature of the social world of post-Revolutionary Paris. It was of its very essence.

The *going* part of this experience is emphasized throughout the first volume of the *Almanach des gourmands*. Grimod is a connoisseur of the geography of food: the *foie gras* of Strasbourg, the oysters of Oleron, the chickens of Bresse. It is always important for Grimod to know where his ingredients come from, and how and when different foodstuffs come into the market. But still more important, Grimod is a connoisseur of the geography of Paris. He was brought up in a great mansion by the Champs-Elysées (on the site that today houses the American Embassy), and though he travelled a bit, once even opening a food wholesaler's in Lyon, the waning years of the Revolution have found him back in Paris, residing in the mansion with his recently widowed mother and a handful of lodgers. He is back in the capital, struggling to make ends meet, a well-known (but under-financed) theatre critic and disbarred attorney as well as a former *négociant*, a friend of actors and playwrights and other artists, and a notorious *bon vivant*, a *gourmand* – that newly celebrated category of eater – who has discovered a new mode of existence. He has discovered the *going* in Paris, here and there, to a cafe, a chocolate shop, a market place, an arcade and, when he can, a restaurant, going partly for the sake of going, partly for the sake of seeing what's there, partly in order to be a part of the crowd of people in the city, and partly to partake, to consume, to enjoy. Half a century later Baudelaire and his contemporaries would make the figure of going about in the city famous as the *flâneur*. But the *flâneur* is a melancholy figure, always at least a little bit estranged from the city in which he makes his way.[8] Grimod imagines himself as one with Paris. Walking about, seeing what there is to consume, and then consuming it, was to be not just a *flâneur*, but also a citizen, actively engaged in doing what good citizens of post-Revolutionary Paris do. No aimless wanderer, Grimod is constantly putting the city into order, centring it around himself and putting it to use. He is submitting the city to the distinctiveness of his desires.

The most famous event in Grimod's life came two decades earlier, when at the age of 24 he hosted a famous waiterless dinner at the family mansion in a black-draped room to seventeen guests and a school of observers (who looked on, eating biscuits, from the gallery), where funereal motifs were matched with Freemason incantations and electricity experiments, dishes were wheeled in on mechanical trolleys, the first of many courses was composed entirely of pork, the second was composed entirely of food prepared with fat, and so forth (though we don't have the details of the later courses). When the guests arrived, they were greeted by a pair of guards who asked them, 'Have you come for Monsieur de La Reynière, the Bloodsucker of the People, or for his son, the Defender of the Widow and the Orphan?' For some of the guests the experience was scandalous, for others a delight, and all of Paris was buzzing about it for months.[9]

He had been born deformed. Both of his hands were missing, and over whatever it was that he had instead of hands he always wore gloves. He had grown up, as the greeting to his guests shows well enough, resentful of the wealth and privilege he was born into. And at the age of 24 Grimod was putting on the performance art of satirical dinners, partly as a kind of protest against the manners of the *ancien régime*. Among the guests at a follow-up black dinner, for those who missed the first one, was Louis-Sebastien Mercier, author of *The Year 2440: A Dream If Ever There Was One*, a utopian novel imagining a social democratic future. He came in the company of fellow novelist Rétif de la Bretonne, another notorious figure of the Parisian scene, who was about to introduce the word 'communism' into modern French.

Grimod's politics at this time appear to have been relatively unformed, but his social agenda was, precisely, a *formularity*. He was expressing the movement of a social revolution through the production of ceremonial form, the dinner. As ever, Grimod was being deliberately theatrical; theatricality was a part of almost everything he did with an eye to the public, which is to say to the presiding spirit of his parents. Sensitive to the form of what he was doing for the sake of form, but also undermining what form was supposed to be about, Grimod was saying to his mother and father, I am of you, but I am not of you. He was saying, I am the deepest expression of all that you stand for – his father, a tax farmer and financier and one of the wealthiest men in France, a liberal-minded gourmand and a connoisseur; his noble mother a notorious adulteress and lady of fashion. Grimod was saying, as the deepest expression of what you are, the novelty in what you are, I am the opposite of what you are as well. I can put on dinners that celebrate death. I can practise baroque hospitality in the spirit not of the triumph of wealth but of saying truth to power. And in the meantime *I can have a good time; we can all have a good time*. In this we shall be exactly like our mothers and fathers and our ancestors before them; but we shall also be absolutely different.[10]

If you were looking for high-minded advances in liberty, equality and fraternity from the French Revolution, then, you are going to be disappointed. Whatever progress has been made in politics, Grimod points out – and Grimod was not very happy about it, even if he was no fan of the *ancien régime* either – what we find now in our social lives is a new order of things where hearts have turned into gizzards, and where the pursuit of *la bonne chère* has become a matter of urgency. On the one hand, *la bonne chère* comes from everywhere. It is one of Grimod's favourite commonplaces that though Paris itself produced no foodstuffs, it attracted foodstuffs from every corner of France and the world beyond. And *la bonne chère* can be found everywhere too. The shops and restaurants are all over the place. Yet on the other hand, citizens need a guide. By the third year of his work as a producer of almanacs of food, Grimod would discover that what the citizens need is even something he calls 'legitimations'; of the products of restaurants and caterers, assessments providing them with seals of approval. What the new world of the Empire needed were forms and formulations that attested to the legitimacy of the post-Revolutionary bourgeois world: gastronomy legitimized, the judgement of taste elevated to a principle of social organization.

To summarize, the late eighteenth century was a period of social experimentation. One outcome was the birth of the restaurant. The restaurant was a new kind of space of private-public eating, with its own formularities. It tended to be posh; lighted with chandeliers, their walls hung with mirrors and paintings, and serving food that was advertised as being especially delicate – above all, the *restaurant* itself, a 'restorative' bouillon served in a fine porcelain cup – it catered to a bourgeois clientele, including bourgeois women. In fact, although the prearranged *repas de commande* formed a good part of its trade, the restaurant catered first of all to walk-ins. It was imagined that people would walk in off the street unannounced to find a tranquil, indulgent environment, where one could be served off a menu and be restored. And if this new kind of institution was a symptom of social change in the late eighteenth century, it was precisely because, on the one hand, it catered to this walking, moving, atomized crowd of clients and because, on the other, this crowd of clients required privacy within a public space, and publicity within a private space, and required it to be *posh*; or rather, it required it in such a way that the space could be located within axes of meaning that included the formal and the casual, the high and the low, the dear and the cheap, and so forth. This was revolutionary in the sense that it marked a fundamental transformation of the modern crowd and the urban space it occupied, and the forms of work, leisure and conviviality that would structure its everyday life. There came to be restaurants for those of limited means as well – casual, low and cheap, like Balzac's Flicoteaux. But that was because an institution was put in place which had transformed the practices of everyday life, and had done so on a model of social and physical differentiations and the stratified distribution of wealth. The restaurant began for the rich, and on the model of service to the rich, it ended up also being for the poor.

Grimod came to writing about the new world of the restaurants and the consumers to whom they catered more or less by accident. He and a publisher friend were thinking about a way to make money, since Grimod's latest foray into publication, a work of literary criticism, had been a financial disaster. The publisher came up with the idea of Grimod writing something about food. Within a couple of months, the first edition of the first volume of *Almanach des gourmands* was out and selling by the thousands. Soon there was a demand for a second edition and a third, and then for more volumes. In fact, everything that Grimod wrote about food from then on followed upon the success of the first edition of the first volume. Thinking about how to write about food in Paris, Grimod came up with the idea of a comprehensive 'almanac' that would include – borrowing an idea from a medieval literary form – a *Calendrier nutritif* or 'calendar of food' as well as a miscellany of items (essays, maxims, news features, anecdotes, verse) and, most original of all, an *Itineraire Nutritif, ou, Promenade d'un gourmand dans divers quartiers de Paris*, an 'itinerary of food, or, promenade of a gourmand in various districts of Paris'.

Though the idea had occurred to him, Grimod did not prepare a simple listing of places to buy or eat food. He did not think of assembling abstract charts and tables or indices, and did not think that what he was writing was simply a directory for consumers to use as they wanted. For Grimod the *Almanach* was a literary endeavour, a jocoserious, even Rabelaisian exposition, full of teasing personality. That's what gave it so much charm, especially in its first volume. It was only after he was well along in his project, when he had received a good deal of response to the *Almanach* from readers (including favourable book reviews), that he came to see that writing about food had a life of its own, and that the consuming public for which he wrote had their own demands. On the one hand, Grimod threw himself into the pursuit of form for form's sake, and form for the sake of the pleasures it enabled; on the other, he found himself trapped into formalities of his own making. At first he would innovate all the more, capitalizing on past success, but then he would give up. Underlying the logic of Grimod's formalization of surplus enjoyment was a fundamental contradiction that he could not resolve and that ultimately he had to escape: the contradiction between eating and writing.

The idea of the *gourmand* and his *gourmandise* was at the heart of Grimod's self-contradictory project. This dispenser and receiver of *la bonne chère* was a new kind of creature, cut off from the authoritative traditions of the *ancien régime*. He had to make things up as he went along. He had to accommodate himself to the new urban space, to its new forms of economic and social activity. And he had to try to do it on his own terms, even if the rules for doing so were still in the process of being established, and the formalities of social life were still a work in progress.

He had to take his food business seriously, too. If it was true that gourmandism (or gastronomy, another new word current in Grimod's Paris, used more or less as a synonym for gourmandism by Grimod) began when hearts had turned into gizzards, and sentiments had turned into sensations, nevertheless, those gizzards were vital, those sensations obeyed an artful logic. Being a gourmand meant knowing how to live lightly, with *humeur joviale*;[11] it meant immersing oneself in enjoyment; but it also meant insisting on the seriousness of the work of gourmandism, and the principles by which the gourmand would endeavour to live.

How so? At several points along the way Grimod tries his hand at definition. And so he writes, in volume three, that it is important to distinguish between the 'gourmand' and the 'glutton': 'The word "glutton" [*glouton* or *goulu*] is reserved to characterize intemperance and insatiable avidity, while the term "gourmand" has come to be used in the world during these past few years with a much less unfavourable, even, dare we say it, a much more noble meaning.' And what is that?

The gourmand is not only a being whom nature has endowed with an excellent stomach and a vast appetite, for all robust and well-constituted men are like that, but also someone who joins to these advantages an enlightened taste, a taste whose first principle resides in a singularly delicate palate, developed over a long course of experience. All of his senses have to be in a constant agreement with taste, for he has to think carefully about his food even before he brings it to his lips . . . [12]

There seems to be an appeal here to something like the man of 'enlightened taste' of the previous century. The idea itself was already commonplace by then, and it had a prestigious philosophical pedigree. It is appears, for example, in David Hume's essay 'Of the Standard of Taste', which Grimod, a fan of philosophy, may have known. Taste is not only born, according to Hume and similarly minded aestheticians; it is also learned. The exercise of taste is an advanced form of sense perception, coupled with habit and thought, which is capable of sensing more, and of sensing more 'delicately' or discriminatingly. 'It is acknowledged to be the perfection of every sense and faculty', Hume wrote, 'to perceive with exactness its most minute objects, and allow nothing to escape its notice and observation'.[13] Twenty years later, the old magistrate Jean-Anthelme Brillat-Savarin, in the famous *Physiology of Taste*, would develop the idea even further with a view to the rational component of taste. While Hume distinguished between the taste for food and the taste for literature, only granting to the latter a rationality of principles and laws and therefore to the wider aims of human progress, Brillat-Savarin said that 'gastronomy is the reasoned comprehension of everything connected to the life of man'. Brillat-Savarin's gourmand, with his 'impassioned, reasoned, and habitual preference for everything which gratifies the organ of taste', was an enthusiast who pursued his passion for food with wisdom, or even with science, having both internalized the standards of taste and learned to generalize them into objective principles.

But all of these ideas – whether of Grimod, Hume, or Brillat-Savarin – seem to make of the gourmand an unpleasant creature, a person of passionate appetites who is also annoyingly fussy. He may be a man of the Enlightenment; he may be a rationalist; he may be an

Epicurean in the classic sense that he knows when to say no; he may be absolutely exquisite, having learned that though to eat is a necessity, to eat intelligently is an art. He may be what was also being called a *gourmet*: a man of exquisite taste. But the man of taste by all these definitions is still a fussbudget, insisting that his fussiness is objective and universal. And that is not what Grimod, for one, really wants to be.

Grimod's gourmand is a *situated* man of taste. And within his situation, he is a *rule-making, form-generating* man of taste. It is within the framework of his situatedness that he finds in the narrator of the *Almanach* a model to follow: the man who goes on promenades of food, making choices, establishing relationships with purveyors, dispensing praise, blame and custom. Grimod's gourmand is always, first of all, *in Paris*. There is no other place for him. He is in Paris on a budget and he is in Paris on a mission, the pursuit of *la bonne chère*, but he is first of all always *there*. But Grimod's gourmand is not passive in his situation, and he is not someone who, like the consumer in classic economics, simply makes choices out of the commodities on hand in order to maximize personal benefit. For he is also someone who tries to generate choices and to fashion a kind of life out of the choices he is helping to generate. Ultimately, therefore, he is not only keen on following rules but on making them, and not only dedicated to keeping to form – the proprieties of the dinner table for example – but also on generating and disseminating it.

The ethic of gastronomy from Grimod's time to our own has in fact depended on a notion of this activity in the face of the necessity of consumption. The sense of the modern-day foodie (justifiably or not) that he or she is *not* a mere bloodsucker of the people, *not* a mere exploiter of the labour of others or the resources of the planet, *not* a mere maker of selfish choices from a variety of commodities, but also a contributor to the general good, as if, in consumption, he or she were also engaged in production – that is what makes gastronomy more than mere self-indulgence. Certainly Grimod came to feel this way about his own role as a gourmand, as well as for the gourmands for whom and to whom he was speaking. And it is what in our own day a number of sociologists have come to think about the consumer in general, including our own *homo restauranticus*: that in a consumer society, the consumer is a constituent of production. A contemporary and acolyte of Grimod's once put this jovially, thinking of the sample day-in-the-life of the gourmand: 'Cuisine, like comedy, with which it has more than one thing in common, must conform to the rules of Aristotle. And the day of the gourmand, which is nothing but one vast meal, must also have its exposition, its climax, and its denouement, which one divides into three acts: lunch, dinner, and digestion.'[14] In other words, the gourmand, the model consumer, manages his existence with a view to the management of consumption, as if in doing so he were the playwright of his own life. A modern sociologist has put this more prosaically: 'it is precisely in the degree to which an individual comes to possess the ability to decide the nature and strength of his own feelings that the secret of modern hedonism lies'.[15] So important is this stage-managing of consumption practice that (for better or worse) it comes to determine the shape of production practice as well.

But we will get back to the twenty-first-century consumer later. The point is that a premonition of this idea is already present in the first major guide to food consumption ever written, both with regard to the general idea of the advent of man the consumer and with regard to the more specific notion of the gourmand. The consumer creates. And, to use my term of art once again, the gourmand *formulates*. The gourmand invents new forms of social action – the black dinner, for example, or more prosaically the gourmet dinners that Grimod would explain to his readership in his how-to writing. He invents his own ceremonies, or what social scientists call 'interaction rituals'.[16] In these formularities there is something very obviously artificial, and to that extent false, which is one of the reasons why Grimod adopts a measure of irony; but there is also something very obviously joyous, which is one of the reasons why, in his irony, Grimod is more comic than satiric, and more supportive than dismissive. Or in other words, the formularities of gourmandism provide one of the main reasons why the gourmand is serious about what he is doing, even if what he is doing is also always funny.

Some of the rule-making, rule-abiding energy in Grimod's project alights upon the smallest of details, the kinds of things associated with etiquette. 'It would be a grand incongruity', he writes, for a guest

at a dinner 'to use a knife to cut off a piece of bread. It is necessary
. . . to content oneself to break it off with one's fingers'.[17] Rules like
this always proliferate in the context of taking meals. But the little rules
contribute to the performance of the big rules – being a good host,
being a good guest, being a good *confrère* or gourmand – which themselves involve not just obeying certain principles and regulations but
also creating occasions in which principles and regulations can be exemplified. The day in the life of a gourmand is rule-driven; but it is rule-
driven for the sake of constructing a kind of comedy. Every day, from
morning to night, is a kind of performance, of which the gourmand is
at once author, director and actor. The gourmand is no fussbudget,
because he spends his day not in finding ways to say no but in finding
ways to say yes. Or, in other words, the gourmand, master consumer
though he is, is also an artist – a secondary artist, perhaps, much as a
critic is a creator of 'secondary' literature, but an artist all the same.

The inevitable egoism of the artist-gourmand has important consequences for gastronomic writing. And here is one of them: when he
turns to restaurants for the first time, Grimod the critic cannot help
seeing the establishments, as it were, centripetally, from the point of
his own artistry as a consumer and a situated man of Paris. Or rather,
he cannot help emphasizing the centripetal force of his own situated,
egoistic presence in the system. The ultimate point of what he is doing
is thoroughly social, centrifugal, out-reaching, universalizing. The
critic reviews for the sake of the greater good. But he does so from
within a particular and highly limited situation. There is therefore a
push and pull in this kind of writing. The gourmand is at the centre
of things, and the gourmand writer doubly so, for his writing redu-
plicates his centrality, publishing it for all the world. He is even triply
at the centre of things because, as it happens, in his own situation
Grimod the gourmand resides at the centre of Paris, and it is in the
centre of Paris that the best food is generally to be found, not to mention its greatest market, Les Halles. But even so, the restaurant
reviewer is obliged to the social world in which his restaurants are
found – obliged to his readers, his purveyors and the system of dining
as a whole. And therefore his writing moves outwards, in 'good faith'
(a term he often uses), in and through the social world it is meant to
serve, on the basis of what are imagined to be universal principles.

So, in his first *Itineraire nutritif*, Grimod goes for a fictional walk, heading from his home, and he goes looking for establishments to say yes to, and spread the word about. He finds what he is looking for in cafes, patisseries, confectionaries, charcuteries and rotisseries (the reader today may be surprised to find that many of the gastronomically delightful elements of modern urban France were already in place in 1803, serving many of the things they still serve today), where a person may pause for an ice or a coffee or take home what he needs for that day's dinner: patés, sausages, roasts, vegetables, bonbons, spices or cakes. But he finds what he is looking for in restaurants soon enough too. Coming down from the Place Vendôme to the Tuileries (just behind the gardens of his house) he comes to the famous Restaurant Véry, which has been in business since before the Revolution. 'We will admire,' Grimod writes, 'the restaurant of M. Véry, where the mahogany panelling, the mirrors, the marble and the bronzes display at every possible opportunity all the riches amateurs would hope for, meriting the establishment's reputation as the most sumptuous of its kind in all of Paris.' Note that the description keeps to the conceit of the promenade, where the visitor, walking, first of all notes the appearance of the restaurant from the outside and then within. Note too that the observation of the restaurant is matched by an observation of the expectations of the observer; what one sees upon entering the restaurant is not only what is there, but what one expects and hopes to find, given what others have said about it. Push and pull: the ego and its objects, the ego and its objectives, the desire of the self and the desire-generating word of others. And the push and pull goes on, as much in the direction of the one as the other, though now not without a bit of sarcasm thrown in: 'We will not doubt but that the excellence of the cuisine is equal to the splendour of the porticos or the brilliance of the dishware, and justifies the enormous prices. And we would be still more certain of this if we saw more daily customers among those who gather there.'

It almost seems as if this first important entry in the first guide of its kind was written without the writer's actually having sampled the food inside. That is unlikely, but the impression is reinforced when Grimod goes on to discuss the restaurant next door, and, pushing and pulling, to make some important distinctions.

If it is a matter of crowds, it is to [Véry's] neighbour M. Le Gacque that one must go, for crowds are to be found there without cease; and here perhaps, at this moment, one finds the Parisian restaurateur who has brought together the richest and worthiest amateurs, although people in general complain about the inattentiveness and rudeness of the clerks . . . Its rooms have nothing sumptuous about them; but the food must be excellent, the wines exquisite, and its prices moderate, given that the restaurant attracts every day so great a gathering . . . [18]

In these first significant entries in the history of restaurant reviewing the food does not seem to need to have been eaten. Certainly the food is not described. Other things are accounted for instead: decor, price, service and above all popularity. We might even suppose that Grimod hasn't eaten at the restaurant of M. Le Gacque either, if he hadn't also added a note to the effect that the cuisine and ambiance must be excellent at his establishment because it has for so long hosted the weekly dinners of 'that amiable and venerable *Société du Mercredi*, whose members are noted for the grace of their wits, and the fineness of their palates'.[19] Of course, the Société du Mercredi was Grimod's own dining club; he had been gathering friends in weekly gastronomic meetings of this kind even before the Revolution. In effect, Grimod recommends the Restaurant Le Gacque by way of a little joke, on the authority of his own authority.

So, in the beginning Grimod hardly bothers with what is the first port of call for any restaurant reviewer today: he doesn't describe the food; it almost seems that he hasn't even sampled it. But this is only a first step. Later on, when he recommends such establishments as the fashionable Rocher de Cancale (famous for its oysters) and the humbler Veau Qui Tète (famous for its *pied de mouton,* 'so marvellously prepared . . . that there is not a gourmand who at least one time in his life has not made a pilgrimage there') he will not be so reticent.[20] But even in his first step into restaurant-reviewing Grimod has alighted upon an essential structure, of which an analysis of the taste of the food is only one aspect among many others. The analysis will push, and the analysis will pull. It will be egoistical; but it will try to be communitarian. And the content of the analysis will turn on a variety of factors at once. We have already seen this in the structure of the restaurant itself. The structure is something that can be, even needs to be *assessed*. For it exists for the patron along various axes of meaning and value. Restaurant Véry, which will always take pride of place in the different volumes of the *Almanach* (though the Rocher de Cancale, owned by a good friend of Grimod's, Baleine, is the almanac's favourite and most frequently mentioned restaurant), is very high, dear and in, but not very now; it is unique and absolutely *there*, at the centre of Grimod's culinary world; but for all this it is also somewhat *exotic* or *unfamiliar*. One does not – one cannot – dine there *daily*. And in all these things it contrasts with its neighbour, except that the neighbour is also at, or rather just a few feet away from, the centre of things.

Another way of putting this is to say that in Grimod's hands, the restaurant review must above all be concerned with the restaurant's *social* function. That function is defined in part by the geography of the city, and in part by reference to the social (and for that matter geographic) location of the gourmand-critic, who among other things organizes dinners at the restaurant just off the centre of the social world of Paris, up the road from his mansion. But the social function of the restaurant depends on many other things as well. Internal characteristics, like the quality of the food and the comfort of the room, are essential. Good eating, *la bonne chère*, is above all what the reviewer wants to say yes to. Yet external characteristics, like popularity, are essential as well. For on the one hand, an external characteristic like popularity is indicative of *la bonne chère*. The best restaurants, Grimod writes in the seventh volume, attract the most customers. 'For the public has an instinct about these things which is difficult to divert; and any restaurateur who attracted a big crowd yesterday will be alone in his shop within a month, if his food stops being good, or if his employees stop giving good service.'[21] At the very least, popularity can become an element in the critic's rhetorical strategy. The critic can *argue* that a restaurant is good or bad simply by *observing* whether it is popular with the public. But on the other hand, popularity is an aspect of the restaurant's social function as a whole, and though the individual consumer may only require good food and service for himself and his companions, the critic has to be concerned with this larger topic. The critic has entered into a social compact. He has become part of a culinary system. He has a variety of interests to cultivate and serve. He needs to calibrate his observations with respect to the public that eats and the public that reads and even with respect to the culinary artists themselves, who are also eaters and readers, and whose own productiveness and artistry can be impacted by what the critic writes. He needs to make clear what saying yes to *la bonne chère* is all about, and to promote the systems and labours of production and consumption that saying yes to it ultimately requires. He thus needs to take price, popularity and the happiness of customers into account, and especially recommend those institutions where fashion, location, decor, service, price, popularity and happiness all find the best conjunction.

It all comes down to the fact that, in entering his social compact and acting as a model and advocate of gourmandism, Grimod is not interested in trying to identify something like 'the best restaurant in the world'. He is trying to provide a guide to restaurants for the rest of us. If our hearts have been made into gizzards and our sentiments into sensations, that is all very funny. But the revolution has also made us into a community, a community of gizzards and sensations, of consumers who need to inform themselves so that once the right moment comes they can say, 'We're going in'. And that great egoist and model bourgeois, the food writer, is at our service . . . up to a point.

That point, that limit beyond which he could not go, however, was reached early on. 'We are far from regarding as complete the list of establishments we have offered here,' he writes in the third volume of the *Almanach* (Grimod loves the royal 'we' in rhetorical situations like this), 'and artists and trades people in the art of food who are not included would be wrong to accuse us of injustice, negligence, or partiality. We have pointed out in good faith those which, in every genre, we have believed to be most worthy of being recommended to the public; and we have spared nothing to try to become acquainted with them all. But we do not flatter ourselves so far as to say we have succeeded, and we will always show ourselves ready to listen to complaints from those who can prove to us that we have not mentioned them in our book.'²² 'We have only endeavoured', says Grimod in the next year's edition, the fourth volume, 'to indicate for each genre those which, *to our knowledge*, have seemed to us the best; and however much the public has shown confidence up to now in the impartiality of our opinions, we are very far from passing judgements without right of appeal. Paris is so vast . . .'²³ This work of reviewing restaurants and other food providers 'requires so much running about for information, so many enquiries, so many cares of every kind the result of which is the discontentment of the parties concerned; for vanity creeps into all stations of life, and on this subject butchers and sausage-makers will soon be as sensitive as actors and poets. Everyone wants to be praised exclusively, often even at the expense of one's colleague or neighbour . . . and ordinarily it is the most mediocre artists who complain the loudest.'²⁴ 'We would have to travel down a very long road if we were to stop by all the good restaurants; for we must avow that there is a great number of them in Paris, and the number of them grows every year'.²⁵

The limits beyond which Grimod the gastronomic writer cannot go are primarily a result of his own situatedness as a critic, but they are also a consequence of the nature of the subject he has come to define as his theme. For once Grimod's project was under way, it took on a life of its own. The dining scene in Paris acquired a public image. It could be imagined (by the public) that there was a totality of food providers in the city, and that there could be a systematic view of this totality, within which all the establishments were rated by qualified critics according to rigorous and impartial criteria. But who could really provide this view? Well, said Grimod at one point, continuing his remark that the number of good restaurants continues to grow every year, 'we will speak here only of the most famous establishments, for those alone are the ones that should concern a gourmand'.²⁶ Or maybe even that is too generous a way of putting it. The number of restaurants, says Grimod in the seventh volume, published in 1810, 'is considerable, but there are few good ones. For our part we will only stop at the best and most celebrated.'²⁷ What else was Grimod to say? Despite his protestations to the contrary, we may suspect Grimod's good faith when he makes remarks like this. The fact is, in all ten years of the *Almanach* Grimod never mentions more than about three dozen restaurants. It may well be that those were the only ones worth 'stopping' at from Grimod's point of view, but we have to wonder what it was in that point of view that was so exclusionary. Grimod may begin by wanting to promote restaurants for the rest of us, but few of us are included in his 'us'. From the beginning Grimod is only interested in the dining scene of central Paris, and in the 'best' places to be found there – the ones worthy of 'gourmands really worthy' – and he will not 'stop' before any establishment that is located outside the peripheries of the central and the best.

Snobbery is not what brings Grimod up short. Grimod has no patience for unearned glory, and his social circle includes actors, writers and restaurateurs as well as individuals of a more respectable social standing. He lives with an actress whose father was a weaver, and as soon as his snobbish, disapproving mother dies he marries the woman. Moreover, he knows perfectly well that good food is not a preserve of the rich alone. 'A good soup is the dinner of a poor man, and the pleasure he has in it is often envied by the most opulent of men.'[28] As for restaurants, in the first volume, Grimod praises a restaurant near Les Halles of one Madame Grappe, for example, 'who every day attracts at her place five or six hundred customers'. For five sous she provides a 'very good dish', he says; in fact, 'she is the Véry of the poor'.[29] Grimod will distinguish between the opulent and the humble, but he will not praise an establishment simply because it is opulent, or condemn one simply because it is humble. He knows that restaurants serve social functions, and he knows there is more than one function worth fulfilling. He will even argue (in volume six) that a good reputation for culinary artistry has to be earned and even continually re-earned. It is a good thing that someone 'obscure, modest, and little known, but endowed with great zeal, may some day be responsible for producing work worthy of the greatest masters'.[30]

But if not snobbery, then, what? The fact is, Grimod cannot get away from the contradictions and constraints inherent to the project of criticism. Art is long, life is short and criticism is long rather than short too. Even if, as a result of his work, an image is generated of a limitless point of view, a totality of a world of dining, where everything and everyone can be rated, and where something like 'the best restaurants in Paris' can be determined, the restaurant reviewer is inherently limited with regard to time, space, labour power and interest, not to mention the resources at his disposal. The reviewer in fact *requires* the limits that are inherently imposed upon his work; he lives upon the limits that make it impossible to accomplish everything he sets out to accomplish. An unlimited point of view, the Divine point of view, simply would not have an *interest* in 'legitimating' the food trade in a nineteenth-century French city. Nor would a Supreme Being operating from the unlimited, divine point of view, have an interest in *writing* about it.

What motivated Grimod as much as anything else was his ungodlike interest in writing in and of itself. He had a utilitarian interest in writing in that he wanted to earn a living as an author, and he had an idealistic interest in it in that he had a genuine desire to promote the progress of gastronomy. But he also had an interest in writing for the sake of writing. Form for the sake of form was part of it. Grimod was given to what Jean-Claude Bonnet aptly calls a 'delirium of form'.[31] His black dinners and his philosophic *mercredis*, his intervention in gastronomy for the sake of promoting what he is not too shy to call 'progress', his explorations of the ethic and comedy of gourmandism, the *légitimations* he set up, where caterers brought in wares to be sampled by a *jury degustateur*, in mockery of the new systems of diplomacy in Napoleonic Europe, and even the new system of law now called the Napoleonic code – in mockery of them, but also in the same spirit as them, the spirit of bourgeois formularity[32] – all this, along with the inventiveness of his gastronomic writing, testified to a project of form for the sake of form. And whether in putting together a discourse on salads, a series of maxims on being a good host or a *promenade nutritif*, Grimod was endeavouring to create a literature and engage in literary play.

But the very consumer culture Grimod helped call into being would have its revenge. His readership forced him to change his style. 'The kind of jocularity proper to the first volume', he writes in his introduction to the third, 'is necessarily very restricting . . .'. 'Above all,' Grimod says, jocularity has to be dropped 'if one wants to avoid falling into farce or affectation'.[33] Farce and affectation, friends to him in his first volume because of what he was making fun of and also because in adopting jocularity he was able to make this new thing, gastronomic writing, into a serious art form, had now become impediments. It would be bad form to continue with the jokes; doing so would dissimulate the underlying seriousness of Grimod's writing, and jeopardize the trust he wants his readers to continue investing in him.

The readership would require changes in the content of the *Almanach* as well, especially with regard to the *Itinéraire nutritif*. In the second volume, no *Itinéraire* was included. Grimod simply didn't have the time or inclination to include one; he had already done that. In the third volume, he finds that he has to take up the food promenade again, though he does so with little gusto. Then in the fourth volume, though he continues to write about restaurants and other food purveyors, he drops the literary device of the promenade altogether. He has found, to his surprise, that the promenade is the most popular part of the *Almanach*. The promenade is the part that has 'excited the most interest, and presented to the majority of our readers the greatest objects of utility. Not only does this Itinerary please those who make the Capital their usual residence; but we know, and cannot doubt, that it has become the compass for gourmandism among inhabitants from the provinces, and even for foreigners who come here for a short visit.'[34] Note the metaphor of the 'compass'; the promenade has now become very much a 'guide', rather than a manual. 'It seems that true gourmands have shown a particular predilection for the two food promenades that are found in the first and third volumes of this work', Grimod reiterates. 'These are the articles that have been read with the most attention, reread with the most interest, and consulted the most often.'[35] For that reason, Grimod expands the guide for the fourth volume. But the literary device of the promenade in that case is too cumbersome. People want information, not a literary diversion. So the promenade becomes a *Petit Revue gourmande*. The literary conceit of a promenade is dropped; and Grimod puts his effort into listing information about different food providers. No more do we see him in Les Halles eyeing the turbots, or walking about the Tuilleries, stopping for ices, or taking a gander into the sumptuous vestibule of the Restaurant Véry. He is all business now, or tries to be.

Reading through the later volumes, one finds that Grimod's personality is irrepressible. Even when he stops walking about and restrains his sense of humour, Grimod continues speaking through a narrative voice full of gentle irony. He is fond of anecdotes about stupendous appetites and gastronomic obsessions. But sometimes even the irony dissipates. Grimod cannot afford to be misunderstood any more; he does not want to be accused of writing 'nonsense', or of not being impartial and, in his impartiality, of not being supportive of the food business. And so, eventually, weariness sets in. 'We cannot hide the fact', he writes at the beginning of volume five, '. . . that the more we advance in this career, the more we feel how difficult it is to proceed with the same measure of enjoyment and originality that people have kindly recognized in our first volume.' It is true that the *Almanach* continues selling well, so Grimod perseveres, but in a minor key. 'After having picked the flower of our subject, we have attempted now to exploit its fruits, and at least then to provide instruction to gourmands, even if we are no longer able to amuse them.'[36]

In the end, Grimod can barely face the task of 'exploiting the fruits' of the *Itinéraire nutritif* any more. The *Petite Revue gourmande* continues to be the most popular part of the *Almanach*, he says at the beginning of volume six. 'It is this consideration that has forced us to give each year a new itinerary, even if it is not and cannot be much changed from before, and is little more than a repetition of what preceded it.' The work is hard, and yet it is repetitious and annoying. 'It is easy to see how the writing of this part of the volume is not what most amuses the author.'[37]

He is even running out of things to write about. Since the last edition of the *Almanach des gourmands*, he says as early as volume five, 'the alimentary topography of Paris has undergone very few changes'. If he keeps on with the *revue* it is only because the food shops and restaurants as well as his readers need it. The *revue* continues to promote providers worth promoting. And it is only for this reason that 'we overcome our repugnance at treating for a fourth time a subject that is useful rather than inspiring, and that gives the writer the mere opportunity of reproducing a lexicon accompanied by reflections, the form of which is very difficult to vary'.[38] On the one hand, the reality of the restaurant and food-shop world of Paris is that it doesn't change very much, not any more at least. It doesn't offer much fresh material. On the other, writing itself, as Grimod is committed to it, requires novelty and variation. Writing is *creative* – and as Grimod is finding out, on its own terms it is more creative than food shops and restaurants can ever be. 'There have been very few changes in the culinary ranks', he thus repeats in volume seven.[39] So this *revue,* this itinerary, 'can scarcely each year afford but the same picture. And yet is necessary to vary its form, and say just about the same thing as before in different words: which, for a writer, is much more onerous than composing new material in prose.'[40]

The food world moves more slowly than Grimod's imagination requires. Cookery and food service do not involve an 'art' whose works can change from performance to performance in the the way that, say, theatre can. (As I urged in the previous chapter, the restaurant of standing has to preserve its institutionalism by always being the *same* as itself.) Man the consumer can keep eating, and keep eating well. And restaurants will keep supplying *la bonne chère.* But the writer will run out of things to say. 'We cannot hide from the fact that however vast the material we are dealing with, we have already ravished the flower of it in our earlier volumes . . .'.[41] Art is long, life is short, the imagination of the 'man of letters' is quick – always varying, always formulating, always eager for new things to write about and new ways to express itself. And yet, in spite of the needs of the writer, food is slow.

And so in the end, Grimod quit the field. He was bored. The gastronomic writing his situation imposed upon him did not provide enough opportunity for creativity. In 1812 his mother died, leaving enough of an inheritance that Grimod was able to acquire an estate in the country, marry his working-class mistress and retire from the city. A lawsuit for libel may have been filed against him; certainly he had made some enemies while trying to be an arbiter of Parisian fashion. Whatever happened, Grimod clearly left Paris with a bitter taste in his mouth. And he never wrote a word of criticism for public consumption again.

We will encounter a number of restaurant critics in the course of the chapters to follow, professional and amateur. Most of them owe nothing to Grimod, for his books are very rare today, even in research libraries, and they have never been translated in full into a language other than French. Grimod was certainly an inspiration to his contemporary Brillat-Savarin, whose often translated and reissued *Physiology of Taste* is much better known today, and who *has* been an inspiration to many food writers. But Brillat-Savarin was not a restaurant critic. And Brillat-Savarin popularized an idea that Grimod could not have accepted: that there is nothing contradictory about gourmandism and gastronomy, that the practice of taste in the modern world does not involve a system of social inequality or a tension between the particular and the universal, between the artist and commerce, and between the needs of writing and the needs of readers. For Brillat-Savarin 'gastronomy' was not an 'art'; it was a 'science'. Nor was it a small part of human life; gastronomy was supposed to govern 'the whole of life of man'. It was as if that which was most absolutely situated about a person – his eating and drinking in a specific time and place, in keeping with a specific structure of social life – could be generalized and elevated into Divine Doctrine, or its secular substitute, Universal Science.

Grimod would have liked to believe something along these lines, for it would have made life easier for him. After all, it was in the practice of gastronomy, and in writing about it, that his gifts were greatest. Moreover, Grimod himself felt the desire to elevate the 'animal pleasures' into something higher and finer, to 'legitimate' the products of consumption and to provide a model of good practices for citizens bereft of its old aristocracy. He tried to insist on principles and objectivity. Writing on food in the Napoleonic era, and even following Napoleonic practices in the pursuit of form, ceremony, objectivity and universality, Grimod was in a way the Napoleon of gourmandism. But Grimod also knew that there was something hollow at the core of his ambition, and something socially self-contradictory in the very practice of trying to act on behalf of the public by trying to write in the spirit of the will to form. There was something *funny* about it even when he had to adopt a tone of objective *seriousness*. To carry on with the ambition was to risk one's integrity for the sake of surplus pleasure – and so, it would seem, he had to quit. He would not be the last restaurant critic in the world to find himself or herself in such a quandary. For eating in restaurants and writing about them are not only dependent on one another; they are also adversaries, each seeking to satisfy needs of its own.

three

Nausea

One hundred and twenty years later we find ourselves in the fictional town of Bouville, on the north coast of France. We are in the midst of the novel by Jean-Paul Sartre, *Nausea* (1938). This is Sartre's first literary success, a landmark at once in the fiction of self-consciousness and in the development of a type of philosophy that was soon to be dubbed 'existentialism'. It is a very intense piece of work although very little, in a traditional novelistic sense, actually happens in it. A man of thirty named Antoine Roquentin has come to this town of Bouville to research the biography of a local political figure, who thrived during the Enlightenment. Roquentin is a loner. 'I live alone, entirely alone. I never speak to anyone, never; I receive nothing, I give nothing', he writes in his diary.[1] He spends most of his time in the library, or else by himself (apart from occasional trysts with a local woman) in the cafes of Bouville, a fictionalized version of the old port city of Le Havre.

But Roquentin has been invited to lunch. A 'Self-Taught Man', a bureaucrat who spends his spare time in the town library reading through all its books in alphabetical order, has asked him to be his guest. Roquentin accepted the invitation hesitantly. He doesn't really like the Self-Taught Man, whose earnestness and suspect sexuality puts him off. (Roquentin is a bit of a homophobe, and the Self-Taught Man, it will be discovered, is homosexually inclined.) 'I had as much desire to eat with him as I had to hang myself', Roquentin writes. But Roquentin cannot refuse, and there they are, at an establishment called Maison Bottanet.[2]

Outside the door to the restaurant a young couple are studying a menu held by a cardboard chef, deciding whether to go in. Meanwhile inside, seated across from the Self-Taught Man, Roquentin has been studying the same thing:

> *Maison Bottanet, cuisine bourgeoise.*
> *Le déjeuner à prix fixe: 8 francs.*
> *Hors-d'oeuvre au choix.*
> *Viande garni.*
> *Fromage ou dessert*
> *140 francs les 20 cachets*

It is interesting that the translator, working in America in the late 1940s, has left this menu in French. It is as if there were no American-English equivalent for it. In other places the capable translator, Lloyd Alexander, has removed the narrator's nonchalant obscenities, *merdre, con, baiser*,* replacing them with more polite English equivalents – for example, turning the verb *baiser* from 'fuck' into 'kiss'. Here he has chosen to put the American or English reader face to face with the foreign, as if the English equivalents of the original French were obscene. And perhaps he is correct: 'middle class cooking, fixed price lunch, choice of appetizers, meat with vegetable . . .' It doesn't sound quite right.

In any case, in a provincial town based on Le Havre, the restaurant is so established that the French novelist can take it for granted. The common restaurant serving *cuisine bourgeoise* is a place where people like the bureaucrat regularly go for their midday meal, choosing to save a little money by ordering the *prix fixe* and buying it in advance by the coupon, twenty coupons at a time. The Bouville that the novelist has recreated is well populated with restaurants and cafes, and Roquentin (who should *not*, by the way, be identified with Sartre) is in his element among them. Nevertheless, Roquentin is not comfortable in the company of the stranger who has invited him here, and even the restaurant Maison Bottanet, so similar to so many other restaurants he has been to, seems alien.

Something dramatic has come over Roquentin over the past few weeks. The whole world has gone strange. He is even strange to himself. His powers of observation have undergone a transformation. He sees and feels more than he used to do. But the things he sees and feels are surreally out of kilter. He has lately been experiencing what he calls 'the Nausea', a sickly sweetish feeling during which it seems that the world about him is, if not reeling, at least disturbingly detached, torn from the context that his normal powers of perception and ratiocination usually place them in, dispossessed of the *meaning* he has been accustomed to give for them. As a psychologist would say, Roquentin's world has become 'de-personalized'. Yet here he is, in a restaurant, like so many other restaurants, a fixed social institution, among other persons.

Two men have just lit cigarettes and got up from the table next to the heater. 'They leave, there they are in the pure air, in the sunlight. They pass along the wide windows, holding their hats in both hands. They laugh; the wind bellies out their overcoats.' At 'the round table near the door' sits a man whom Roquentin recognizes. 'From time to time he looks at me, attentive and smiling; but he doesn't see me; he is too absorbed in his food.' On the other side of the room, 'two squat, red-faced men are eating mussels and drinking white wine', laughing among themselves. The choice of mussels is for the novelist an important detail. 'Near the window, a slight, dark-complexioned man with distinguished features and fine white hair, brushed back, reads his paper thoughtfully . . . He drinks Vichy water.' So, the restaurant is populated. Customers absorbed in their own lives, aware of each others' presence yet not quite *seeing* one another, politely animate the room. Eventually the young couple will come in, announcing themselves to the room with the automatic courtesy: 'Messieurs, dames', the young man will say.

It is time to order something to eat. Ordering off the *prix fixe* menu limits Roquentin's choices. 'I am allowed one hors-d'oeuvre: either five slices of sausage or radishes or shrimps, or a dish of stuffed celery. Snails are extra.' Roquentin is not bothered by the fact that his options are limited, and orders the sausages, but the Self-Taught Man takes offence. He wants his guest to order something less parsimonious. 'Isn't there something better?' he interjects. 'Here are Bourgogne snails.'

'I don't care too much for snails.'

'Ah! What about oysters?'

'They're four francs more', says the waitress.

'All right, oysters, Mademoiselle – and radishes for me.'

'Blushing', the Self-Taught Man explains to Roquentin, 'I like radishes very much'.

Again, the choice of foods is significant: sumptuous, slimy oysters ('slime' is important in the world of Sartre's philosophy of existence – hence the mussels as well)[3] versus humble, crunchy, bitter radishes. The choice of the items is significant both with regard to the nature of the items in themselves, and with regard to their expense, the Self-Taught Man awkwardly trying to show hospitality by ordering the dearest item he can. The Self-Taught Man's presumptuousness in choosing what Roquentin will have to eat is significant too. Instead of being content with what Roquentin desires, the Self-Taught Man operates according to a higher law of hospitality, which paradoxically rejects the desire of the person to whom hospitality is being shown. The Self-Taught Man insists upon being identified with this higher law, which says to the guest, I will spare you nothing, I will make you this gift, which you cannot repay, which you can only enjoy, and in order to do so I will compel you to desire what I desire you to desire. Nor does Self-Taught Man relent in imposing his higher hospitality for the following course. Ordering *boeuf en daube** for himself, which tempts Roquentin as well, the Self-Taught Man insists on ordering for his guest a *poulet chasseur,** which is the only meat dish on the menu that costs extra. Moreover, he insists on ordering wine (a cheap *rosé d'Anjou**), though when he does so the waitress sassily protests 'Well! Times have changed. You never drank any before.'

One hundred and twenty years after the last edition of the *Almanach des gourmands*, we can see that the restaurant has become a site not only of consumption but also of a host of social transactions. According to our topology of the restaurant, the Maison Bottanet is moderately priced yet sophisticated (inclining toward 'the high'), familiar and common yet not unfashionable, somewhat *casual* yet very much *now*, and certainly very much *here*. But what does all this mean? From the point of view of our observer, the alienated Roquentin, all of this is upside down. He has the sense of being in a place that is all too expensive (since the cost is so high to him, the acceptance of a display of hospitality he does not want to accept), that is unfamiliar rather than familiar (since everything is so *strange*), and that has nothing to do with anything so potentially seductive as fashion. This restaurant, in addition, is actually formal rather than casual (since it makes so many demands on courteousness, on the observance of ceremony), and it impresses on him a need for resistance, a feeling, as it were, of wishing to be, or perhaps actually being, *not now* and *not here*. The food is not what disturbs him at first. What rankles is the way the people in the restaurant are entering into their transactions with themselves and others. This common and not unpleasant establishment has come to be a pretext for the exercise of what Sartre in his major philosophic work, *Being and Nothingness*, would come to call 'bad faith'.[4]

'Bad faith' is Sartre's term for moral self-deception, and the Self-Taught Man's egregious hospitality is only the most obvious example. Bad faith is a way of escaping from oneself by lying to oneself about who one is and what one does. In the case of the Self-Taught Man's clumsy hospitality, bad faith enters into what the man does so far as he attempts to tell himself and all those around him that he is a naturally generous man. What is wrong is not only that he trying to impress Roquentin and the waitress, but also that he is trying to impress himself. His awkwardness betrays him, but it is not the awkwardness itself that constitutes bad faith; rather, it is the lie that the awkwardness betrays.

There is more bad faith in other aspects of the Self-Taught Man's behaviour and more bad faith, generally, in the dining room. The Self-Taught Man tells Roquentin about himself and his principles. He is a humanist and a socialist. He loves humankind. He loves learning, wit, poetry, science. He strives very hard to impress all this upon Roquentin. And again, as Roquentin will come to see, while the Self-Taught Man is involved in all these protestations in order to get something out of Roquentin, it is only because he is trying at the same time to get something out of himself. With regard to what he wants out of Roquentin – recognition, empathy, friendship, admiration, obligation – the Self-Taught Man is operating for the sake of what *Being and Nothingness* calls 'being-for-others'. But with regard to himself, with regard to what *Being and Nothingness* calls a person's 'being-for-self', the Self-Taught Man is endeavouring to continue playing a game of deception; he is pretending to himself to be what he is not.

It is only gradually that all of this dawns on Roquentin. There are other scenes of transaction. The couple walk in, and they are the cynosure of everybody's gaze – youthful, attractive, well-dressed. And the couple enjoys the experience: 'They are quiet, happy at being together, happy at being seen together.' There is of course no hiding in a restaurant this size, in the middle of the day. Being in a place where it is impossible to hide, as Roquentin realizes, is part of the attraction of being in a restaurant, if also one of its pitfalls. Roquentin is caused to remember the time he spent with his old girlfriend Anny in London some years back: 'Sometimes when Anny and I went into a restaurant in Piccadilly we felt ourselves the objects of admiring attention. It annoyed Anny, but I must confess that I was somewhat proud.' In the here and now, in Bouville, the people in the restaurant glance with longing at this young couple in their own way. The man with the newspaper gives them a 'profound look'. The waitress meanwhile struggles to give them professional attention. 'Before the waitress, who had run up to help [the young man], could make a move, the young man slipped out of his raincoat . . . The waitress, a little disappointed, turns to the young woman. But once more he is ahead of her and helps the girl out of her coat with gentle, precise movements.' Roquentin, for his part, is caused to reflect on himself while also carefully observing the couple as they sit down at the table next to him, recognizing that although he too has an impulse to admire them, he does not admire them. He only observes. 'I am at the age to be touched by the youth of others. But I am not touched.' Indeed, watching them flirt with one another – he has already deduced that the couple is just getting acquainted – he is repelled. 'They are touching [to me], but they also make me a little sick. I feel them so far from me . . .'

The young couple is engaged in the transaction of courtship, and Roquentin is by turns moved and disgusted – *touché** and *écoeuré** – by the spectacle. 'They are comfortable, they look with assurance at the yellow walls, the people, and they find the world pleasant as it is just as it is, and each of them, temporarily, draws life from the other. Soon the two of them will make a single life, a slow, tepid life which will have no sense at all – but they won't notice it.' Their 'not noticing' is what disturbs Roquentin. Apart from being affected by his own melancholy (this novel was originally entitled *Melancholia*), a depression which makes him find, like Hamlet, that 'all the uses of the world' are 'weary, stale, flat, and unprofitable', Roquentin is sadly learning that most people, himself included, go through life without paying attention to what they are actually doing, and so pretend to themselves that they are actually doing something else. They are in bad faith. 'They annoy me,' he comments after a while of eavesdropping on the couple's conversation. 'They're going to sleep together. They know it. Each one knows that the other knows it. But since they are young, chaste, and decent, since each one wants to keep his self-respect and that of the other, since love is a great poetic thing which you must not frighten away, several times a week they go to dances and restaurants, offering the spectacle of their ritual, mechanical dances . . .'

Roquentin's observations anticipate one of the three main examples that Sartre will use in *Being and Nothingness* on the matter of what he calls 'bad faith': a man and woman (in a restaurant, apparently), where the man makes quietly aggressive gestures of seduction and the woman pretends that she does not notice or understand what the man is doing. The woman pretends that her companion is not trying to seduce her, in order not only to make a kind of impression on the man (saying to him, in effect, 'I politely decline to acknowledge your gestures of seduction – so far') but also to make an impression on herself (saying to herself, 'I am not here in order to be seduced by my companion'). It is harmless from the point of view of conventional ethics; it may even be wisely utilitarian, a good way of paying homage to the reality principle. By pretending not to notice what the man is doing – holding her hand, among other things – the woman is keeping the peace. But so far as she really believes that she is not noticing what the man is doing, she is acting in bad faith. She chooses not to know what she knows. She makes an active choice to be inactive, and impassively allows him to grip her hand without responding.

The young couple in Bouville are actually *mutually* in bad faith. They are doing the kind of thing people have to do in order to get through life. 'After all,' says Roquentin, 'you have to kill time. They are young and well built, they have enough to last them another thirty years. So they're in no hurry, they delay and they are not wrong. Once they have slept together they will have to find something else to veil the enormous absurdity of their existence.' But Roquentin wonders, 'Still . . . is it absolutely necessary to lie?'

He is concerned, at last, with the fact that this kind of self-deception is universal. Consider the restaurant as a whole. 'I glance around the room. What a comedy! All these people sitting there, looking serious, eating. No, they aren't eating: they are recuperating in order to successfully finish their tasks. Each one of them has a personal difficulty which keeps him from noticing that he exists . . .'

Roquentin's 'what a comedy' may remind us of the nineteenth-century gastronome who made much the same remark, though for less cynical purposes. In the French *La Nausée*, however, Roquentin actually says, 'C'est une farce!'*

A comedy, whether the comedy of the day in the life of a gastronome, or the 'human comedy' of Balzac, or the comedy of social life that sociologists like Erving Goffman call our attention to, is something to rejoice in. For Balzac as for the sociologist of everyday life, 'all the world is a stage' and all of us are 'players'. As a 'comedy' social life is a kind of game through which we attempt to achieve a series of happy endings. The restaurant, as Goffman pointed, is just that kind of game, a theatrical event, divided between a front-of-house (where servers serve and diners eat) and a backstage (where cooks cook and servers and cooks have to deal with one another). At front-of-house and backstage alike the actors are playing, though according to very different rules. Front-of-house is a place of decorum, service, courtesy and hospitality balanced against self-interest and self-indulgence. Backstage is another matter: restaurant kitchens are notoriously scenes of bad manners, practical jokes, insult, obscenity and rage. But both the refined scene of the dining room and the unrefined scene of the kitchen are theatres where a kind of comedy is being acted. Happy endings are sought; playacting is required; and everyone seems to understand this. To be in a restaurant, in any capacity, is to play – and in this respect I think it would be right to consider the idea of 'play' both in terms of the pursuit of enjoyment and in terms of the theatricality or gamesmanship through which the happy ending is sought.[5]

But Roquentin says, 'What a farce!', and a 'farce' is something different. It is 'a ridiculous or empty show, a mockery', say the dictionaries, talking about the wider use of the word to which Roquentin appeals. On the stage a farce differs from a comedy in that the former is played for laughs alone; in a farce it doesn't much matter if anyone has a happy ending, or if the audience goes home reassured about the aims of life. The relevant article in Wikipedia adds that a farce tends to show people as being 'vain, irrational, venal, infantile, and prone to automatic behaviour'.[6]

What a farce! Roquentin's outlook is a challenge at once to himself and to the world. What would one have to *be* and what would one have to *do* in order not to participate in a farce, a ridiculous performance of bad faith? How would one have to *live*? How would one have to *exist*?

Just in the context of the world of the restaurant Roquentin's outlook poses a challenge. If all the world is really a stage, and the restaurant is one of its scenes, is all the world, and the restaurant along with it, really a farce? Or is there some alternative? What would it mean for a restaurant *not* to be a farce – for the people in it, through which it exists as a continuing social performance, *not* to show themselves 'vain, irrational, venal, infantile, and prone to automatic behaviour', and engaged in a 'mechanical ritual'? What would it mean for *homo restauranticus* not to live in bad faith? What would it mean to use the restaurant in *good faith*? And what would it mean not simply to 'recuperate' but *really to eat*, as Roquentin puts it? How might we might reassure ourselves that the restaurant is or at least can be the *comedy* we prefer it to be?

The scene continues. Roquentin and the Self-Taught Man converse, Roquentin trying simply to get through this lunch without causing offence, the Self-Taught Man endeavouring to reveal his soul, and to enlist Roquentin's support. The humanist talks about his humanism, his socialism, his love of humankind. He makes a confession, but Roquentin isn't buying it. 'All men are my friends', the Self-Taught Man says. But Roquentin has noted that the Self-Taught Man is a loner, and that his affection toward 'men' is probably sexually motivated. This confession is false: more bad faith. The problem isn't humanism, socialism or love. The problem is that the Self-Taught Man's lofty sentiments are hollow and inconsistent. 'His eyes question me', Roquentin says; 'I nod approval, but I feel he is a little disappointed, that he would like more enthusiasm. What can I do? Is it my fault if, as he speaks, I recognise the lack of the genuine article?' Inside the soul of the Self-Taught Man Roquentin sees the spirits of a whole company of different kinds of humanists, socialists and philanthropists, all making lofty but contradictory claims, demanding recognition and enthusiasm. In fact, the different men inside him 'all hate each other: as individuals, naturally not as men. But the Self-Taught Man doesn't know it: he has locked them up inside himself like cats in a bag and they are tearing each other in pieces without his noticing it.'

Not content with making his confession, offering Roquentin that one additional gift of himself, along with the oysters and the *poulet chasseur*, that cannot be reciprocated, the Self-Taught Man tries to wrest from Roquentin a similar confession. Of course he does not want Roquentin genuinely to confess; he wants Roquentin to say, 'Yes, I am a man just like you. I feel just like you. I agree with everything you say'. The Self-Taught Man, to put it in philosophic terms, wants confirmation of his own selfhood in the selfhood of the Other. I have told you my beliefs and feelings, he says in effect; now you tell me yours; but tell me them in such a way that what you are doing is really mirroring my own beliefs and feelings. And that is not all: confess yourself in such a way that I can assimilate you, annihilate you. Do not assert yourself as you really are. Rather assert yourself only so far as I can eat you up. It is all 'a trap', writes Roquentin, and if the Self-Taught Man wins at the game he is playing, 'I am immediately turned round, reconstituted, overtaken . . .' You can't even protest against him. 'If you oppose him head on, you play his game; he lives off his opponents. There is a race of beings, limited and headstrong, who lose to him every time: he digests all their violences and worst excesses; he makes a white frothy lymph of them.'

All resistance is futile. 'You will excuse me,' the Self-Taught Man says with a laugh, presumably at the comedy (and not the farce) being performed in the dining room, 'but when I think of the depth of my love for people, of the force which impels me towards them, and when I see us here, reasoning, arguing . . . it makes me want to laugh.' By this time the two interlocutors are on their dessert course. Roquentin has bravely made his way through his *poulet chasseur*, which he had allowed to go cold and sticky. Now he has ordered cheese.

'I keep quiet', Roquentin says, 'I smile constrainedly. The waitress puts a plate of chalky Camembert in front of me. I glance around the room and a violent disgust floods me. What am I doing here? Why did I have to get mixed up in a discussion on humanism? Why are these people here? Why are they eating? It's true they don't know they exist. I want to leave, go to some place where I will be really in my own niche, where I will fit in . . . But my place is nowhere; I am unwanted, *de trop* . . .'

The Self-Taught Man goes on, insisting that deep down Roquentin too really loves humankind. 'With difficulty I chew a piece of bread which I can't make up my mind to swallow. People. You must love people. Men are admirable. I want to vomit – and suddenly, there it is: the Nausea.'

The question raised by *Nausea* is two-fold. What would make the theatre of the restaurant into an occasion of good faith rather than bad, of comedy rather than farce? And what at the same time would make eating at a restaurant really *eating*? Or in other words, what would prevent us from responding to the restaurant with nausea?

It doesn't matter that few of us who frequent restaurants think of ourselves as acting in bad faith when we do so. Much less does it matter that few of us respond to eating in a restaurant by existential nausea, a feeling of detachment and contempt, of apprehension and disgust. Nor does it matter that though Sartre raises these questions for us, he doesn't answer them, neither in *Nausea* nor in any of his subsequent works. Sartre was never able to compose a study of 'existentialist ethics', even after his 1943 magnum opus, *Being and Nothingness*, suggested that an ethics was the next thing required of the pattern of thought he had embarked on.[7] What matters is that the question is there, the question exists, whether in the context of the modern restaurant or any other scene of modern life. How is it possible to live *in society*, with *other people*, Sartre wants to know? And how is it possible *to live*? Indeed, how is it possible *to be*?

One of the problems with food studies and food writing in general is the temptation to use a love of food as a pretext for an escape from seriousness. Of course, there are subjects in food studies that are always treated with seriousness, like world hunger and environmental degradation. (These are the kinds of subjects, by the way, that the later Sartre would exhort us to take a stand on, and for the sake of which to engage in civil disobedience.) But eating oysters? Drinking *rosé*? Much of the best food writing is created by people who choose to write about the enjoyment of food as the *other dimension* of life, that is as *play*. Nor would it seem that they are wrong to do so. Sartre himself is a believer in play for the sake of play. Sartre in fact warns us against adopting the opposite disguise of high-mindedness, the seriousness of the moralist or reformist, which may serve as yet another mask behind which bad faith may prosper. A 'principal result' of his work, he says at the end of *Being and Nothingness*, 'must be to make us repudiate the *spirit of seriousness*'.[8] The contrary spirit of play is essential in all things human, even if play in many circumstances can be a pretext for fleeing from the authentic business of the self.

But here, then, is a deeper matter. How do you separate comedy from farce, good play from bad play, joy from flight, engagement from disengagement? How do you know that your play and your enjoyment is undertaken in good faith rather than bad, that it is in effect *comically serious play* rather than *farcical dissimulation*? What do you have to think, do, and be in order not to be disgusted by the whole thing? How can we *continue playing* in view of all the doubts that we can raise about its motives, purposes, and results? How can we go on eating our oysters and drinking our *rosé* (or, all right, our Chablis Premier Cru) when it is obvious that doing so is a pretext for a transaction of bad faith? How can we *really eat* when we know, for example, that in doing so we are accepting the hospitality of a stranger whose hospitality is really a dissimulation and even a kind of con game. *I will give you those oysters, I will enlist the help of a whole room of strangers in order to give you those oysters, including an attentive waitress, so I can eat you up* . . . On the one hand, giving and receiving hospitality is of the very essence of the world of the restaurant. On the other, the rigour of the moralist and the philosopher cautions us that the giving and receiving and all the other activities within the context of the restaurant are inherently farcical. We may well demean ourselves whenever we play the game. Certainly we may well dissimulate when we play the game, hide from each other and hide from ourselves. It is possible that we are not even really eating.

Sartre would never have devoted himself to analysing restaurants and restaurant behaviour in and of themselves – semiotics was not his thing, although he admired the work of Gaston Bachelard and at the end of *Being of Nothingness* calls for a 'psychoanalysis of objects'. But Sartre was very much, like Roquentin, in his element when inhabiting the world of restaurants. It is important to remember that, lest we mistake his meaning. Sartre was famous for being a regular patron of several restaurant-cafes on the left bank in Paris, as was his alter ego in the *Roads to Freedom* trilogy, the Parisian philosopher Matthieu.[9] And he seems to have been an avid consumer of comestibles, although he was not a gourmet. In *Being and Nothingness*, one of his other main examples of 'bad faith' involves a homosexual who will not admit to himself that he is homosexual, like the Self-Taught Man in *Nausea*, who goes on about his love of mankind instead of his love of men. But Sartre's other, most famous example is a waiter in a cafe:

Let us consider this waiter in the café. His movement is quick and forward, a little too precise, a little too rapid. He comes toward the customers with a step a little too quick. He bends forward a little too eagerly; his voice, his eyes express an interest a little too solicitous for the order of the client. Finally there he returns, trying to imitate in his walk the inflexible stiffness of some kind of automaton while carrying his tray with the recklessness of a tight-rope walker by putting it in a perpetually unstable, perpetually broken equilibrium which he perpetually re-establishes by a light movement of the arm and hand. All his behaviour seems to us a game. He applies himself to linking his movements as if they were mechanisms, the one regulating the other; his gestures and even his voice seem to be mechanisms; he gives himself the quickness and pitiless rapidity of things. He is playing, he is amusing himself. But what is he playing? We need not watch long before we can explain it: he is playing at *being* a waiter in a café.[10]

We have seen a little bit of this over-compensating behaviour in the waitress in *Nausea*. She finds herself distressed when the young man removes his own coat instead of letting her do it, and once again distressed when the young man removes his date's coat before the waitress can do so. The artificiality of her behaviour, the fact that she is *playing* at being a waitress, though not perhaps aware that she is doing so, is made evident in a situation where her role is undermined by people who *do not play along*. I am here to take off your coat. Why are you not letting me take off your coat? What else can I *do*? Otherwise, of course, the waitress in *Nausea* does not give us this impression of over-compensation. Roquentin never comments on her the way he comments on the other people in the dining room. She shows herself to be so competent that her behaviour never seems to need commenting on. She even allows herself to get a little sassy with her customers, as when she talks back to the Self-Taught Man.

But the waitress's apparent competence, her apparent naturalness in her role, should not distract us from noting the possibility of bad faith in her own existence, nor from noting the possibility of bad faith in other people's responses to her. It is significant that the novel only calls her 'the waitress'. It is one of the conditions of her existence for the purposes of the story being told that she does not have a name, and apparently does not need one either. She is playing her role successfully. If the waiter in the cafe engages in a kind of 'pitiless rapidity', and so plays at being a waiter, the waitress too engages in gestures of performativity; her sassiness is in fact a part of her performance.

There are several issues involved here. One is the issue of the *signifier* of bad faith. The cafe waiter signifies his artificiality by his overweening attentiveness to what he is doing, his being too quick, too stiff and so on. The waiter's automatic behaviour, when one observes it, *signifies* bad faith. Similarly with the waitress in the restaurant; her distress in one situation and her sassiness in another betray bad faith. But being overweening in one's performance of a social role is not *itself* bad faith. That is only its signifier: what betrays the bad faith in the eyes of the other. Caught in the gaze of the other, a disciplinary kind of gaze as it were – Sartre and Foucault are not dissimilar on this topic – the waiter and the waitress show off their bad faith, even if that is not their intention.

But there are other issues to consider then besides the nature of the signifier. For in fact, even if the waiter and the waitress succeeded in altogether disguising the artificiality of their behaviour, even if they played their roles to perfection, with the naturalism of a professional actor, they could still be in bad faith. Bad faith is something underneath any sign of it which we may detect, what Sartre will later call 'an inner disintegration in the heart of being'.[11] We *see* it in the waiter and waitress, for their roles involve a certain kind of acting. But the bad faith is not *in* what we see; it is in what we infer to be inside what we see, and therefore actually invisible; it is in the servers' relation to their own selves. However the servers play their roles, they can and perhaps must be living in bad faith, for no one can really *be* the social role he or she plays, according to Sartre, and the more successfully anyone performs that role the more alienated the person probably *is*. Moreover, Sartre is not talking about something to which servers are particularly prone, or which we are only likely to observe in a small number of cases of waiting and waitressing. Sartre is talking about a general condition. 'There is nothing there' in the waiter's behaviour, he writes, 'to surprise us. The child plays with his body in order to explore it, to take inventory of it; the waiter in the café plays with his condition in order to *realise* it.'[12]

Bad faith is a condition of human action; for it is in the nature of every human being, as Sartre puts it throughout *Being and Nothingness*, to be what one is not, and not to be what one is. And therefore you will find bad faith just about anywhere you look. As for the cafe waiter, or his ally the waitress in the Maison Bottanet, what we are observing is a particular instance, a particular mode, of the human necessity. It is a necessity that attacks us from all sides, for what the waiter does is both *internally* and *externally* required. Having a role to play, internally, required to be what he is not, the waiter is playing with the role he plays. That allows him to 'realize' it, and therefore also to represent it, to show it to others. And from a certain point of view we will want to commend him for it. Compare him to the server in a restaurant who is too shy to do her job, who hangs back languorously and waits for the customer to take charge (I encounter this a lot with young servers in Britain) or with the server who is fearless but inobsequiously off-key. You encounter the latter a lot in America. 'Hi, I am Bob, I'm not feeling well today, I've got a cold, and you won't believe what my sister said to me this morning, can I take your order?' The waiter who plays with the role he is playing – who self-consciously toys with a role that he is obliged to play in any case – is more likely a good waiter than a bad one. He is the kind of waiter you want! And for his own part, too, you can see, 'he is amusing himself'. Everyone who has ever worked successfully in the service industry has had to learn what Sartre's waiter has learned: in order to be happy in your job, you have to do a *good* job, and to do a good job you have to embrace what you are doing, you have to be amused at your own performance.[13]

But the 'obligation' in all this, Sartre insists, is two-sided. The waiter is obliged to himself to play with the role he is playing. He is obliged to play it internally, for the sake of being happy in his job. But he is obliged externally to the public and his employer as well. On the one side, the waiter has to play with playing in order to *be* what he is playing; on the other side, he has to play with playing because that is what his customers (and his boss) *demand* of him. They demand that he *not* be what he really is. 'And this obligation is not different from that which is imposed on all tradesmen', Sartre adds. 'Their condition is wholly one of ceremony. The public demands of them that they realise it as ceremony; there is the dance of the grocer, of the tailor, of the auctioneer, by which they endeavour to persuade their clientele that they are nothing but a grocer, an auctioneer, a tailor. A grocer who dreams is offensive to the buyer, because such a grocer is not wholly a grocer.' The case of the dreaming grocer is similar to that of the waiter who suffers from a cold and a hurtful sister, or even (to cite a proverbial case which I think is unfair but which in its unfairness helps illustrate the point) a waiter who shows himself to be dreaming of becoming a famous actor on Broadway. 'Society demands' that the tradesman be a tradesman, 'that the grocer limit himself to his function as a grocer . . . There are indeed many precautions to imprison a man in what he is, as if we lived in fear that he might escape from it, that he might break away and suddenly elude his condition.'[14]

Two-sided, and ambiguously so. Sartre is sliding around a little in his discussion, but as he does so, he comes upon the extremely important issue of social coercion. This is a topic that goes back for us to the 'slaves' who are required to feed the members of the gastronomic eating society in order that the latter can be free, and to beat each other up in order to establish a hierarchy of submission. But Sartre's critique of social coercion itself gets a bit ambiguous, for it actually involves a condemnation of two different things without pausing to make a clear distinction between them: subservience and ceremony. The problem with the grocer who dreams, or the waiter who wants to be an actor, is partly the problem of a failure in subservience: the grocer or the waiter who is *more* than just a grocer or a waiter makes a claim of equality. Bob the waiter avidly insists on it. 'I am *not* a waiter', he says. 'I'm Bob!' Sartre would thus condemn the obligation in question because it is an obligation of servility, where the customer can be *someone* and the servant cannot be *anyone at all*: the servant cannot be what he or she is. However, in refusing to confine themselves to the frame of subservience, the dreaming grocer and Bob the suffering waiter are also breaking ceremonial form. They are acting as if their interaction with the customer were not a matter of ceremony but rather a matter of informality and friendship. But just as no one can be the friend of a waiter who has only just now introduced himself, so no waiter can actually be the friend of the customers he is serving for the first time. In most cases, even after long acquaintance, most people cannot really be the friends of their servers; they can only be friendly with those others *in their capacity as servers*. Nor can servers ever really be friends with their clients, except *in their capacity as clients*. Sartre appears to be condemning this too, criticizing our modern-day imprisonment in the ceremonies of commerce. It would appear that for Sartre waiters and waitresses can never be free so long as they are waiters and waitresses, first because they are trapped in a system of inequality, and second because they are trapped in a system of ceremony, which coerces them into *playing* at what they *have to be*.

The restaurant on this view is both unfair and unconscionable. To be sure, bad faith need not have anything to do with either inequality or ceremony. Sartre also finds a good deal of bad faith in the cult of sincerity. He finds bad faith in that sincere reformism he despises, that posture of political do-gooding undertaken in the 'spirit of seriousness'. But in the theatre of the restaurant, inegalitarianism and ceremonialism go hand in hand: indeed, they cause one another. Restaurants are inegalitarian *because* they are ceremonial, and they are ceremonial *because* they are inegalitarian. We require of our restaurants that they collude with social coercion, and at the same time, and for that very reason, to collude with bad faith. If there are all kinds of ways for people to deceive themselves, and thus for them to be what they are not and not to be what they are, the restaurant provides an especially rich theatre for the practice. The Self-Taught Man is a prime example, for he *shows* himself to be the post-bourgeois man of seriousness he needs to know himself to be. He *shows* himself; but he *is not* in fact what he shows himself to be. And by the same token, whether in the early nineteenth century or the 1930s, we can see how a restaurant worker will find himself or herself precisely *as a worker* in the venue of the restaurant. It is only the *worker in service*, identifying with his or her role, who can be disappointed in not being able to take off someone's coat, is it not? Perhaps certain kinds of exceptions can be found. But what Sartre's analysis in *Nausea* and *Being and Nothingness* encourages us to see is not only that the institution of the restaurant rests upon certain forms of social coercion, but that the coercion itself rests upon bad faith. The restaurant provides a theatre in which the dominating and the dominated can play at being what they really are, the dominating and the dominated; but in the theatre of the restaurant, they can play at dominating and being dominated in a playful drama of bad faith.[15]

Nausea needs to be looked at too. Sartre is not talking about actually vomiting. He is talking about feeling an uncomfortable indeterminacy, a feeling whose outcome may or may not be an actual bout of vomiting. He is talking about that in-between state where one is neither at rest with the insides of one's body nor in the act of rejecting them. And he is not talking about this condition merely metaphorically, or clinically. There were critics who originally thought that the nausea was mainly to be understood metaphorically, or allegorically, and there are wags in the world of criticism today who have argued that what Sartre is really talking about are panic attacks, or that the background of Roquentin's nausea was really Sartre's own experiments, in 1935, with mescaline.[16] Actually, I do not doubt that the appeal to nausea has metaphorical value, and I do not doubt that experiences of panic or of menacing hallucinations could have been inspirations for Sartre's representation of 'the Nausea'. But in *Being and Nothingness* Sartre himself argues that anguish or anxiety (*l'angoisse*) is at the core of human existence as it really is. Rather than being a pathological condition aroused by neurosis or drugs, although it can also be that, *l'angoisse* is 'consciousness of freedom'; it is for the human being 'a certain mode of standing opposite his past and his future' in which the person's freedom in the face of the past and the future is revealed.[17] As for 'nausea', Sartre states unambiguously that nausea is a constant of human experience, and an important part of the human awareness of self-existence. 'This perpetual apprehension on the part of my for-itself of an *insipid* taste which I cannot place, which accompanies me even in my efforts to get away from it, which is my taste – this is what we have described elsewhere under the name of *Nausea*.'[18]

There is certainly something distasteful, as it were, in Sartre's portrayal of the human condition. Anxiety, nausea; two psychosomatic states that ought to be at the margins of our consciousness, feelings that are aroused by pathological conditions – fear without an object worthy of being feared, disgust caused either by a disorder imposed by environmental factors on the perceptual system (as in seasickness) or by the ingestion of a toxic substance – are brought by Sartre, following Kierkegaard, Nietzsche and Heidegger, into the centre of philosophy, as if they were the secrets of human existence. There is something intolerable about the idea. But Sartre would claim that the mere fact that the idea is intolerable is an indication that it is true. We spend our lives trying to escape from anguish and nausea. For in anguish we perceive our freedom, and in nausea we perceive something upon which our freedom rests, and which is therefore distasteful: the contingency of our existence.

It is in fact in order to escape from anguish that Sartre believes that most of us are constantly fleeing into bad faith. We lie to ourselves, we escape the anguish of who we are, and so we prevent ourselves from knowing something about ourselves that is too painful to know: the fact that we are free. As for nausea, 'we look for the pleasant or for physical pain to free ourselves' from it. We are constantly trying to avoid this nausea. But we cannot ever really avoid it, for this 'dull and inescapable feeling perpetually reveals my body to my consciousness'. It is impossible to be conscious, as a human being, without being conscious with, for, and through a body. It is impossible therefore to be conscious of one's self, in other words *self-conscious*, without depending on the body's sentience, that is without sensing the body's own signals to itself. And therefore this 'insipid taste', this 'my taste' or even this 'taste of myself' is inescapable, even if what this taste alerts us to is our contingency of being.

Up to a point the advent of nausea in the restaurant scene is melodramatic. The nausea comes to Roquentin just as he is getting *fed up* with the Self-Taught Man. It comes too at a moment when Roquentin discovers that he doesn't *belong* in this restaurant, since he doesn't live a life like the other people in it, and indeed since because of who he is, and the circumstances of his life, he doesn't belong anywhere: 'my place is nowhere; I am unwanted, *de trop*'. In the melodrama, Roquentin is getting disgusted with life and everything about it, and he is starting to panic. Moreover, as the nausea begins to come over him Roquentin himself reads the moment melodramatically: 'A fine climax: it shakes me from top to bottom. I saw it coming an hour ago, only I didn't want to admit it.' But the melodrama fails in the next instance, for his next words are these: 'This taste of cheese in my mouth . . .' It sounds a little absurd, even when it is read in context, but that is because Roquentin is rediscovering, at the moment of panic, not panic itself, nor anguish or despair, but absurdity: the absurdity of his own existence. Seeing that he is *not* one of these people around him, that he does not live in the bad faith in which they are immersed, and therefore that he has no place among them, he discovers neither good faith, moral action, a meaning behind the absurdity of the lives around him nor the horror of the Medusa-head of bare life staring back at him, but his own superfluity. He is not *needed*. So though the revelation seems melodramatic, coming as a climax to an attack of anguish or despair, and it 'shakes me from top to bottom', it only amounts to the 'taste of cheese in my mouth'.

At this point, Roquentin has to get up and leave. That he makes a fool of himself in so doing does not escape him. It is impossible for him to excuse himself; it is impossible for him not to cause offence; it is impossible for him not to disturb the peace of all those restaurant-goers and -workers around him, including the unfortunate Self-Taught Man, whose hospitality has ended up in disaster. But it is even impossible for Roquentin to bother feeling foolish or ashamed. He gets up and leaves as soon as he can, as abruptly as he can. For Roquentin has, as it were, an appointment with Being. He has to confront, appreciate and come to terms with this contingency of being which is not only himself but also all of Being.

For our purposes, however, we need not follow him out of the restaurant, but we need to think some more about the nausea that makes him leave. Sartre shows us that Roquentin's nausea is fundamentally a resistance to bad faith. To get away from the lies that the theatre of the restaurant seems to require Roquentin to inhabit, he has to experience that nausea. But why nausea? Why, of all the emotions or physical states that the philosopher-novelist could have called upon, is nausea chosen? The resistance to unawareness that nausea signals could presumably be triggered by other feelings, and other sense-perceptions. A blinding saturation of colour might have done: and in fact, Roquentin does experience alterations in his relation to sight at some points. But the philosopher-novelist chooses nausea as his theme, as if to say something about our relation to food and drink, as if to pinpoint existential disgust not at a high level of moral reprehension but at the day-to-day level of the tongue and the palate.

Nevertheless, there are philosophic reasons for Sartre's choice of the sense of taste and what he calls nausea. Sartre chooses taste and nausea in the first place because he perceives that taste involves a form of auto-sensation. I do not know of any other philosopher who has paid attention to this, apart, perhaps, from Michel Serres.[19] Taste for Sartre is similar to the sexual auto-sensation that Luce Irigaray calls attention to in her famous essay, 'This Sex Which is Not One'.[20] The woman, for Irigaray, is anatomically 'in touch with herself' in a way a man cannot be, and this provides a kind of ground of feminine self-awareness. Sartre by the same token calls attention to a gender-neutral form of self-awareness: the awareness of oneself, prior to the consumption of any food or drink, as not just a creature with a mouth and a tongue, but as precisely *this self*, this self one feels, tongue against one's palate. Prior to any self-conscious observation of the matter, one is aware that one *is*; for among other things one senses the interior of one's mouth, and the tissues and fluids in the inside of one's mouth, and one senses oneself as this being which is 'in touch' with oneself. In fact one both touches and tastes oneself. One tastes oneself continually. And the taste, the flavour of the saliva and mucous membrane, is 'insipid'; it is an insipidity in my 'perpetual apprehension'. Eating and drinking can be thought of as a certain kind of escape from oneself precisely in the challenge they pose to insipid self-apprehension. The *rosé* washes the insipidity away. The *boeuf en daube* overtakes it, filling the mouth with textures and flavours, engaging the tissues and fluids along with the muscles in the mouth in what Sartre, without irony, could call a 'project', a project not only of digestion and appropriation but also of having sensations.

Slimy and chalky, cheesy substances – viscous things – operate somewhat differently for Sartre. They are not fluid like wine or solid like beef, and my response to them – 'oh, this is slimy' – is not merely an expression of aversion that goes without saying but an apprehension of something about the world and my relation to it as someone with a mouth, a tongue and a gullet. I *appropriate* the wine and the beef while, at the same time, I use them to help me flee from the inertia of insipidity. But I cannot do quite the same thing in the same way with viscous substances. For viscosity is a condition of things on the border between the liquid and the solid, and my body, my self-conscious body, is aware of this. It finds that the slimy, as it were, defies both liquidity and solidity as I attempt to consume the object, and it therefore defies my attempts at appropriating it. It can't be gulped like a fluid, or chewed like a solid and then swallowed, and there is something in it that seems to stick to me, that will not allow itself either to go away or, more happily, to be assimilated by my digestive apparatus, and therefore to become me. The slimy is 'a fluidity which holds me and which compromises me . . . it clings to me like a leech'.[21] The idea may seem a little strange out of context, but it is important for understanding Sartre's notion about being human and being therefore a being whose 'initial projects' include a choice of what kind of foodstuffs to eat, and where and how. Towards the end of *Being and Nothingness* the following sequence of ideas is developed, some of which may again seem strange but all of which, in the context, add up to an important idea: a) that 'slime is the revenge of the In-itself'; b) that 'the slimy is *myself*'; c) that 'to touch the slimy is to risk being dissolved in sliminess; d) that the slimy arouses 'horror'; e) that 'the horror of the slimy is the horrible fear that time might become slimy;

and finally, f) that when one tries to consume and appropriate the slimy, 'the sliminess is revealed . . . as a symbol of an anti-value; it is a type of being not realised but threatening which will perpetually haunt consciousness as the constant danger it is fleeing, and hence will suddenly transform the project of appropriation into the project of flight'.[22]

So, the 'taste of cheese in my mouth', the cheese being a viscosity for the Sartre's purposes in *Nausea*, and as it were then a stand-in for the self, the insipid viscosity of one's taste of oneself, is not an arbitrarily chosen token for Roquentin's encounter with his own absurdity. The taste of cheese is a sign of a certain horror – a horror of the very sticky, banal insipidity of the self.

But let us go back to the *rosé* and the *boeuf en daube* for a moment. For they too can harbour a certain horror, though a horror of a different kind. For the teetotaller the *rosé* can elicit disgust. For the vegetarian the *boeuf en daube* can do so. This is well documented. For myself I can attest that during a period of over a year, in 2003–4, for reasons of health and conviction, I neither drank alcohol nor ate meat, and during that period, before long, I could find myself repelled by the proximity, the sight and the smell of alcohol and meat. That is not to say that some part of me did not still desire them; but I had internalized a prohibition, and my body as well as my mind were *écoeuré* by the prohibited substances.

One of Sartre's two main points about food, drink and nausea relies on the analysis of experiences like mine: 'Tastes', Sartre argues, 'do not remain irreducible givens; if one knows how to question them, they reveal to us the fundamental projects of the person'.[23] 'What wine does one drink?' asks the poet of the sublime, Wallace Stevens. 'What bread does one eat?'[24] It was a fundamental project of my *self* back then not to 'appropriate by destruction' any foodstuffs that derived from the slaughter of animals, or for that matter any fluids derived from the fermentation of fruits and grains. Or to put it positively, it was a fundamental project of mine to *desire* vegetarian fare and such beverages as bottled water, coffee and fruit juices. And let me add that now, the times having changed, I do not have that reaction at all. I would be delighted with a good *boeuf en daube*, if one were offered to me, and I would be glad of a nice glass of rosé, or better yet a nice bottle of Châteauneuf-du-Pape to go with the beef. I have a different *project* now. Sartre explains to us that such choices, whether involving a whole culinary ethic or something as simple as a preference for garlic, is a choice of a self in relation to the world. 'What I accept or what I reject with disgust is the very being of that existent [the food chosen], or if you prefer, the totality of the food proposes to me a certain mode of being of the being which I accept or reject'.[25]

Food and drink is one of the sets of objects which the self, in its freedom as well as in necessity, chooses to make its own, to assimilate to itself. For that reason any choices of any food or drink, 'if one knows how to question them', may reveal a fundamental project as to what I have decided to be. It will reveal a serious choice of consequences, so far as one is aware of them: for example, a choice to eat only organically produced vegetarian items, so as to promote a healthier environment; or, conversely, a choice not to bother, since after all one person's eating habits will never make or unmake a planet. And it will also reveal a choice of a 'mode of being': for example, a choice of oneself as a person who eats lightly and spiritually, taking pleasure in fruits, vegetables and grains; or, conversely, a choice of oneself as a person who indulges his heartiest appetites, and goes for the beef and beer. Moreover, what Sartre says about the choices of items can also be said about choices of modes of production and consumption. If I *choose not* to eat at places like McDonald's, because I do not like the effects of McDonald's on the environment, or the corporation's employment practices, its encouragement of 'McJobs', I make a choice based on consequences.[26] But if I choose not to eat at McDonald's because I do not like the food and the service or because I prefer to eat at a trendy bistro, I am expressing an original project as to what kind of person I will be, what kind of sensations I will indulge in, what kind of institutions I want the self I have chosen to be to patronize.

Now as a public intellectual Sartre again and again exhorted people to think seriously about consequences. One chooses organic produce because one believes that *it is good for the planet*, regardless of whether it is *good for me*. One chooses to avoid McDonald's, if one is making a moral decision, because one believes that *it is bad for the planet*, not because one does not care for burgers and fries. But in his early work, Sartre focuses rather on that 'mode of being' whom one chooses to be.

For it is in that mode of being that one chooses oneself, in good faith or bad. It is in that mode, indeed, that one chooses how to *play* at being oneself. One chooses fruit and vegetables because one is a fruit and vegetable person – that is, because one chooses to play at being a consumer of fruits and vegetables – a vegetarian. Or one patronizes certain kinds of restaurants – 'I only go to the finest restaurants, darling; I have my *standards*' – because that is the being who one plays at being, in good faith or bad. You can choose to act morally by the standards of the moral imperative – do for others as you would have them do for you; do for the planet as if it depended on your stewardship; do for the future what you would have done in the present. You probably should. And therefore you might well question whether you should patronize *any* restaurant at all, whether McDonald's or Alain Ducasse, since either restaurant may be said to participate in a system of exploitation which it is your *duty* not to support. But Sartre says: first choose to be the kind of person you are, and choose to be who you are in good faith. Do not *lie* to yourself.

Which brings us back to 'the Nausea' one more time, the nausea and slime. The problem is that from Sartre's point of view it may well be impossible to be in good faith. 'Man is a useless passion', says Sartre at the end of *Being and Nothingness*. On the one hand Sartre exhorts us to be free, exhorts us to *be* the freedom which we already *will be*. But on the other hand, Sartre's philosophy is fatalistic. For one can never *be* what one is, and one *will* never be what one is or would want to be. The very idea that one *can* be what one is, or already is what one is, or is on a trajectory toward being what one will be, is the false premise of sincerity. It is the other side of the lie of bad faith: the waiter in the cafe, the woman on a date, the homosexual in denial. Or it is the seriousness of the self-reformer, the narcissistic moralist, the vegetarian in the cafe. Nor is there really much hope in what is sometimes taken to be the countervailing ethic of authenticity. Sartre alludes to authenticity in *Being and Nothingness*, but in his notebooks of the late 1940s, where he was trying to sketch out the ethics that his philosophy required, he observed something that his philosophy already implied. 'If you seek authenticity for authenticity's sake you are no longer authentic.'[27] On the contrary, 'the one and only basis of the moral life must be spontaneity, that is, the immediate, the unreflective'.[28] When Roquentin encounters the nausea and the slime, the taste of cheese in his mouth, he encounters not a project, not a distaste for this or that, not a choice that he has made, but a fundamental absurdity that is his self, and that restores him to a condition of spontaneity. Unfortunately, in his spontaneity he is also de trop, just as existence in itself is de trop, and he has no *place*, not even in a welcoming restaurant, where people are trying to be hospitable to him.

What about the rest of us, though, still in the restaurant as Roquentin departs for his spontaneous encounter with Being? How can we ourselves remain in the restaurant, or work in or patronize any restaurant, or transact our social lives in any restaurant, after having been mocked by the behaviour of the alienated historian, who flees from us with contempt, and insulted by the existentialist philosopher? How can we work as waiters or cooks, how can we remove people's coats and cook their food, or how can we be customers at our tables, eating oysters and radishes and holding forth on the meaning of humanity, or simply holding hands and gazing into one another's eyes, in the face of the challenge of existentialism?

Late in the novel Roquentin goes to Paris to visit his old girlfriend, Anny. He and Anny are alike in many ways, but Roquentin recoils at what seems to be Anny's solution to the absurdity of existence. She spends her life in pursuit of 'perfect moments'. There are times when the world crystallizes for the subject into an ecstasy of gratification. Mystics have their trances, and secular materialists have their encounters with a beautiful painting, a beautiful sunset or a beautiful meal. A dinner of grilled lamb and potatoes with the local rosé at the Colombe d'Or, for example, a restaurant that Sartre came to know in Saint-Paul de Vence, on a mesa above the Mediterranean, where the walls are decorated with original Chagalls and Mirós, and where on the terrace you can sit under the twilight, with a view of the surrounding hills – that would be a perfect moment, if one were ready for it. And what else can we expect out of life? What else should we do but pursue such moments, to stage our lives – again, as if they were comedies – in pursuit of momentary perfection?

For Roquentin these perfect moments, unfortunately, are only so much escapism. And so it is for his author, Jean-Paul Sartre. Sartre himself, besides having taken a few relaxing vacations in the Côte d'Azur, and being a regular patron of restaurants in Paris, was an advocate of 'the masses', including workers in service, and a compulsive eater and drinker.[29] He was not opposed to a good meal, with a view of a beautiful sunset, in Saint-Paul de Vence; or a blissful blitzed-out night of cake, brandy and cigarettes in a cafe on the Left Bank. For long stretches in his life he was an alcoholic and a drug addict, popping amphetamines to keep himself going. Sartre liked to get high. So far as Sartre was concerned, along with his creation Roquentin, there was nothing *wrong* with the pursuit of such perfect moments, and nothing wrong with experiencing them. But they could never be solutions to the problem of existence. What do we really want? What do we really need? What bread shall we eat? What wine shall we drink?

It may be impossible to answer questions like this, except in the negative. For we will always be what we are not, and not be what we are. But in terms of the restaurant, a minor case of the larger problem, we may at least be able to invoke a few conditions that need to be satisfied if we are to avoid bad faith.

1) The restaurant will have to be a comedy and not a farce.
2) The idea of hospitality will have to be freed from the logic of bad faith. It will have to be possible to give in good faith, even if giving also requires making certain demands on the recipients of the gift.
3) The restaurant will have to be assimilated to the condition of art.
4) The workers in the restaurant will have to be *really cooking* and *really serving* (in the spirit of comedy, hospitality and art, which is to say in the spirit of unalienated work), and the customers in the restaurant will have to be *really eating*.
5) The restaurant will have to be a project of freedom.

It's a tall order, especially when one considers that all of this will have to be accomplished in a spirit not of seriousness but of play. And it would seem to have become even harder after the heyday of Sartre and existentialism, when the world of consumption took on another dimension, and the theatre of behaviour at the restaurant, and the hospitality and artistry and the conditions of production and consumption and even the very possibility of projects of free-dom all have become more difficult as the world moved on, more complicated, obstructed and compromised . . . even as the world became more *affluent*, and the world of the restaurant spread further and further . . .

four

Her Majesty the Consumer

The child shall have a better time than his parents: he shall not
be subject to the necessities which they have recognized as para-
mount in life. Illness, death, renunciation of enjoyment, restrictions on his own will, shall not touch him; the laws of nature
and of society shall be abrogated in his favour; he shall once
more be the centre and core of creation – 'His Majesty the
Baby', as we once fancied ourselves to be . . .
SIGMUND FREUD, 'On Narcissism'[1]

Big and Little Bloggers

As it happens, I visited Le Havre once in the summer of 2005 and dined
at a restaurant similar to the one where *Nausea's* Antoine Roquentin
ate in the fictionalized Le Havre called Bouville.

My wife, stepdaughter and I had come to the end of a brief holiday on the Normandy coast. The next morning we were to take the
ferry from Le Havre back to Portsmouth; so there we were for the
night. It was a warm Sunday evening, and the three of us left our hotel
in the city centre and went upon our restaurant walk in search of a *bel
endroit* where food could be had – an odd walk because it was Sunday, and almost everything was shut, and also because Le Havre itself
is odd. It is not the muddy foggy ornate town of Sartre any more.[2] Le
Havre was bombed heavily by the English on the occasion of D-Day;
five thousand people were killed, and over twelve thousand buildings
were destroyed, leaving a hole where the city centre once had been.
Where Roquentin had dined, watching the wind off the English

Channel 'belly out the overcoats' of pedestrians – all of that is gone now. In its place rose a modernist confection, built from the designs of famous architects out of pre-poured concrete, making Le Havre the Brasília of France. Much of the centre was composed of block after block of white, grey and pinkish tenements of four or five stories. It was like being on the campus of a 1960s university, the sterile University of Illinois at Chicago, say, or the outsized University of California at San Diego. And yet much of the centre retained the smallish footprint and dimensions of the old city, and in spite of the modernist construction daily life was still organized as in an old French town, with storefronts and cafes lining the narrow streets – all shut now in a sigh of relief before the coming of Monday morning.

We wandered about looking for somewhere hospitable. I had at that time long since forgotten Sartre's novel, although it had made a big impression on me in my youth, and the only associations going through my head had to do with my growing hunger and my growing astonishment at the oddness of this town. We passed a few unpromising establishments and then came out to the plaza of the covered market, *Les Halles*. Almost every city in France has its *Les Halles* – a city-run covered market, newly built usually but modelled after the old *Halles* where the French used to do so much of their food shopping and now do their *terroir* shopping – the local oysters and sausages or trout and pâté, the traditionally favoured salad greens – from well-kept, individually owned and operated stalls. The *Halles* too of course was shut, but we had learned by then that the markets often attracted a good restaurant or two. Whenever in a strange town in France, we had come to look for a place called something like Le Restaurant du Marché, where the establishment would specialize in offering a 'market menu of the region', made from ingredients purchased from the stalls that day. So we walked about. My wife was sceptical, my stepdaughter was cross, we had to go an unexpectedly long way, but there it was, eventually, just across from the plaza and a car park: Le Bistrot des Halles.

We went in. The restaurant was on the ground floor of a homely modern brick building that would not have been out of place in East London, but it was done up inside and out like a belle époque concoction – in fact, though I didn't realize it at the time, it was done up on the model of an early twentieth-century Lyonnais *bouchon*, a kind of bistro at once bourgeois and homey. It had a red-painted wooden exterior and mahogany-like panelling inside; it had ivory tablecloths and claret-coloured banquettes and old-fashioned posters and bric-a-brac on the walls, along with chalkboards on which daily specials and wine offerings were listed. There were a few tables on the pavement outside, occupied with cheerful diners; inside the restaurant was about half-full. The atmosphere was lively, in a sultry, summery sort of way. It was not cheap, and the customers were well dressed, wearing polo shirts and linen slacks or wan-coloured tight linen frocks, but prices weren't out of line either. For €26 you got a *prix fixe* meal, a half-litre of wine included; or you could order à la carte and spend more and take advantage of a wine list about which the restaurant trumpeted its pride.

We were greeted and served by a young busy waitress, who assured us that the food was good and the *prix fixe* wine was spot on and she had a nice table for us, in the back near the bar. We followed her to our appointed place. I do not remember what my wife or stepdaughter had, but sitting there in the back, looking longingly at the people with tables by the open terrace and hence fanned by the summer breeze, but digging in contentedly all the same, I had a whole grilled Atlantic sea bream and a carafe of cold white Beaujolais. The sea bream was one of the best pieces of fish I had ever had. It was charred and crisp and spicy on the outside, and warm and sweet and tender and smelling of the sea on the inside, just barely cooked through, the flesh the colour of an apple blossom. The wine, something of a rarity outside of the area in which it is made, was fruity and dry, with a hint of almonds, and a very good match for the fish. When the dessert course came I chose the cheese option, and was presented with three wedges of local, traditional cheese, a Livarot, a Pont-l'Evêque and, yes, a chalky Camembert. Each cheese was presented at just the right stage of maturity, a few hours before turning toward the wrong side of decay, at just the right temperature, on a warm evening very slightly cool, and as I bit into the Camembert and felt that chalk in my mouth I remembered why, like all Jewish-American gourmands with limited means, I never really wanted to live anywhere but France. I was experiencing something like one of those 'perfect moments' mentioned at the end of *Nausea*. It was a materialist's ecstasy, at once paradisal and artificial; it seemed as if I leapt out of the *angoisse* of myself and arrived into a kind of dream.

Of course, the feeling passed. But the memory of that meal and the sea bream and the Camembert has never left me. I suppose I should have known better. I should have been alert to the fact that there was after all something contrived about my experience – a Lyonnais *bouchon*, with early twentieth-century decor, transported into a bombed-out city rebuilt according to the dogma of a post-war aesthetic, and presenting, apart from the Beaujolais wines, perfectly prepared samples of the traditional food of Normandy. (My stepdaughter had an *andouillette de Caen*, I have been told by an authority on the subject.) I should have known, but I didn't. It was only when I started doing research for this book that I became aware of the artificiality of my experience. It came when I looked up the restaurant on the Internet, and came up with a listing of 'reviews' by blogging consumers on the website www.fra.cityvox.fr.

'Un très bel endroit', said the first entry, 'typique. Une jolie brasserie, mais le service difficile, une impression de gêne'. (A very handsome place, in the right style. A pretty brasserie, but the service is a problem, a feeling of being a nuisance). The grade awarded was one out of five for the welcome and the service, three out of five for the decor and the ambience, and one out of five for quality and price, for a total of two out of five. And the criticism goes on: 'An inviting exterior, a welcome that leaves you cold, service more than sad and in view of the quality, exorbitantly costly. Too bad the meat is good, the wine list well selected but prohibitive . . . Easy parking, even in the city centre.'

I like that last remark about the parking, made as if the writer, in spite of it all, were trying to demonstrate the disinterested objectivity of a contributor to the Michelin Guide. But this was not the only caustic review. The next one was even worse, awarding the establishment only one out of five:

> The wait between starter and the main dish is very long, forty-five minutes, with stupid looks and grins all around. We had to help with the preparation of our *digestifs* (really impressive, not a drop more by the glass!) In sum I do not recommend it at all.

I am not sure what this last entry means about helping prepare one's own drinks, or the establishment not having 'a drop more' to offer (I suppose the writer means the drinks the party helped pour were stingy!), but the overall impression is clear enough. Service was maddeningly slow. The clients couldn't get their Calvados. When they got it there wasn't enough. And, like the entry before, the blogger is certainly an out-of-towner with a story to tell. He came from somewhere, looked up, went in, and now he has an announcement to make. Don't go there! I'm angry!

The next entry, still very negative, is more expansive and discursive. The writer had invited people there for a business dinner and again the service was awful. They didn't get what they thought they had ordered, the plates were cold, part of the order came very late, everything was expensive all the same, and no apologies were forthcoming from the staff, nor was restitution offered. 'I was embarrassed', the businessman says. 'It would have been better to bring my guests to a kebab shop; at least the people who worked there would have been welcoming.' In fact, he had the impression that the staff at the restaurant were making fun of him. 'This is the worst joint I have ever been to, considering the price.'

Nevertheless, some good reviews follow, from older entries. 'I've been dining at the Bistrot des Halles for years', writes one, 'every time I've passed through Le Havre, and it's always at the same high quality, the prices are reasonable, the welcome perfect, the decor pleasant, all one could ask for and come back for.' This time the restaurant scores a four out of five. 'What shall I say', begins another. '[This is] one of the few restaurants worthy of the name in Le Havre. Service is always very professional, always an excellent address.' Grade? This time it's a five out of five! And a few still older entries, whose objectivity is suspect, are still more glowing. 'You have to go there!' says one. 'The service is impeccable . . . The ambiance is convivial and the dishes well garnished, the food succulent!'

Le Bistrot des Halles is not an old-style bistro, evidently. It is a postmodern bistro, a parody of an old-style bistro, inhabiting a world of simulations and simulacra, where a replica of the belle époque of Lyon can be injected whole, without irony, or at least without much irony, into the concrete veins of the French Brasília.[3] And recently, in keeping with its status as a postmodern bistro, and moving into an era which can now be called not only postmodern but also 'hypermodern', it has become absorbed into a secondary system of consumption: the world of restaurant bloggers. Once upon a time diners dined in places here and there. Now the diners still dine, but the 'place' where they dine is also a kind of 'non-place', with no real roots in its actual geographic situation.[4] And there is more. Once upon a time, diners communicated their needs and feelings in the space of the restaurant. They spoke to the waiter! They still do, but now they are also communicating their needs and feelings in the placeless spaceless, 'hypermodern' world of the Internet, which has assumed a life, or the simulacrum of a life, of its own.

In the case of the response to Le Bistrot des Halles in this placeless, spaceless, hypermodern venue of the Internet, a clear pattern develops. The more recent entries, from mid-2007 to 2009, are uniformly hostile; the older entries are almost uniformly enthusiastic. Obviously, the statistical sample is small – I do not think any conclusions about the restaurant tomorrow or the day after can be drawn from it. Obviously, too, the wiser reader of review blogs will understand that when people go to the effort to write, like students giving their course evaluations at the end of term, they are more likely to do so either because they really loved the experience or really hated it. People are less inclined to go to the trouble to take laptop in hand and announce to the world, 'It was okay.' In the world of restaurant reviews, as in the world of student course evaluations, there appears to be a statistically significant dearth of threes out of five. Moreover, it is important to keep in mind that blogs come to have a life of their own: bloggers are communicating to each other, elaborating, confirming or taking exception to one another, and nothing would seem to stimulate a blogger more – Internet communication has been known to be like this for quite some time – than to find an opportunity to take exception. But there is nevertheless a clear pattern here, as reviews turn from the glowing to the glowering. Something has gone wrong – but how?

Underneath this one pattern, it almost goes without saying, other norms and structures are pressed into service. Consider an issue I brought up in the first chapter of this book, the problem of the nature of a restaurant's reliability. I said that this reliability is in large part a function of the activity of awarding grades concerning reliability. The activity makes an assumption: a restaurant should always be the same as itself. All of our bloggers adopt this assumption, and all but one make a corollary assumption, that the restaurant, as experienced on a single occasion, is what it is and is what it always will be. *One* experience there is therefore equal to *all* experiences there, and *all* experiences are reducible to *this one*.

Yet as I also suggested earlier, one may well ask what has to be *done* in order for a restaurant to be consistently itself. Is it not possible, for example, that our bistro in Le Havre could have turned over its personnel several times between 2005 and 2009? Could the good waitress of 2005 not have gotten ill, or pregnant, or simply quit, and been replaced by her evil twin sister, or a stranger from Pas de Calais? Or suppose the staff remained the same. Could the staff members have nevertheless changed, as individuals, or in relation to one another? Could the waitress and the cook, say, have begun to suffer marital problems, and been arguing some nights? Or could the cook have begun drinking on the job? Or worse still, could the cook have begun *not* drinking on the job? You will say, in answer to the question as to what has to be *done* for a restaurant to maintain its standards, that it will have to have been supervised by a determined owner, directed by a sturdy management team and very possibly operated by the same talented head chef and support staff over the years. But perhaps the conditions of running a neighbourhood bistro, even an expensive and slightly hokey one, in weird Le Havre, do not quite involve a 'management team'. And perhaps too – we will be looking at this possibility later – not all customers are alike either, or end up eliciting the same response by the staff, with or without a management team.

In any case, it is noteworthy that in all of the recent, negative reviews of the Bistrot des Halles, the complaints are waged about service, price and timing from the kitchen, and no one has anything bad to say about the way the restaurant looks and feels, for it is *typique*, and few have anything bad to say about the quality of the food. One of the critics even betrays himself with the remark, 'Too bad the meat is good.' Either it's too bad (*dommage*), because if the service weren't so atrocious it would be worth dining there; or else, ambiguously, it's too bad because then my review would be more consistent: I wouldn't find myself awarding an establishment a two out of five when after all the food is good. So, if the bloggers assume that the restaurant always has to be the same as itself and are more likely to express either great satisfaction or great discontent rather than any less extreme emotion, they are also, it turns out, less concerned with how good the food is than with something more nebulous, the quality of the experience as a whole in view of the demands they have placed upon it.

And what are those demands, precisely? That is what I am mainly interested in here. These blog reviews, obviously, tell us as much about the people doing the reviewing as about the restaurant itself. They do not often tell us much about *who* these people are, exactly. For it is a condition of this new blogging culture, where people enter information on a public page, that the bloggers remain anonymous. Call them little bloggers, who add to someone else's public page, as opposed to big bloggers, who run their own pages, and who may or may not be anonymous. The little bloggers *reveal* themselves through their blogging, but they also *conceal* themselves – an important point, both because the simultaneous revealing and concealing is a condition of participating in the culture of little bloggers, and because a parallel revealing and concealing is operative in the very act of consumption at a restaurant, the act of *being a customer*. To *play* at being a customer in a restaurant is to conceal and reveal one's being. But if the blogs do not tell much about who the people are, it tells us a great deal about *what* the people are as bloggers and customers. They tell us what postures they adopt as diners and critics and communicators; they tell us what social roles they imagine themselves entitled or called upon to *play at*. And so, too, the blogs tell us what *demands* are placed upon the culture of the restaurant by consumers.

Within the context of these demands, the little blogger makes a double assumption. On the one hand, the restaurant will always be what it is. (Hence among other things the indignation of some bloggers, who are arguing among themselves as to what this or that restaurant *is*, and complaining that the restaurant simply *is not* what others would lead one to believe.) But on the other, I, the little blogger, concealing and revealing myself, have a very different kind of character. For I can change. I can be different. I can move on, going from restaurant to restaurant. I can make choices. I can go back to a place I like, or I can warn the public never ever to go places I don't. 'To avoid at all costs!', I can say. I can pass judgement! I can whine! I can throw a tantrum! And meanwhile, tantrums apart, given my immunity as a semi-anonymous consumer from being subjected to scrutiny or judgement, I can live as the hero of my own life story, like Dickens's David Copperfield, and all the experiences along the way, can be the materials for building up the ironic maturity of my self. And why not? Sartre calls this 'appropriation'. In a famous Egyptian novel, *Midaq Alley*, a young man challenges a friend to be ambitious, and find out about the world beyond the cramped quarter in working-class Cairo where they have grown up. For the young man, seeing the world is all about accumulating experiences that are not available in a life confined to the inner city. He puts it to his friend like this: 'You've never lived. What have you eaten? What have you drunk?'[5] Life for the sake of a life accumulated is the idea – experience for the sake of the accumulation of experience, pleasure for the sake of the accumulation of pleasure, and the accumulations adding up to a life of which one can be the hero. What have you eaten? What have you drunk? A kind of curiosity that is not only gastronomic but also scientific and romantic and indeed what Sartre calls 'initiating' can lead one from town to town and from restaurant to restaurant in search of a *bel endroit*. It can arouse one into trying the local Camembert at a fake *bouchon* just a few miles up the road from where they actually churn and set and age the stuff, not to mention having a sea bream just a harbour away from where the ships go out and wrest the few good fish left to be caught in the depleted deep of the English Channel. But this curiosity, this passion (*useless,* as Sartre says, but also vital, and vital in its very uselessness) is based for the majority of bloggers on a perverse assumption about themselves and their relation to the world. They are consumers. They change, they grow, they do their thing and get their kicks. But the world for them must always be as it is (innovations in gadgetry and planned obsolescence apart), providing them with the commodities they require. 'Illness, death, renunciation of enjoyment, restrictions on his own will, shall not touch [them]; the laws of nature and of society, are to be abrogated in [their] favour.'

'Man the consumer', I have said, was born at about the time of the French Revolution, and I am sticking to my story. And I am sticking as well to the idea that, for better or worse, humanity in the modern, post-Revolutionary world, for all the tensions and contradictions and even the wars that have been associated with it, has been on a mission of joco-serious appropriation. *La joie de vivre,* the French call it, which goes along with *savoir vivre*; there are no words for either expression in English. Grimod de la Reynière was one of the tragicomic heroes of the *joie* and the *savoir.* But since the Second World War those of us in the developed world have been said not only to be consumers, but to live in what is called a 'consumer society'. The basic idea is that where society once included a provision for consumption, and things were produced in order to be consumed, we now live in a society that is all but entirely organized for the sake of the production of consumption. 'Our enormously productive economy demands that we make consumption our way of life', said Victor Lebow in 1955; it demands 'that we convert the buying and use of goods into rituals, that we seek our spiritual satisfaction and our ego satisfaction in consumption'.[6] But even more, from a more radical and recent point of view, the structure of society involves a system of *compulsory* consumption, and even, as Jean Baudrillard originally put it, the compulsory *consumption of consumption.*[7] It is no longer the case, the argument goes, that increased productivity demands increased consumption, but instead that increased consumption demands a redoubled production of more consumption. I consume not in order *to have* but in order *not to have.* I consume in order not to have consumed, that thereby I may consume all the more. Did you ever think that I would *stop* at the 32-inch TV, when the wall in my house is fifteen feet wide, and Samsung has introduced a new picture technology for its 50-inch screens? Did you think I would stop, if I could help it, at a white Beaujolais, when a more costly and elegant Pouilly Fuissé was available too? Maybe today I'll stop, but wait till tomorrow: I see a Pouilly Fuissé in my future. And if this fake *bouchon* provided me with a perfect moment, so be it; one of these days I'm gonna get my ass down to Lyon and have the *real* thing. And I'm gonna *tell* everybody about it too!

The consumer at the restaurant, consuming in order not to have consumed – that is, in order not to have changed the world, but only to have changed and confirmed herself through the appropriation of commodities – since the Second World War, and especially since the 1970s and the coming of postmodern culture, is commonly guided, so far as restaurants are concerned, by a primary fantasy, a Freudian fantasy: Her Majesty the Consumer.

She – let me call her she, for many of my examples are female, though she is a he as well – hell, sometimes she is *me* as well – is looking, again and again, for the perfect moment. Again and again she wants it. And again and again, either she doesn't get it or, having got it, she needs to get it all over again, only differently. 'The main course was a *pavé* of salmon', says one of my favourite amateur big bloggers, about a restaurant in Cassis on the Mediterranean coast in Provence, 'which was silky and luscious, but really, it's just salmon. The only thing about this dish that I'd have trouble duplicating at home is the extra-crispy skin, and I suspect if I just used a ton of butter, I'd eventually get it done.' Disappointment. This blogger calls herself both 'An American in London' and an 'R. W. Apple Wannabe', and she is quite delightful. But the spirit of the real, late R. W. Apple, a famed journalist for the *New York Times*, is missing. Apple made a name for himself by reporting on the civil rights movement and the Vietnam War before becoming, in his later years, a travel journalist, exploring the less well-known cuisines of the world, getting to know the people behind the food as well as the food itself. Our anonymous blogger is a consumer, pure and simple; she is motivated not by curiosity about the precarious world through which Apple travelled, but by a hunger for the kind of consumer goods available in the stable world of goods through which she tours. And so, for lack of genuine curiosity, she is capable of world-weary disappointment even in something she knows to be worthwhile. She could make it at home, that salmon. And that is disappointing because of the nature of her expectation – her expectation of something more out of her travels, what Sartre would call transcendence.

To actually go through the blogger's self-effacing, mildly ironic, unpolished yet serviceable prose, adorned with photographs not of herself but of the dishes she eats, one might not think that something so sublime as 'transcendence' is what she is after. She tells us herself, in her introduction to her blog, that she is really only, well, a consumer:

I'm an American who moved to London in August 2005 with my husband, also an American.

Our goal in London is to make new friends, eat, drink, and see Europe while our jobs provide the moolah to keep the fun and games going. We try to travel outside the UK at least once a month, and I'm keeping this blog to share the good, bad and ugly, with a slight focus obsession on the food front. (Subtext: Here's yet another amateur who fancies herself a food and travel writer.)

This is a consumer writ large: she lives and works in order to 'keep the fun and games going'. What she or her husband actually do she doesn't say, and it doesn't matter. All that really matters (for the present) is that she is rich, or rich enough. Indeed, there is no other *purpose* in her writing at all except the matter of keeping the fun and games going. Or to put it another way, whatever she does for a living, and whoever she actually is apart from her role as a traveller and a blogger, the fun and games is her purpose.

But the demand for transcendence in her fun and games is everywhere. She 'fancies herself a food and travel writer'. She fancies herself, as Sartre would put it, as being what she is not. In point of fact, a good many professional food and travel writers, freelancers most of them, lead fairly marginal lives. The pay is poor. Security is non-existent. One has to beg one's bed and board, or sell oneself out for bed and board. One is lucky to earn a little something on the side teaching a night-time course at a community college on 'How to Be a Food and Travel Writer'.[8] These professionals have made an unusual wager: in order to be able to freelance and travel and see and eat the world, they will devote themselves to a profession that doesn't usually allow one enough money to see and eat the world. They have chosen a kind of danger.

Obviously there is no danger in being An American in London. In London she and her husband ('Jon') have high-paying jobs. But in her capacity as a semi-anonymous big blogger, our 'wannabe' transcends herself. She becomes what she is not: no longer a privileged Londoner from America, earning vast amounts of money in the City, but a food and travel writer. She becomes, that is, what she 'fancies' herself to be, rather than what she really is. Moreover, in her fun and games as a wannabe writer, racing from restaurant to restaurant, she goes in search of the ineffable, the un-duplicable perfect moment. On one level, the problem with that *pavé* of salmon was the fact that, as a work of art, it did not excel. It was only okay. (And I trust An American in London on this level: she has good taste, and good taste is not to be despised.) But on other levels, the problem was not whether it was good or not; the problem was that the dish could easily be duplicated. The problem was that it was *familiar.*

Now again, the problem of having the familiar delivered to you can be the problem of artistic expression. Whether it is the purpose of art, as Russian formalists once said, to 'de-familiarize' reality, or rather merely to quicken the senses, and allow us to see and feel the world anew, a *pavé* of salmon that is only a *pavé* like every other *pavé*, though it may succeed as an artefact, will absolutely fail as a work of art. It neither de-familiarizes nor quickens. And An American in London is looking for art. But the category of the familiar and the unfamiliar has other dimensions, and An American in London is looking for more than art alone in her quest for unfamiliarity. All restaurants (again) can be located along axes of the familiar and the strange in relation to the consumer; that is one of the ways in which the restaurant operates as a commercial institution. So it is not just 'art' that is in question. There is a certain kind of business here, of production and consumption. Moreover, as all Freudians know and all literature students are nowadays taught (yes I know, it's a bit dogmatic), the idea of the familiar has a number of decisively psychic implications – for at the bottom of our psychic lives the familiar, the *heimlich*, is inevitably intertwined with that which is uncannily unfamiliar, the *unheimlich*, and both harbour primary and therefore inescapable desires and fears. We must always be oriented toward the world as through a regress and a progress, a regressive return toward what it primordially familiar, and a progressive (potentially anguished) advance toward what is strange. The *pavé* in this light was wrong because, in its bland familiarity, it failed not only on the level of a project of consumption and satisfaction, but on the level of psychic demand. In the first place, it gave our blogger, in what was supposed to be exotic seaside Provence, a food that was familiar and customary for her at home in London. Categorical expectations were thwarted: I expected *exotic Provence*, and all I got was *salmon*, an un-Mediterranean fish, cooked the way *I* could cook it. (In fact, salmon was the only thing on the menu.) But in the second place, then, the salmon failed to satisfy a deeper craving, the craving of a consumer in search of transcendence. In all its familiarity and duplicability, the *pavé* was incapable of satisfying the primary fantasy of Her Majesty the Consumer: the fantasy of infinite reward.

'Primary narcissism' is an essential part of becoming human, psychoanalysis teaches. A human is a self-regarding creature: it not only looks after its needs, but looks after it*self* as a being with needs. Infancy teaches us to be self-regarding just so far as it puts us in a loving crib, under the supervision of a loving family, and teaches us a lesson: my needs come first, and they come first not just because they are needs, but because I am me. In fact, it is just when I am most satisfying my needs, *giving* myself the most love, that I also *receive* the most love, the most attention, the most smiles. 'Look at me! I'm eating!' In the end, my self-regarding thus shades into exhibitionism (looking toward myself, I make sure that others are looking at me, doubling my gratification). I get what I love, because I love myself, and everybody loves me in return, as if to say, 'Yes, your Majesty, we love it too. We love it when you love yourself.'[9]

I am not criticizing An American in London for having been afflicted with the universal condition of primary narcissism. In a sense I am not criticizing her at all. She only is what she is, and what our society has trained her to be – which is to say, she is only, also, what she is not. But the secondary narcissism that An American in London exhibits (though again, not with regard to who she really is, about which I know nothing, but about what she constructs herself as being in the guise of a 'Wannabe R.W. Apple', a would-be journalist), which she constructs before us not in her own right but as a wholesale representative of us all, the 'Number Six Ranked Blog' according to the blog site Urban Spoon – that is something different. This secondary narcissism, so publicly displayed, though under the guise of semi-anonymity, so generally extolled as a model of conduct, an object worthy of emulation, is a form of regression. Instead of living in the present, with its good and its bad, its compromises and its inevitable mixture of happiness and unhappiness, its precariousness and its historicity, the subject acts as if she lives in the ideal past of infancy, under circumstances where the world is magical, dissatisfaction is intolerable and absolute happiness is the only option.

This is perhaps a form of *necessary* regression. For decades social critics have been arguing that the consumer society makes us all into narcissists.[10] The conditions of the consumer society turn consumption into regression, a quest for infinite infantile reward, and since we all have to be consumers, it may be that we all have to regress. We have to respond to the consumer goods on offer to us as vehicles of a magical transcendence to which only an infant, fixed necessarily in a dynamic of self-love, is really entitled. For there is no other way to respond. But there is an ideology at work in this too.

'I pay for all meals and trips', continues An American in London, 'using my own hard-earned cash, and I'm motivated to write this blog because I enjoy talking about travel/food for its own sake and I have a consumer-advocate streak.' Of course – I *deserve* my meals and trips. I paid for them! It is no secret that the ideology of the consumer society, especially in its American form (the form that I was brought up in, too), tells us that in modern life one *gets* what one *deserves*. If one pays more, because one earns more, one obviously deserves more too. And of course, having deserved what I have got, I am *motivated* in two mutually complementary, justifying ways: out of *enjoyment*, and out of *altruism*. 'I have a consumer-advocate streak.' As she goes on to say, 'If a hyped-up resto stinks, I'd hate to think someone else wasted their money there, and on the flip side, if a resto is excellent, I'd love to encourage everyone to go and "support" delicious food, attentive service and proportional-to-quality prices.' A key feature of the ideology of the consumer society is that though gross consumption is gross, informed consumption is altruism. To give strangers a tip about a restaurant, in the hope that they will 'support' it (the scare quotes are the blogger's, not mine) – and you can see strangers exchanging tips all the time on blogs like our wannabe's or like Urban Spoon or the granddaddy of them all, Zagat.com – is to perform a *public service*.

All of these aspects of secondary narcissism and the ideology of consumption are evident in the French blogs about Le Bistrot des Halles (including the obviously male ones) no less than that of An American in London. To blog is to perform a public function. To blog is to 'altruize', as it were. And in performing that public function – since one would *hate* to see other people *waste* their money – one encourages others to mirror the ego of the blogger, to provide yet more confirmation that what one enjoys is really enjoyable, and that what one gets in the course of enjoyment is what one deserves. The logic of the blog and the ideology behind it even go so far as to turn a disappointing experience into injustice. Our businessmen in Le Havre, not having received a proper *welcome*, nor the proper attentiveness and deference, have been *humiliated* by the bistro, and hence they will justly – *justly* – (a) prevent other people from undergoing the same humiliation and (b) throw a tantrum and get their revenge. 'To be avoided at all costs!' If you don't get what you wanted, haven't received what you deserve, that can only be because you have been victimized by an injustice, for which, luckily, word of mouth in the old days and blogging in the present allow you to exact a measure of redress. It is tantrum time. And if a disappointing experience is an injustice, a good experience is by the same token an expression of *justice*. Our American in Paris thus tells us that the restaurant in the town of Cassis, La Petite Cuisine, which served her luscious silky salmon that was only salmon, but which delivered nice service along with a view of the sea, managed to 'fit the bill'. An interesting expression when you think about it: to 'fit the bill'. In Britain people traditionally say 'fill the bill', going back to the original meaning of completing the bill (filling out the bill) of a theatrical performance, the list of entertainments on offer; and the general meaning of either version, American or British, to fit or to fill, is 'to be suitable for a particular purpose'. The *Oxford English Dictionary* thus cites a passage from Somerset Maugham, writing in a 1954 novel, 'He felt that he owed it to himself to have a mistress he could love, and whose position would add to his prestige. He decided that Alexandrine Daru, Pierre's wife, would fill the bill.' (The squad behind the OED is not entirely without a sense of humour.) There is an inevitable selfishness in the use of the term, since it involves a willingness to engage in exploitation. La Petite Cuisine, like the fatal Alexandrine Daru, can be *my object*, since *I owe it to myself*; I deserve it because I am me. When An American in London uses the term, financial connotations resonate too. 'Fitting the bill' comes to mean both 'suiting my purposes' and 'being worth what I am prepared to pay'. What is ultimately at stake therefore is the satisfaction of a demand according to the consumerist version of the principle of the *lex talionis*. 'For a leisurely lunch, La Petite Cuisine fit the bill. While the bistro's lunch menu options were uncreative, at least they were well executed. You could find much worse perches from which to while away a sunny afternoon.' It is not only that one gets what one pays for, in a case like this; it is also that one gets what one deserves. And one deserves, in return for €40 and all the *good will* one exerts in simply being there . . . at least this much: a perch overlooking the Mediterranean, with good service and well-executed food . . . although of course one actually deserves a little bit more than that. In fact, one deserves transcendence.[11]

This secondary narcissism is something that the restaurant encouraged from the outset. The individualized service that the original restaurants provided, such that though one was in a crowd of people, benefiting from an economy of scale, one could be personally catered to, according to one's desires, and in a sense as if no one else was also in the room   this individualization was an outcome of the *generalization* of entitlement during the advent of modern capitalism. (Years later, Ortega y Gasset would refer to this as 'the revolt of the masses'.[12]) One no longer had to be actually entitled, seated at the dais at the head of the hall, in order to be majestic. In this newfangled public-private space, even humble little you, if you could afford it, could be treated as a king; or, in other words, as a baby.

This was not exactly what Grimod de la Reynière was trying to promote. He preferred a more social relationship to restaurant dining: the diner was in a social relation with the people who fed him. Moreover, for his own part, he preferred his weekly Société du Mercredi gatherings, in a group of seventeen friends, on the occasion of some quasi-philosophic premise; intimate dining at a table set apart held fewer charms for him. And again, as a critic, Grimod was concerned in large part with the way in which dining could be elevated into an art; in nineteenth-century fashion, he was concerned with progress. His writing was meant not just to inform potential customers about where to go, but also to encourage restaurateurs to keep improving their offerings, and gourmands to keep improving their palates. But the restaurant of the nineteenth century already provided well-known opportunities for the expression of what we may now call secondary narcissism. Balzac shows us a number of examples of it, as in the story of Lucien de Rubempré; so does Zola, in novels like *The Kill*, where narcissism at a restaurant leads to incest – committed in a private room of an actual restaurant, the Café Riche, on the Boulevard Poisson-ière.[13] In the early twentieth century, in furtherance of the tradition, Sartre shows this as well: whatever else the diners in Bouville are looking for at Maison Bottanet – for example, food – the main protagonist apart from Roquentin in the little drama, the Self-Taught Man, is looking primarily to confirm his narcissistic self-image. He needs food, but what he craves is attention and affirmation.

Clearly, however, our postmodern age differs from earlier periods in that secondary narcissism has been promoted into a virtue. In the first place, a great many more opportunities for the expression of majestic consumption are available, in restaurants as in other sites of consumption; and a great many more people have the resources to take advantage of these expanded opportunities. This remains the case even during serious economic downturns, like the one that began in late 2008 and that, as I write, is still very much with us. Employees are discharged, homes lost, the stock market drops, budgets are cut, banks and nations are faced with bankruptcy, services cut, lives ruined . . . and still restaurants stay in business, and opportunities for majestic consumption continue to proliferate. The party goes on because, even if the economy tanks, the system remains, and the system is geared toward the proliferation of opportunities of consumption, majestic consumption included. And in the second place, as the opportunities have multiplied, the exploitation of consumption opportunity has been elevated into one of our highest and most cherished values, even among 'the rest of us', the vast majority who actually *cannot* take advantage of what the wealthy take for granted. Narcissistic consumption is no longer deviant: it is the norm. And when you put the two together, the opportunity and the value, or in other words the material means and the ideology, even though the means are actually only for the minority and the ideology is what is oppressing the majority, you get the illusion that the purpose of life itself is the pursuit of infinite reward, the transcendence of the material and the ideological in the infantilized moment of consummate consumption. In the case of the American in London, if one wanted to be unkind, one could say that the blog serves the purpose of justifying a classic case of conspicuous consumption, and indeed even of generating a condition of conspicuous consumption. The big blogger, posting all her trips and meals online, in photos as well as in words, makes her consumption conspicuous. There she is, in her costume, in her disguise, concealing and revealing. There she is online! There's where she ate! There's even *what* she ate![14] And then, having made her consumption conspicuous, the blogger adds, Here's what *justifies* my conspicuous consumption: (a) I enjoy it, I enjoy my surplus enjoyment; (b) I am a consumer advocate. I am doing this for the public good!

But there's no point in complaining about the blogger's duplicity here. The American in London is simply what she is. She has been trained to live her life as if it were a partly hidden, partly exhibited romantic pursuit in search of the infinite reward she deserves, since after all she is . . . her*self*.

M.F.K. Fisher

As I was first putting together this chapter, I thought that the best example I could find for the narcissistic fantasy and regression that restaurant dining can entail would come from the American food writer M.F.K. Fisher (1908–1992), because she was so achingly voluptuous a writer. Since she wrote repeatedly about herself and her adventures in food, I believed I would find in her work an especially seductive example of secondary narcissism. I remembered a couple of passages about her dining at Aux Trois Faisans, a respected restaurant in Dijon, in the 1930s, a time when Dijon was one of the culinary capitals of France. In one passage, she wrote about her first meal there. She was barely 21 years old, and newly married to a man not much older than she, an American graduate student at the University of Dijon, and this was also her first meal alone with her husband in a French restaurant anywhere. 'We were really very timid', she wrote.

> The noisy dark staircase; the big glass case with dead fish
> and lobsters and mushrooms and grapes piled on the ice;

the toilet with its swinging door and men laughing and buttoning their trousers and picking their teeth; the long hall past the kitchens and small dining rooms and Ribaudot's [the owner's] office; then the dining room . . .

'Shyly', she wrote, she found herself seating, to be served by a 'small bright-eyed man' with thinning, waxed hair.

His name was Charles, we found later, and we knew him for a long time, and learned a great deal from him. That first night he was more than kind to us, but it was obvious that there was little he could do except see that we were fed without feeling too ignorant. His tact was great, and touching. He put big menus in our hands and pointed out two plans for us, one at twenty-two francs and the other, the *diner de luxe au prix fixe*, at twenty-five.[15]

The other passage comes about six years later, when she returns to Aux Trois Faisans with a new lover, and is served by Charles a monumentally old and rare, oddly bottled and exceptionally smooth *marc de Bourgogne*.

I had remembered those passages. I had remembered being seduced by them. And here, I thought, would be the best examples I could possibly come up with of the experience of surrendering oneself to a waiter and a restaurant, in return for which one received a kind of infinite reward. One is never so much a baby as when an excellent waiter at an excellent restaurant shepherds one through a transcendent rite of fine dining. I remembered these passages in concert with a work of literature of the Italian Renaissance that I had written about years before, Francesco Colonna's *Hypnerotomachia Poliphili* (1499). In one episode the protagonist of this long dream of a romance

finds himself a guest at the banquet of a queen, seated amid beautiful women, in a palace of costly and exquisite design. Every guest was tended by three servants – themselves beautiful women. One of the servants fed the guest, a second 'interposed a plate beneath the food so that nothing should fall, and the third, on the left, elegantly wiped the guest's lips with a white napkin, soft and perfectly clean.' This table service 'was observed diligently for each of the guests, so that no one touched any of the food, but was fed willingly by the servant, except for the cup.'[16]

'Fed, tended, wiped', as I said, the guests at this dinner 'made a perfect return to infancy'. Even the erotic charge of being tended in this way by beautiful women would be a part of the infantile fantasy. The *unfamiliarity* of dining so luxuriously is of course completely *familiar* so far as it represents, at bottom, a return to the mother, and all the eroticism that the feeding child and feeding mother invest in the exchange bonding them together.

But as I read through Fisher a second time, I realized that Fisher was not, in her work, a narcissist. She expressed sensuality and desire and somewhere lingering in the back of it all must have been any of a number of primal wishes. But she did not, in her writings, regress. The writings I am referring to were all produced between 1937 and 1949 and they were collected into a volume called *The Art of Eating* in 1954. The texts, including *Serve It Forth, How to Cook a Wolf* and *The Gastronomical Me*, are full of ironies and regrets as well as appetites, and the realm of the tragic is never far removed from them. The two accounts of her experience with Charles the waiter are about initiations, ageing and leave-takings. Fisher does not surrender to Charles, she does not imagine herself being fed by him, and she does not look to him for infinite reward. She 'learned' from him. In her account of the very old *marc de Bourgogne* she juxtaposes the *marc* with Charles himself, who in fact had just been fired from his job of many years, due to his alcoholism. Fisher was to be his last customer in Dijon. What is universally acclaimed as Fisher's finest work, *The Gastronomical Me* (1943), which includes the story of her first meal at Ribaudot's under the guidance of Charles, is certainly about a 'me'. But the book is not about a consumer, much less a majestic one.

What I hadn't realized the first time I read Fisher's work was that none of this writing up to 1949 was produced before the great leap forward of the following decades into the world of the consumer society. It was possible to be a majestic consumer in the age before the triumph of consumer society; one could always, for example, participate in that conspicuous consumption that Thorstein Veblen documented in *The Theory of the Leisure Class* in 1899. But Fisher was never a member of the leisure class, and she was never, in any case, interested in enjoying merely what could be called leisure, or the fruits of leisure, much less to do so for the sake of broadcasting her social status. There was I think something Nietzschean in her project of becoming a 'gastronomical me', or existentialist, if you prefer. Her project was a struggle against the big Nothing. She did not inhabit, in any case, and so she never accepted nor rejected, a triumphant consumer society, and majestic consumption was never her aim. All of those major texts from 1937 to 1949 inhabit a world of scarcity: the depression years, the war years, the post-war scarcity years. And as she lived through her times, she did not and could not assume that the world was always as it was, so that only she could change and grow. On the contrary, she saw the world in danger of slipping away from her, and she in danger of slipping away with it as well. *The Gastronomical Me* is about a woman trying to discover and satisfy her hunger in situations where the discovery is likely to be thwarted, and satisfaction denied: Prohibition-era Protestant America, for example, or France during the drift into the Second World War, and then the circumstances of having a lover and husband whose health has collapsed, and who in despair at the pain he constantly suffered would eventually kill himself. Her brother, for no apparent reason, would kill himself too – perhaps it was a copycat suicide, modelled after the death of Fisher's lover – and it is with an oblique reminiscence of the ineffability of her brother's life that this gastronomical book actually concludes.[17]

If I missed the tragic and existentialist dimension of her work the first time around it may have been because I took it for granted and, having taken it for granted, I had eyes only for what was new and luscious in it – fine dining in pre-war Dijon. Or it may have been because, even if I understood the story of wartime *angoisse* so well that I could take it for granted, I had not yet opened my eyes to the transformation in life expectations that the coming of post-war consumer society has meant. I perhaps assumed that I too would have a life of fragile expectations as M.F.K. Fisher had had. Since I was relatively poor during my first reading of her work, and had no job security, my own expectations were in fact quite fragile. The wolf that Fisher immortalizes in her 1942 work, *How to Cook a Wolf*, was really at my door. But my expectations were not fragile in the same way as Fisher's, and the wolf who threatened me had acquired new disguises. For I lived, insecure though I was, in an era of affluence, of the easy availability of goods and services. I did not appreciate that then. I had forgotten about the revolution I had taken part in – America in the 1960s – a revolution that started out as a protest against conformity and injustice and ended up as a democratization of majestic consumption.

In the world of *The Art of Eating*, fine dining is a very old tradition, whose rules and protocols and delectable pleasures have long since been established. The problem is that in America people have been cut off from that tradition; they have to go to Europe to enjoy it, or at least learn with diligence to cook the wolf themselves. A similar frame of mind can be found in the work of other American gastronomes of the time, such as that of the journalist A. J. Liebling. In fact, you will find it among a whole host of 'Lost Generation' and Depression-era writers from America, from Ernest Hemingway to Henry Miller, or such other figures of wealth and patronage as Sara and Gerald Murphy, as immortalized in Calvin Tomkins's work *Living Well is the Best Revenge*. And then you will find the same idea in British writers of the post-war years like Elizabeth David or, more recently, Peter Mayle. The American experiment (and the British experiment too, though on a lesser scale) had failed to provide genuine prosperity, even if during some decades it had succeeding in generating a great deal of money, material comfort and surplus gadgetry. It had failed to provide *joie* and it had failed to provide *savoir*. But there, in old France, was what seemed to be a whole civilization that had long since been dedicated to nothing but joy and the knowledge of it. So old and well-established was this tradition, as the expatriates understood it, that it was probably already in decline, and perhaps – for our sins – in danger of vanishing.[18]

It should be added of course that Fisher was faced as well with the constraints of gender. For a woman of the 1930s or '40s to assert her 'hunger', which is what Fisher said she was doing, was to assert an uncommon autonomy: the autonomy of appropriation. I will devise and determine the law of myself as someone who stands before the world in order to appropriate it. For what have I eaten, what have I drunk? What has any woman eaten or drunk, or been given licence to do so? Fisher quotes the philosopher George Santayana in the motto of *Gastronomical Me*: 'To be happy you must have taken the measure of your powers, tasted the fruits of your passion, and learned your place in the world'. But how was a woman to do this, and how was a woman to do this in an era of Prohibition, depression and war? In France, though the position of woman in society was no less subordinate to that of men vis-à-vis political and economic power than in the English-speaking world, there was at least a licence to *joie* and *savoir*.

Far from being an expression of consumerism and its demands for infinite reward, then, the early and most important work of M.F.K. Fisher represented a kind of plea on behalf of autonomy. This is a plea that continues in her underappreciated novel of 1947, her only published full-length work of fiction, *Not Now But Now*.[19] The heroine of the work, whose narrative world resembles that of Virginia Woolf's *Orlando*, is seeking freedom and only freedom – 'not now but now' refers to the free flight in the air of a parachute jumper – but she can never find it because she doesn't know how to correlate (to use Sartre's terms) her being-for-self with her being-for-others. To put it another way, although she strives in every way for something like free flight, she does not know exactly how to manage things when she inevitably lands on the ground and has to operate in society. Others will not allow her to be for herself. (Therefore she complains about everyone else being 'selfish'.) She is made into an object of jealousy, idealization, servitude and prostitution. At one point a group of men actually place wagers on who is going to keep her as a mistress, as if she were a race horse, although all along she has believed herself to have chosen the men who are wagering on her. She had convinced herself that she was in complete control over the men who have all along been controlling her for their own selfish ends.

You get the picture. This novel depicts a woman with a great appetite for food, drink and sex as well as for wealth, beauty, prestige, admiration, adoration and maybe even love. But she cannot stand in relation to the world from which she wants so much as a consumer in search of commodities. Her world is not like that. Her world is never really *for* her; it is always for others. And it is never simply what it is;

it is always changing, always slipping away. Literally it slips away. For in the conceit which she no doubt borrowed from Virginia Woolf, but which she develops in her own way, relieving it of the suggestion of cultural progress inherent in Woolf's vision, the world lacks historical solidity. The story literally jolts from an imaginary present to 1938, then to 1847, then to 1927, and then to 1882, until it returns to another moment of free fall in the present. (It also jolts from Switzerland to London to small-town Illinois and then to San Francisco, all locations that Fisher herself had known.)

Gael Greene and Ruth Reichl

One has to jolt forward into the world of the consumer society, during a period when Fisher was past her prime as a writer, to find a preponderance of majestic customers and critics in search of infinite reward; to food writers like Gael Greene, for thirty years the restaurant critic of *New York Magazine*, and Ruth Reichl, who was food critic for the *New York Times* for six years before going on to be editor of the now-defunct but much beloved and missed *Gourmet*. I choose to call attention to these writers because of their importance and their excellence, as well as for the symptomatic role I think they both have played in the development of post-war gastronomy. Both of these women played leading roles in what is sometimes thought of as the food revolution in America that began in the 1970s – a period when, to quote the awful title of a book dedicated to the subject, America was transformed from a land of the dull, the bland and the industrial into *The United States of Arugula*.[20] ('Arugula', or 'rocket', stands for the choice of interesting, unusual, artisanal and natural ingredients that characterizes the new foodie culture in America.) But both of them played these roles in the world of the triumph of the consumer society.

The whole story, as its participants and historians usually tell it, is a kind of providential narrative, not unlike the narrative of the pilgrims at Plymouth.[21] Up until the 1960s, or perhaps even later, the American palate was persecuted by the High Church of corporatism, convenience and insipidity, and genuine gourmets were left to wander in the wilderness. Then a few pioneers led the way to a new world:

Craig Claiborne at the *New York Times*; Julia Child, author of *Mastering the Art of French Cooking*; Alice Waters, founder of Chez Panisse, the restaurant that invented California cuisine; Wolfgang Puck, chef and restaurateur, most notably of Spago in Los Angeles, a stage set of movie stars and baby vegetables. Before long, gathering chefs and entrepreneurs and food warriors to its cause, the United States of Arugula was born: a place where a gourmand could really eat, and critics like Greene and Reichl could really write about really eating, and where the business of being a 'foodie' was not only recreational and profitable but also creative, ethical, oppositional. It is important to understand the fact that whether they were hippies like Alice Waters, sybaritic gays like Craig Claiborne or glamorous libertines like Gael Greene, the leaders of the movement were originally part of subcultures rather than the dominant culture of America, and understood their labours in gourmandism as countercultural work. This story, or the participants' understanding of it, is not altogether untrue. If it was found out in the 1970s that the revolution would not take place, and the walls of capitalism and corporatism were not going to be brought down, it was also discovered that people did not have to eat Wonder Bread and Swanson TV Dinners any more, or otherwise limit their appetites to the pallid offerings that the corporate state and conventional morality were trying to foist upon them. There were pot stickers and *shao mai* out there, and sashimi with daikon radish threads and Roman oxtail soup and *pain levain* and tomatoes that looked and tasted like tomatoes, if you had the countercultural wherewithal to seek them out. Gael Greene could allow herself to be called 'The Insatiable Critic' and write a memoir called *Insatiable*, the idea being that the *refusal to be satiated*, the ever-renewed demand for more and better in the realm of the senses, could be extolled (at least by a woman writer in this age of second-wave feminism) as an imperative. And why not? Who is to say no to such a force of nature in search of carnal knowledge? But the story is obviously a lot more complicated than that. One of the complications is that this countercultural revolt coincided almost exactly with the triumph of the consumer society and the accession of Her Majesty the Consumer. And the coincidence was not a mere coincidence. Both the countercultural gourmet and the mainstream consumer of mass-produced commodities are pledged to a system of hedonism for its own sake. It's Alice's Restaurant all over again, except this time it's the Alice of Chez Panisse.

Things were different in the United Kingdom. The consumer society came later, delayed by a post-war austerity that lasted into the mid-1950s, and the food revolution came later too. America, an extremely prosperous country with a highly mobile population, long used to dining out in restaurants, was taught by a bohemian fringe to turn its needs up a few notches and to appreciate more and demand more as well. The country was food-crazed by the 1980s, experimenting with all kinds of fusion, ethnic and regional cuisines, though led in spirit by southern French and northern Italian customs. The United Kingdom, by contrast, a struggling former empire which for a long time found itself as the odd man out of Europe, where dining out and fine dining were traditionally monopolized by the upper classes, was led out of the wilderness by working-class chefs, upper-middle-class connoisseurs and hardscrabble television personalities, who basically tried to get Brits of all classes to emulate the upper-middle-class French.[22] It was not until the mid-1990s that the movement was in full swing, and it has been taking even longer for the movement to percolate down to diners in the provinces and those lower down on the social scale. It has never been led by a bohemian fringe, though it has depended on the creativity and labour of artistic-minded immigrants along with the working-class boys, and it has not been affected much by the input of restaurant critics in the press. If Britain has had a number of highly talented critics, its critics have never played an iconic role in the national food culture, as Craig Claiborne, Gael Greene and Ruth Reichl were to do in America.

Claiborne first and then Greene and Reichl would do what Grimod did: they would promote the progress of gastronomy, a progress that involved both the provider and the customer. They were not only expressing taste; they were making taste, and the taste they were making was a revolution of the senses. But Greene and Reichl (Claiborne's case is a bit different) earned their keep as representatives working on behalf of the interests of consumers and consumerism. They were the voices of the new consumer, and they were at their best precisely when they best exemplified the extremities of majestic consumption and the bad faith majestic consumption inevitably entails.

The problem, the lurking bad faith, is everywhere discernible in the memoirs they have written, Greene's *Insatiable* and Reichl's trilogy, *Tender at the Bone*, *Comfort Me with Apples* and *Garlic and Sapphires*. Interesting books, all of them, and entertaining, but they jolt us a major episteme away from the world of *Gastronomical Me* and its tragic self-revelations. We are now in a world without suffering, or at best where it is believed that suffering is unnecessary, that there is no *need* or *justification* for it any more. We are in a world bursting at the seams with surplus enjoyment, and it is only a shame when one finds oneself born to the wrong mother, or married to the wrong husband, or temporarily out of a job. We are in the world, too, of simulation – where for lack of scarcity and suffering, nothing need be as it seems, and nothing need seem to be exactly what it is. Reichl openly confesses that her memoirs have been fictionalized, as if fictionalization were better than the mere dry facts of a real life, and even truer than real life. ('Everything here is true, but it may not be entirely factual.'[23]) The real Ruth Reichl is the fictional Ruth Reichl. As for Greene, for her the purpose of a memoir apparently is to play a game of hide-and-seek, both with oneself and with one's readers. Now you see me, now you don't, and in fact the real me is the one who you see and don't see at the same time. Greene's trademark image – rendered on the front cover of her book, repeated several times within the covers of her book, and reproduced yet again at a focal point on her recently launched web page (www.insatiable-critic.com, a blog that apart from its state-of-the-art professionalism is not much different from the one by An American in London), is of a woman in a wide-brimmed hat, staring straight at you, except that the brim of the hat covers her eyes and casts a deep shadow over her face down to her nose. You are supposed both to recognize her and not to recognize her.

The game of concealing and revealing that both critics play has a literary pedigree that goes back to André Gide and Vladimir Nabokov and moves on through the work of such luminaries as Phillip Roth and J. M. Coetzee, not to mention younger figures like Josip Novakovich and Dave Eggers. Our restaurant critics are postmodernists. The game they play is also part and parcel of the kind of restaurant criticism they have been practising. This is the criticism, now institutionalized in many places (above all by the *New York Times*, not to mention the legendary legions of critics for the Michelin Guides), where the critic is always supposed to be unknown to the establishment being evaluated.[24] So our leading critics today, writing in an age of prosperity, are both postmodernists and quick-change artists. They travel through life incognito, they tell us, mixing fact with fiction yet coming to a certain kind of truth all the same, a taste-making self-making truth.[25] The concealing and the revealing is what *enables* their truth-generating writing. But it is also what allies them most closely to the consumer whose interests they represent. 'Look at me!' they say. 'I'm eating!' Only, 'Don't look at me!' they also say. 'I'm passing judgement and I require my anonymity! I am busy being an exhibitionist who has to hide sometimes.' Like a Renaissance king, we might add, or like the Calvinist God.

An absurd and joyous spectacle is made out of this by Gael Greene, who is after all a glamour-addicted and starstruck journalist, working in what for her is almost always a glamorous New York. She *knows* that it is all a game. She *makes fun* of glamour. But she also *celebrates* it. (Fashion, as I have said, can only be properly taken seriously in the spirit of play.) She finds, while living through the American food revolution in one of its capitals, New York, that sensual pleasure is not simply sensual pleasure; it has its lows and highs and its hierarchy of privileges and orgies. So it is important for her to tell us about the celebrities she has slept with – including Clint Eastwood, Burt Reynolds and French chef Jean Troisgros – with the implication that sex with a glamorous celebrity is somehow better than sex with almost anyone else. Sex with a celebrity *signifies*; that indeed is what makes it *better*. And the same goes with restaurants. The experiences she is most happy to tell us about are always celebrity moments. There are the orgies of feasting that she indulges in as a guest of French food industry, and a playmate of great French chefs, or as a special patron (once her disguise has been penetrated and she is well known for the critic she is) of what she doesn't hesitate to call the 'best' restaurants of New York, beginning with the celebrated and exclusive (though now defunct) Le Cirque, that playground for the rich and famous and especially the power elite of New York, with whose chef de cuisine she has an affair. The pleasure in such circumstances, in a word, is transcendent. 'Look at me, the best chefs in the world are feeding me like a child. Some of them are even fucking me.' And in the restaurant world of New York City this special treatment takes on even more significance because the restaurant world there is ultimately all about special treatment. It is all about the surplus enjoyment of *surplus service*. Some time in the history of the restaurant the players in the posh restaurants in New York City, perhaps imitating their betters in Paris and London, invented the idea of the best tables for the in crowd and their opposite, 'Siberia', the worst tables for the outcasts. The players, customers and providers alike, invented the idea that the distinction expensive restaurants bestowed upon their customers depended not only upon the fact of eating in the restaurant but upon public acts of favour, as if the servers in the restaurant were the patrons, and the customers their clients, beginning with where the customers were seated. Gael Greene likes to make fun of this circus of favours bestowed or withheld, and its reversal of the natural order of things, since after all service workers are here bestowing prestige upon their patrons, rather than the other way around. But Green also likes to take advantage of it when it comes her way, and she never finds anything wrong with it – so long as, now and then, the power lunchers and foodie elite of New York sitting at the best tables and benefiting from the best service do their part and contribute to charity. (Her favourite tax-deductible charity is Citymeals-on-Wheels, which she helped found: and where, thanks to the generosity of wealthy restaurant-goers and restaurateurs, people who are immobile and poor are delivered non-restaurant food by way of non-restaurant service.[26]) 'It seems to me it's endearing', she writes, 'though some might think it's pitiful – that New Yorkers . . . are never quite sure they count until they get *that* table.'[27] But Greene, it turns out, needs to occupy *that* table herself, even if, as a restaurant critic, she is supposed to be *in hiding*. Living in what is essentially a world without scarcity, Greene can only keep finding grounds for not being satiated, for never quite having *enough* of *that*. For she is consumed – glamorously consumed – with consuming consumption.

Ruth Reichl is much less comfortable with this situation. In her twenties Reichl found that she was well suited to a career as a food critic; she enjoyed it and she was good at it. But she was raised in an intellectual household in Greenwich Village; she came of age living among artists in a commune in Berkeley, California; and she can never quite convince herself that writing restaurant reviews is a worthwhile or respectable way to make a living. 'Let me get this straight', says one of her fellow communards, when she is first recruited to be a reviewer. 'You're going to spend your life telling spoiled, rich people where to eat too much obscene food.' 'You're wasting your talent', says her sculptor husband.[28] Reichl can never quite disagree with these sentiments. But she shows herself being seduced into the life of fine dining and high-end journalism, and once she is in it she finds herself stuck. The 'trouble', she is told by Alice Waters, who has similar reservations, is that 'once you're successful at something, it just sort of follows you around and haunts you'.[29] *Garlic and Sapphires*, recounting her six years as critic with the *Times*, delineates a continual struggle between a good Ruth who gets seduced into high-end life and a bad Ruth who enjoys it: a struggle that never gets entirely resolved, since Reichl cannot bring herself to believe in the existence of two Ruths or the dichotomy between them: she is after all a postmodernist in her outlook, and so remains suspicious of the very binary oppositions with which she constructs her account of herself.

At one point she wrote a piece in the *Times* with the following headline:

WHY I DISAPPROVE OF WHAT I DO
It's indecent to glamorise a $100 meal. Or is it?

Her solution was to appeal to what she took to be a *democratization* of restaurant culture in the United States. In effect, she was appealing to the theme of this book, and like the author of this book she was all in favour of democracy as opposed to elitism. You don't have to be an elitist to enjoy restaurants any more, or take a critical attitude toward what they offer. But the democracy Reichl supported was a little more vexed than she wanted it to be. She could not make status and glamour and elitism go away. In fact, she could only confirm them.

'Going out to eat used to be like going to the opera', she wrote in the article, trying to save her position from elitism; 'today it is more like going to the movies'. Indeed, 'Everyone has become a critic.' Because 'American food has come of age', one no longer has to go to a very expensive restaurant in order to have a good meal. And because of this general democratization of fine dining, the critic is no longer herself an elitist; she is just like the rest of us, a critic like everybody else. Therefore go forth, eat and criticize. But in spite of her longing for the *dēmos,* Reichl is really trying to have it both ways, and she knows that too: 'deep down I knew there was something basically dishonest about what I had written . . . I was making excuses'.[30] The problem of course is that Reichl (a great fan of M.F.K. Fisher, whom she came to know personally) cannot escape the fact that she is labouring, if not on behalf of the rich (although in fact she is labouring on their behalf as well), then on behalf of Her Majesty the Consumer and the demands the narcissist with money places on the world.

She operates *sympathetically* on behalf of Her Majesty, to be sure, even *empathetically.* For in a brilliant exploitation of theatricality, Reichl disguises herself as other people, as 'Molly', 'Miriam', 'Chloe', 'Brenda', 'Betty' and 'Emily', complete with wigs and carefully chosen character-establishing outfits. Reichl pretends to be someone else – a dowdy tourist from the Midwest, or an older, poorer woman from upper Manhattan, or a glamorous blonde in stilettos. She does this in order not to be known to the restaurant staff as the critic of the *New York Times.* But other motives develop as well. As she disguises herself, she also learns something about the women she imagines herself to be, and get first-hand experience of how the social world responds to dowdy tourists, elderly women or blondes. In effect, she multiplies herself, and begins to view restaurants from a multiplied perspective. No longer simply The Critic, she is now, democratically, the critics that all people are, waging their own revolt of the masses.

Early during her career at the *Times,* to turn to her most brilliant incident in disguise, she is Molly at Le Cirque, New York's most elite restaurant, dining with an elderly friend. And then she makes comparisons. She compares Molly's experience of the restaurant with her own experience as the young and attractive Ruth Reichl, yet unknown to New York restaurateurs but very much herself. Then she compares the two experiences to her experience when, though still unknown to the people who run Le Cirque, she dines in the company of a well-known editor of the *Times,* who gets VIP treatment. And finally she compares her experiences with that of a Ruth Reichl who has been outed, recognized by the staff at Le Cirque as the restaurant critic of the most important newspaper in town, and who thus gets the very very VIP treatment. It almost goes without saying that Molly, an older and unassuming woman, gets the worst service and food, and ebullient Ruth Reichl, the recognized restaurant critic for the *Times,* gets the very best. The critic promptly gets the best table, oversized and upfront, attended to by the head waiter and the maître d' alike; gets lavished with special *amuse-bouches*, truffles and chocolates, not to mention exquisite little dishes of black bass and the like, made to show off the kitchen's ingenuity and versatility. The Midwestern matron is treated with indifference. She is made to wait until well after her reservation indicated she should have to wait; she gets the worst table, cramped and set in the back amid smokers, although she requested non-smoking; she has the wine menu snatched out of her hands, because a more important customer needs it; and is generally made to feel unwelcome. The food is lavish, in spite of the rude service, but it all seems a bit 'brown', lacking spirit and colour. An excellent curried tuna tartare comes with 'flabby pieces of "toast"'. A pallid fillet of halibut with mushrooms is served with 'soggy rounds of potatoes' and topped with a single sprig of chervil, 'the lone spot of green'. And in the end, 'Molly' finds herself wishing that 'when the maître d' asked if I had a reservation, I had just said no and left'.[31]

'Molly' gets her revenge, however, when the restaurant critic speaks up for her, lambasting the restaurant for its treatment of ordinary paying customers, and demoting Le Cirque from four stars (the *Times'* highest rank) to three. Not all of the readers of the *Times* were happy with the review, it turned out. Some were appalled by its hubris, or its coyness. But others let Reichl know that they felt 'it's good to know that we finally have a critic who's on our side', or a 'spy in the house of food' working on behalf of the 'silent majority'. When Molly gets her revenge, a whole segment of the population gets its revenge. It is no longer 'silent'.[32]

But in speaking out through the ventriloquism of the professional critic, 'Molly' shows herself to be little different, at bottom, from the businessman in Le Havre, or the American in London visiting Provence. For what is it that she *wants*? What is it that this member of the silent majority feels herself entitled to *play* at being? We can all feel that 'Molly' is right to be offended at the treatment she received at the exclusive restaurant – no less than the Frenchman who had to pour his own niggardly *digestif* was right to have taken offence. Because she was *unknown*, apparently powerless, female and dowdy, the restaurant excluded her from its exclusiveness. It made her feel unwelcome. And on one level, on the level of universal consumerism, according to whose *lex talionis* one is supposed to get what one pays for, she is *entitled* to feel disappointed, cheated, humiliated, and we to feel indignant along with her. But why should we *expect* that the restaurant would *not* treat her that way? Why in other words should we expect that the restaurant perform a surplus service that the society as a whole will never perform for her? Why should we expect a restaurant designed, noted and patronized for its exclusivity not to be exclusive, and to do for the Mollys of America what America itself refuses to do? Le Cirque – the regular dining spot of ex-presidents and media moguls, the gathering place of an in crowd, who in fact become an in crowd precisely by gathering, precisely, *there* – existed on a social level as an institution of the powerful, for the powerful and by the powerful. That is what Le Cirque was *for*. If the restaurant made people who lacked the special kind of power it was made to confirm feel, in a word, powerless, then it was succeeding, not failing at its mission.

To this 'Molly' has a reply in protest, a protest that we can sympathize with. But should we? For her protest corroborates the very position she is trying to object to. It tells us precisely that the problem with Molly was not that she didn't belong to the world of Le Cirque and the power elite of America, but precisely that she did. She belonged to it as a dutifully majestic (if sometimes frustrated) consumer who knows that she can demand to get what she deserves. 'I did not come here simply to eat', 'Molly', in character, tells her dining companion at Le Cirque, in anger at the service. 'I came here for glamour. I am willing to pay for the privilege of feeling rich and important for a few small hours. Is that too much to ask? I have come here looking for a dream.'[33]

five

Dining Out in Paris
and London

> The diversity of our opinions does not arise from some being
> endowed with a larger share of reason than others, but solely
> from this, that we conduct our thoughts along different ways,
> and do not fix attention on the same objects.
>
> RENÉ DESCARTES, *Discourse on Method*

I first learned about the cultural dichotomy between Paris and London
in matters of food well before I had ever set foot in England, and when
I was only first getting acquainted with life in France. It was from a
book, George Orwell's Depression-era *Down and Out in Paris and
London*.[1] Orwell places two accounts of living in poverty side by side,
and it is hard to choose between them: living in Paris, working eighteen-
hour days, hopelessly, among filth; or living in London, hopeful but
not working at all, holed up at night in sterile shelters for the home-
less, and left to wander aimlessly during the day. A vivid contrast of
the quality of life comes out in Orwell's memoir, all the same, where
Paris, apart from the terrible working conditions, has to be the winner.
Paris is a reverie of food and drink and sex, even for the poor, or perhaps especially for the poor; London is a prison, where the poor are
made to live on tea, sugar, margarine and toast, in the hope that they
will learn to improve themselves.

Still, the stereotypes have prevailed, and not without reason. The
first time I arrived in Paris, in 1974, I found myself surrounded by
the sight and smell of wonderful things. The shops and stalls were full
of them, the bins, the shelves and the window displays: crusty breads
and freshly baked flans and quiches lorraines and tarts, pear and

strawberry and raspberry and kiwi and mixed, the fruit fanned in layers over a thick *crème pâtissière* like precious jewels; whole cheeses – hard cheeses, runny cheeses, white and yellow and blue cheeses, smelly and mild – from every *département* in the state, and even a few from abroad; pâtés of all kinds, hams and terrines and fresh-made salads of seafood and vegetables and potatoes and tubs of just-beaten mayonnaise, rich with egg yolks and voluptuously leaking oil; fruit stands along the pavements with bins of fruit so fresh and colourful you wondered if any painters could ever do them justice, and so fragrant – you could smell the apples from yards away – that you knew they couldn't. Pavement stands were hawking oysters on the half shell, fresh roasted chestnuts, hot *crêpes* made to order, spicy Merguez sausages served on long crunchy rolls with demonically hot mustard and *sandwichs tunisiens*, made with tuna, olives, potatoes, oily peppers and a sprinkle of hot sauce, packed into a thick chewy roll. You walked around the town and even in the coldest weather people were sitting outside in the fashionable cafes sipping inky coffee and fruity *kirs* and having snacks of pastries or of baguettes with olives and pickles and with slices of pâté or ham. Meanwhile, behind the glass walls of the closed terraces of the brasseries you saw diners at all hours seated at tables with white linen tablecloths digging into *soupe à l'oignon, choucroute garnis, rognons à la crème, steak au poivre* with *frites*. The first restaurant meal in Paris I treated myself to, being on a budget, was a salad and a Franco-Italian pizza, the latter served in a way that I, a New Yorker and also a Chicago guy, had never heard of till then: very thin and airy and crispy with a whisper of tomato sauce, fresh mozzarella and thin slices of fresh tomato, the pizza served whole on a dinner plate, to be eaten with a knife and fork. Pizza tasted different that way. I was forced to eat it more slowly, and think about the little layers of dough, crust, sauce and cheese that I was chewing.[2] I later watched with admiration as a gentleman sitting a few tables down from me ordered a banana for dessert, just a banana, and proceeded to peel and eat it too with a knife and a fork, and savour it forkful by forkful like a dish of hot apple pie.

My first time in London, many years later, in the early 1990s, could not have been more different. Still a budget traveller, I wandered the streets, looking for a place to sit down and have a bite to eat. The streets were fine. London architecture is heavier, less sinuous and ornate than Paris's; but the streets of the West End and the City are still handsomely lined with chiselled limestone and glass, and the sidewalks are still buzzing with pedestrians moving hurriedly in all directions. But there were no real outdoor cafes, no food stalls, no patisseries, no roasting chestnuts, no oysters, no fruit stands and no smell of anything but exhaust fumes and perspiration. I passed chain restaurants serving hot-table buffets of all-you-can-eat pizza and pasta, the metal trays of doughy pizza and bins of soggy pasta left to sweat and expire under heat lamps, and several other establishments offering uncooked sandwiches of dull white bread with a few thin slices of meat and cucumber and 'salad cream' inside, wrapped in plastic, along with a smattering of Wimpy hamburger restaurants and several other American-style fast food chains. Until I learned how to wander into the back streets of the town, that was about it. My first restaurant meal was at an Indian restaurant off Trafalgar Square. I had heard a lot about London's Indian restaurants, and had already learned to enjoy Indian food while in Chicago, but this one served food that was overcooked, unbalanced and loveless; the lamb in my curry was chopped up into ridiculously small bits and even so was stringy, the *raita* was sickly sweet, the rice was dry. Even the chutney was dull, more of a mango jam than a condiment with character; the curry sauce itself tasted like it came from a jar that had been left open a little too long. And this was not to be the worst meal I would have in London then or on subsequent trips. It wouldn't even be the worst Indian meal I would ever have there.

I should probably mention the eggs Benedict my wife Marion and I had recently, in the spring of 2009, in a restaurant with an Italian theme close to Euston Station. It came on a huge round white plate. Four muffin halves were arranged on the plate face up, like the four corners of the globe. On top of the muffins were rounds of bright pink lean bacon-like meat that tasted of dishwater and decay; on top of the bacon-like meat were four overcooked poached eggs, their yolks broken during the poaching and cooked through to a pale chalky yellow and their whites spread out like the extremities of a continent on a *mappa mundi*; on top of everything, and underneath everything, the eggs, the bacon-like meat and the muffins, was about a quarter-pound of hot melted butter. There was no hollandaise sauce, just the ocean of hot melted butter, and I am not exaggerating. We couldn't eat it, but we decided not to complain either. It was clear to us that no one in the restaurant had a clear idea of what eggs Benedict actually was.

Okay, things are better now, for the most part, everyone is agreed. In fact, outside of Euston Station London vaunts itself today as one of world capitals of cuisine. In twenty years, though there still exist establishments that serve eggs Benedict in a puddle of butter, and curries made with bottled sauces, London has gone foodie. There's nowhere better, Londoners like to say. London is where you go for innovation, variety and excellence now. *All* the adventurous food in the world is to be found in London these days.[3] Michelin stars abound in London, and unique experiments in modern eating abound there too.

And I should also mention a recent meal I had in Paris, whose reputation in many quarters has gone downhill since my salad days in the 1970s. On a hot lazy summer evening in 2006 I went with Marion to a neighbourhood seafood restaurant in the twelfth arrondissement. We sat outside; we and one other couple, who sat inside to take advantage of the air conditioning, were the only customers that night. This was no amateur restaurant, however – it had been established for quite a while, and offered delivery of fresh oysters and other crustaceans to other caterers as well as to private parties. You could get a dozen number three *fines de claire* to go. I ordered the grilled sea bass. It came to the plate fine, fresh, filleted, but slightly overcooked and only mildly flavourful, the skin limp rather than crisp, and accompanied by noodles – tagliatelle, I think it was. There was no sauce for the fish and no sauce for the noodles. There wasn't even any lemon or butter. I am not under-reporting. That was all there was, slightly overcooked sea bass and a small mound of boiled noodles. Fortunately there was a saucer of sea salt on the table with a little spoon so you could sprinkle it on the austere comestibles like drops of holy water at a benediction. Never much of a religious man, I wasn't impressed. But it got me thinking.

In Search of a Method

This is the place in the book where, having brought my readers from Grimod de la Reynière to Her Majesty the Consumer and the New York critics who serve her, I ought to do some criticism of my own. Show you how it really ought to be done. Show you what it's like to be a consumer without consumerism, and a critic without narcissistic pride. But I can't. I don't have the stamina to be a critic, or the resources either. And I'm not really interested, to be honest. I would never want to let that story of which I and only I am the hero – my life – be overtaken by a programme of systematic consumption and evaluation, so that I have to busy myself day-to-day with the job of feeding myself with a notebook in hand and a duty not of enjoying myself but of awarding points or stars for the benefit of others. My hat goes off to anyone who can do it – after all, someone has to – but I want restaurant-going, when I have the time and money for it, to be kept in my own corner, in my own little project of freedom. I want it to be about where I am and what I am doing. I want to be an amateur. I want to continue being one of the rest of us.

I am not opposed to *professionalism*, let me add – far from it, either when it comes to restaurant critics or restaurateurs. There is a great deal of professional expertise involved in running a good shop, even when it's on a side street in Collioure, or Columbus, Ohio, just as there is enormous expertise in being a good critic. One of the problems with restaurant culture today, especially in America (but also, as it turns out, in Britain and France), is that when big business takes over, and you have a restaurant reduplicated by the hundreds from one corner of the country to the other, the labour at the restaurant is deprofessionalized, and the tastes of customers dumbed down. Chili's Restaurant, a chain with over 1,400 locations worldwide (the chain started in Dallas in 1975 and today has over two hundred locations in Texas alone) offers an appetiser plate where the diner may choose three items from among the following, all served with 'dipping sauces': 'Big Mouth® Bites' (miniature hamburgers); 'Boneless Buffalo Wings'; 'Southwestern Eggrolls'; 'Chicken Crispers®'; 'Wings Over Buffalo®'; 'Crispy Onion String & Jalapeño Stack'; 'Hot Spinach & Artichoke Dip'. This offering must make sense to the people who work in Chili's, as it must to their millions of customers. It represents, one might politely say, a triumph of culture over nature. But it is not the food of professionals, serving a knowing clientele.

So I am not opposed to professionals, whether restaurant workers or critics. I rather embrace what they do. But my job, as an amateur, as one of the rest of us, as a literary historian and a cultural critic, is *not* to become one of them. It is instead to look at the whole of restaurant culture from an oblique angle. It is to examine the assumptions of the culture. And it is to try, at the same time, to look at the restaurant whole. To see restaurant culture from the point of view of the professional critic, who would of course skip Chili's and anywhere like it, and who would most likely skip Columbus, Ohio altogether too (the city of 750,000 does not have a full-time restaurant critic – and why would it? why would it even have a part-time critic? even the 'best' restaurants there, as voted by Internet little bloggers, are outlets of national chains)[4] – to see the restaurant culture of the world from the point of view of someone whose job, after all, is to seek out the most noteworthy restaurants around, is to see the culture in part, the good part, or the apparently good part; it is deliberately and creatively to ignore the Big Mouth® Bites of the world. It is therefore also to ignore the *dēmos*, the many, and therefore also to ignore the plight of the many. Try getting a good meal in Columbus, Ohio. Try getting a meal that has been prepared for you by a *professional*, with love . . . his own personal speciality . . . But never mind that, the critic is off to El Bulli, where all the Bites are small, but one is dining in ONE OF THE BEST RESTAURANTS IN THE WORLD.

Anyway. It is obvious that even to think about 'restaurant culture as a whole' is to engage in making a number of assumptions, from the fixed point of view of the individual making the assumptions. I have tried to remain an amateur, even while I have been thinking about 'restaurant culture as a whole', because one's engagement with the culture is determined by class, wealth, education and opportunity. Professionalism obscures that. The critic whose father was a printer, the chef whose father worked in the mines – when they move into the big city and become a critic or a chef, they leapfrog out of their stations; they eat and learn about eating just as well as, or even better, than the plutocrats they serve. So, they are experts. But they are experts from the point of view of plutocracy, the rule of the rich – even if in their heart of hearts they are democrats, and liberal and generous and wonderful in all other kinds of ways.

What does 'restaurant culture as a whole' look like from the point of view of the many? It is hard to say, because there are many versions of the many. I have looked at the ethnology of restaurant culture. It is very interesting, but all good ethnology begins with the assumption that culture is local, unique to the places and people among whom it is found. So there is no whole. I have looked at the sociology of restaurant culture. It is extremely disappointing. It purports to be about 'society', but it is usually rather about something like suburban Melbourne, Australia, or Preston, Lancashire.[5] Perhaps there is no way into this subject matter that is not already partial and biased. I have tried up to now to show a number of the angles from which restaurant culture can be examined – historical, philosophical, geographical – and some of the ways in which this examining gets put into language. I have tried to be theoretical, too, drawing conclusions from observations, making deductive assertions about the nature of the restaurant as a cultural artefact and an economic institution. But what is my position, really? My *position* . . .

Once it occurred to me that I might write a book about restaurants, I had to ask myself, what did I really know about them? I had travelled a bit and eaten a lot and I had formed a lot of opinions. I had formed what seemed to me to be some rather *clear and distinct* ideas about them. But what did I really know? On what basis could I ever be said to really know anything about restaurants? Having moved up to a small city in north-west England – which is not entirely a culinary desert but which is not a nursery of culinary excellence either – I had to think about my isolation. I had to take into account the fact that I wasn't *there* where the culture really was. I wasn't even there where the *discourse* about restaurants was being formulated – all the buzz, and the anti-buzz.

So I thought again about Paris and London, cities to which I sporadically travelled for business and pleasure, but about which, so far as their own whole restaurant cultures were concerned, my ideas were obscure and vague rather than clear and distinct. I thought about George Orwell and the old stereotypes of the two cities' culinary cultures, and about the change of fortunes each city's culture had apparently undergone. I thought about the buzz itself. Where did it come from? What was it really about? Having been educated, as a literary critic, in the hermeneutics of suspicion, I was disposed not to believe the hype and the buzz (London, now a World Capital of Cuisine, etc.) but to place it in brackets, to suspend my belief about it, and to wonder not only what truths might underlie the hype and the buzz but also what lies. What was the hype and the buzz trying to *hide*?

I thought too about the food journalism that had been transporting my mind and affecting my ideas about restaurants ever since when. For many years I had been reading items in the *New York Times* like 'Thirty-six Hours in Bordeaux', 'Along the Waterfront in Lerici, Italy' or R. W. Apple's last piece for the *Times,* 'An Epicurean Pilgrimage: Meals Worth the Price of a Plane Ticket' – which featured restaurants from Buenos Aires to Shanghai. I read these articles and I was *envious*. I felt *deprived*. What had I eaten? What had I drunk? And for London and Paris, the articles were countless. No one could try to do London or Paris in 36 hours and believe that he or she had really *done* them. There are articles all the time on neighbourhoods, and sub-neighbourhoods, and public squares and intersections and streets, all with their own eateries, their own buzz. I thought about all this, which I had been putting my faith in, these expert guides to what it is like to visit or live in a city which were as much fantasies as realities for me. Thirty-six hours: JUST GIVE ME 36 HOURS. ANYWHERE. I WANT TO EAT!

Or did I? It was time to put into doubt my own inclinations toward gourmandism, and to think about what it meant for me to be so enthusiastic about fine food, to be so caught up in the buzz about fine food, and to dream about weekends in Bordeaux, or Buenos Aires or Shanghai, eating and drinking. It was time for me to think about who and what I was trying to be when I got caught up in the fantasy world of the foodie, and the buzz of food and travel journalism. And it was time to think about what it was that the restaurants were doing to me, what kind of identity they imposed upon me as I walked through the doors. For as I said in the beginning, the restaurant is an institution for which we diners are the media: 'we are the vehicles through which the restaurant conducts its business of giving sustenance, joy, distinction, and aggravation'.

London

For London I raised a little money, and bought myself a little time: five days and nights, to be exact, and £600. I had my usual research associate to accompany me, Marion Scott Appelbaum. Together we laid our plans carefully. We would stay in a budget hotel in a residential area, a little off the beaten path but convenient enough for the restaurants and shops we wanted to visit. To save money, we would do most of our major dining at lunch time, and take advantage of lunch-time specials. We would visit as many different kinds of places as time allowed, although we were especially interested in the new things and the most popular things among knowing Londoners – for example, that hybrid form of social life known as 'modern British cuisine', and those newfangled chain restaurants (the like of which one seldom finds anywhere else) that their proud corporate parents call 'mid-range'. We would also visit shops and markets, and study street life: I hadn't narrowed my study down entirely to restaurants yet. What was the phenomenological, material and symbolic place of food, the situation of food in modern London?, we wanted to know. We took along notebooks, a laptop and a Dictaphone, along with a *Time Out Guide to Dining in London*, 2007 edition, and observations culled from various Internet sites, including the online Zagat survey and the annual list of the World's Fifty Best Restaurants, as featured in the London-based *Restaurant* magazine. Knowing how limited our resources were, we knew not only that our findings would be partial, tentative and somewhat arbitrary, but that our project was following less in the footsteps of Franz Boas and Bronislaw Malinowski, or even R. W. Apple, than freelance journalists desperate for a byline in a respectable publication that might actually pay for the article.

And so . . . off we were. We were out on the streets within moments of checking into our hotel. We were in Kensington, not a 'typical' London neighbourhood one might say, but what is 'typical', and why? Kensington is very wealthy and residential; it has its own high street with small and large shops. It is not a major destination for either locals or tourists, although there are a number of hotels (we got an excellent deal, in a comfortably shabby establishment, it being offseason) and there were plenty of tourists on the streets. It is not a place where one goes out of one's way to dine, but it is not an area where one cannot dine either. At the time of my research there, an old department store was being converted into a very large new Whole Foods market, the first outpost in Britain of the American organic-gourmet food chain, and, it has been said in the press, sure to change food retailing in Britain utterly. Perhaps we were researching a 'before', with an 'after' to come. In any case, the sociological model of that which is statistically 'typical' in the context of a vast, diverse, cosmopolitan and always rapidly changing metropolis is almost certainly irrelevant. What is typical about London is its variety. Or not quite: for even if London has lots of variety in its social and cultural life, it has variety in its own way. It has its own way, one might say, of distributing variety, and what one encounters when one visits the city, is not only what is unique about unique places, institutions, and people, but perhaps even more importantly, and certainly more noticeably, are its systems of what may be called continuity-in-variety. These are systems inscribed in its architecture, its structures of transportation and communication, its patterns of work and leisure, of production, distribution and consumption. The guidebooks direct the tourist to 'landmarks' like the Nelson column in Trafalgar Square; the restaurant guides direct the gourmand-tourist to places like Le Gavroche or Sketch, the former a French-run London institution with the usual Michelin stars, the latter 'the most expensive restaurant in London', as almost all references to the establishment have been quick to mention.[6] Yet though the unique is everywhere promoted, it is the 'everywhere' itself that really presses upon experience.

Out on the streets, in Kensington, following the route of a tourist-*flâneur*-gourmand, passing along a route from Kensington Road to Kensington High Street, sensing the continuities of London life – the architecture, the pace of the traffic, the smell of the air – we looked for food. And at first, we didn't see much. London has historically been a city of eating behind closed doors, and as for food shops, whatever the situation may have been in the past, by now they have almost entirely been absorbed by a handful of big 'multiples', the large corporations like Tesco and Sainsbury's, which have placed almost all the food available for consumption inside big brick boxes with little outdoor display. This is the first thing to know about the continuity-in-variety of the culture of food in London. It is almost entirely hidden from view. You do not encounter vegetable stands on the streets of London, or food stalls, or the smells of cooking, or the sight of people dining (except sometimes through plate-glass windows, especially the floor-to-ceiling windows common to cafes and sandwich shops), though you may well encounter that in many sections of many other large cities in the world. You can go for miles on the streets of London, in other words, without encountering a tomato. (The few vaunted outdoor food markets are in fact quite tucked away, the most famous of them, the Borough Market, being hidden under a viaduct in a non-residential area.) What you encounter everywhere are establishments through the doors of which, or behind the plate-glass windows of which, food is to be found. And not just any establishments: as a corollary to the fact that food is behind closed doors and windows, the second thing to know is that the London food scene is almost entirely dominated by large corporations, with multiple locations – signages, brands, doorways to enter, open doorways sometimes, but doorways all the same, or else glassed-in eating areas that, instead of being terraces open to the city, as in (say) Paris and Rome, are almost always, rather, very much glassed-in. So the largest of corporations, the multinationals, have dotted the terrain with McDonald's and Pizza Huts. Smaller, local corporations, specializing in all sorts of food, from Japanese to Portuguese to a hybrid called 'world food', have bred multiples too: Wagamama ('pan-Asian', nineteen), Ask (Italian, twenty), Balls Brothers (wine bars, fourteen), Zizzi (Italian, 35), Yo! Sushi (Japanese, 22), Nando's (Portuguese fast food 'Peri-Peri' chicken, 54), Giraffe (fifteen: an establishment where you are promised 'world food' but where the main attraction appears to be the English breakfast). Even restaurants that aspire to fine dining can come in multiples. There are now six branches of Bertorelli's. There used to be ten of Fish Works, though now they are down to three. Famous chefs, like Gordon Ramsay, strive to own multiples as well.

But I hadn't taken stock of all that yet. My knowledge was in brackets.

So we were out on the streets, on a bright but chilly early spring day, looking for a culture of food. We passed a number of imposing eighteenth- and nineteenth-century buildings, what the English sometimes call 'mansions' though they are actually blocks of flats and townhouses, and the imposing facade of a genuinely unique institution, The Milestone Hotel, with a restaurant inside. The hotel is 'five star'. Every reference you find to it in guidebooks or on the web makes that assertion, and comments from customers on websites like Trip Adviser consistently confirm that the hotel is 'perfect' or nearly so, that it is a 'true five star', and so forth. Certainly, the hotel, composed out of a pair of Victorian 'mansions', was handsome; at first, I thought it was a private club, and I imagined it as a place where the Prince of Wales would feel at home. (And after all, it is just off the street called Prince of Wales Terrace.) But it is just a hotel, albeit an idiosyncratic and expensive one, with rooms starting at about £250. And anyway, we were interested in food. A very handsome plaque indicated a restaurant inside, and displayed a menu. Called Cheneston, it had items like a starter of 'Terrine of *foie gras* with toasted brioche and pear chutney' for £17 and a main course of 'Pot roast supreme of guinea fowl with celeriac and parsley mash, morel mushroom sauce' for £24; 'Tournedos of Aberdeen Angus beef, galette potato and burgundy shallot sauce' for £29.50; and for the vegetarian, a 'Pea and mint risotto with seared scallops and minted foam' also for £29.50. Expensive, in other words. This was all during the height of the economic boom that would bring along the economic crash of 2008, and the pound at the time was almighty, so that a plate of risotto cost the equivalent of $58, or €42. In any case, devoted as this example called Cheneston was to a conventional if a little updated British-Continental style of eating, the restaurant already stood for me as a representative of the hazards of triumphant London cuisine. Heavy and rich food this was; if not unappetizing (some of the dishes seemed very promising), it was nevertheless bulky. Above all, it was mish-mash food, French ingredients, cooking techniques and terms (galette, tournedos), combined with a few Italian and Spanish tricks (the risotto, the 'foam'), vying against Asian condiments (chutney, but made from an English fruit), British ingredients (Aberdeen beef) and un-ironic allusions to bland English home cooking (pot roast and mash, rather than *daube* and *purée*). Triumphant London cuisine going back to the heyday of the Empire has ever been thus, featuring a vocabulary that is hybrid, and a style of eating that is heavy rather than light, organized around the consumption of big hunks of meat with sauces, starches and condiments, along with the proverbial overcooked veg, which is nowadays not overcooked so much.

We went on, down Kensington Road. An Indian restaurant nearby boasted a 'fusion' cuisine, which on the evidence of the menu mainly meant large portions of meats – roasted beef, braised lamb and stir-fried chicken portions, served in sauces made with raisins, garam masala and chilli. We next saw a convenience shop, a narrow and shallow emporium where one could buy cigarettes, liquor, newspapers and urgent foodstuffs like fruit juice, soft drinks, canned beans and eggs. I went in to buy a newspaper, and stood in line at the high check-out counter behind an American woman. She was nervously studying the display of confections below the cash register – Cadbury's Dairy Milk bars, Mars Bars, KitKats, Snickers, Toblerone, those sorts of things, at least 50 different kinds. She looked and looked. A heavy-set woman in her forties, she was perturbed, while both I behind her and the clerk in front of her huffed and puffed, waiting for her to make a decision. Finally, she blurted it out, expressed her desire and befuddlement. 'Don't you have any English toffee?' she asked. The clerk, a young man, an immigrant from the east, paused before answering. Like most Englishmen, I am sure he had never heard of 'English toffee'. 'Only have what here', he said. The woman tottered away, indignant, and I bought my paper.

Out on the streets, as we reached the corner of Kensington Road and Kensington High Street, we finally found a row of colourful establishments, One Restaurant, an Iranian establishment, a Prezzo, a Strada, a Caffè Uno (three similar 'Italian' chain restaurants, specializing in pizza and pasta), a Starbucks, a Giraffe, Utsav, an Indian takeout, Stick and Bowl, a Chinese noodle house, and then further along, off Kensington High Street, two places with a bit more allure, Bar Cuba and Arcadia, the latter a genuinely local – which is to say individually owned and operated – Italian restaurant, the former a Cuban theme establishment with both a restaurant and a dance bar. The scene was starting to seem hopeful for this particular missionary. But then as I turned back up to Kensington High Street I found that this small strip of restaurants was pretty much the end of it. Most of the rest of Kensington High Street, and the side streets immediately off it, apart from some chain outlets like the 'Italian' place Ask and the sandwich cafe Pret A Manger, was devoid of culinary culture. Big clothing stores predominated, the kind one would find on almost any high street in all of Britain: an Accessorize, a Topshop, a Gap. In fact, if you were blindfolded and driven about for a bit, and let out in the middle of Kensington High Street, apart from the Tube station, it would be very hard to know where you were. It is almost indistinguishable from at least thirty different high streets across the United Kingdom. And apart from that small strip of colour and promise, the food was not only behind closed doors, but phenomenologically absent. By the Tube station is a Marks & Spencer with a small separate doorway leading downstairs to the food section. I was reminded of Joseph Conrad's description of the steps down to the anarchist-pornography shop in *The Secret Agent*. The speciality down the stairs at M&S is prepared meals in cardboard boxes, supplemented by prepared sandwiches available in cardboard and cellophane containers. Further down the street, on a raised ground floor, is the one genuine supermarket of the area (in advance of the opening of Whole Foods), a Waitrose, which also pushes a lot of prepared meals and sandwiches, along with a cornucopia of bottled mustards, honeys, chutneys and what the British call cooking sauces, ranging from Tikka Masala to Bolognese.

Off the high street, you are in the midst of the old empire. The architecture is elaborately costly, large and brawny; the residential buildings bespeak not only wealth but patriarchal glory. Marion very inconveniently decided, as we wandered past powerful 'mansions' and town houses and even some detached houses, done up in white painted limestone, or in brownstone and parti-coloured brick, that she wouldn't mind living in these parts. But the high street itself is unimpressive, and the restaurant scene is small. Where did the wealthy eat? Clearly, either at home or in a different neighbourhood. Clearly, in the eighteenth and nineteenth centuries the wealthy almost always dined at home, from meals cooked by servants. And the food shops and stalls of the high street were the shops and stalls where servants were the main social actors. Now the servants were gone, and so were the shops and stalls. In advance of the opening of a Whole Foods, there was little beside chain restaurants specializing in generic 'Italian' food and a pair of food emporia, Marks & Spencer and Waitrose.

After our wander through Kensington, it still being too early to eat, we searched for a pub, and we didn't have far to go. Just off the High Street, mingled with small service shops, was a handsome old Victorian pub, The Prince of Wales (that name again!), with wooden floors and panelling and very high ceilings. We found a seat in the back, partook of a couple of pints and observed the natives. The pub encouraged dining. It had many tables suitable for dining, crowded together, and there were menus everywhere. At four-thirty in the after-noon the pub was noisy and busy, and as workers from nearby shops filed in after five, it got even busier. What one mainly observed was that almost everyone was drinking beer, and that the main buzz of the place was the struggle to find a table. We saw several confrontations over table space. Meanwhile, we studied the menu. In addition to fish and chips and scampi and chips, there were potato wedges with cheese, nachos, salmon fish cakes, 'posh bacon and eggs', steak and ale pie, Chicken Kiev, chicken tikka, hamburgers and, for the vegetarian, mushroom risotto. The fact is, food like this (featuring bits and pieces of the cuisines of seven national cultures) is available in pubs all over London and in much of the rest of the UK too, and much of it comes no less pre-made than the takeaway meals that dominate the shelves at Marks and Spencer. Much of it too is virtually inedible.

'London food is both centralized and distant', I wrote in my journal next morning. 'Food is something you go to', I went on. 'It is never simply at hand. Organized into zones – zones of circulation, "neighbourhoods", "financial districts", "entertainment districts" – this city. Food is in the entertainment district or else it is hidden from you, and one way or another you have to go to it. So you go . . . We need to go to Soho. There is nothing out here in Kensington for us. We're on our way.'

I have since been informed that I went to the wrong place. I should have gone to East Ham, where the Indian restaurants are. Or I should have gone to Clerkenwell and Shoreditch, where there are establishments as diverse as Fifteen, the Bistrothèque, the Bacchus Pub and Kitchen and the Song Que Café. (Actually I did visit the East End, though not any of the restaurants I just mentioned, and will report on a couple of East End establishments below.) I should have gone where Londoners in the know go when they want to dine. The beaten path for the local *homo restauranticus*, even if it is off the beaten path for *homo touristicus*, is where any happy eater ought to aspire to visit. But notice the logic in the suggestion. In what might be thought of as 'the whole' of restaurant culture in towns like London, there is a distinction between restaurants for locals and restaurants for visitors, or for people in the know and people ever out of it. Duly noted.

But being off the tourist's beaten path, or being 'ethnic', is no guarantee of excellence or even digestibility in London – I have memories to prove it, from the East End and the West End alike. And in any case, two further points need to be made. In the first place, though the local and the touristic are indeed completely separate, if you are in fact either a local or a tourist, in the texture of a capital city the local and the touristic are completely intertwined – economically, culturally and even for the most part geographically. Arbutus, a new but beloved institution in Soho, serving swank French bistro food, is just up the road from a Gourmet Burger Kitchen, a Nando's and a Bertorelli's. Tourist expenditures both *support* local culture and *mitigate* it. Tourist tushes fill up the seats at Arbutus and Nando's alike, and the untrained youth who gets his first job at Nando's may well work in Arbutus, or his own equivalent of Arbutus, some day. So the local-tourist distinction is a fit subject for a little bit of old-fashioned deconstructing. It would seem that locals are the opposite of tourists, but at bottom all tourists are locals, and all locals are tourists. And in the second place, whatever the objective facts of dining in London actually are, if you are in possession of those facts as a local expert, I was visiting London precisely as a tourist, or a tourist in brackets, as well as a journalist in brackets and a social geographer in brackets. I went where, given my limits of time, space and resources, and the brackets I had put around the whole operation, I had it in me to go.

Off to Soho, then. Or almost. Our first meal for the trip took us to Chinatown, just down the road from Soho, where I learned an important lesson. On a pleasant night, we walked the distance from Kensington to the central entertainment district; it seemed to take about an hour. Having decided on Chinese food for our first meal, we then walked the Chinatown walk. Many of the restaurants are centred around a festive, brilliantly lit plaza, the pedestrianized Gerrard Street. This is a manufactured Chinatown rather than the real thing. That is to say, first someone came up with the idea of planting a Chinatown in the district, and then Chinese restaurateurs and workers followed.[7] It was a *commercial* idea, promoted by an entrepreneur, rather than a neighbourhood where Chinese immigrants preferred or were obliged to live. But it has grown to attract an expanding Anglo-Chinese community, and it is a fun place, where the kind of Chinese food you don't get in most of the rest of England is available. I had jellyfish salad in a small establishment there once.

But where should we go for this taste-testing meal? A friend, buzzing good-naturedly, had recommended a modest place, The Crispy Duck on Wardour Street. (It has since moved to Gerrard Street.) *Time Out*, also buzzing, had recommended a new Sichuan establishment, Bar Shu, a '2006 Runner-up Best New Restaurant': it is not 'London's first Sichuan restaurant', the guidebook said, 'but it's the first to have recreated Sichuan food so successfully'. We had trouble finding it, though; my research assistant was getting cross; I was getting cross. And when we finally found it, I for one was unimpressed. The menu did not seem adventurous or for that matter especially Sichuan, and it was surprisingly expensive, with all the interesting main courses at £20 or more. It was not within our budget. (Much to our prejudice, I was later told.) So I insisted that we walk back to the centre of Chinatown, which made my assistant even more cross. Where to go? There were so many. So many of them seemed alike, with menus on the pavement set on stands in glass and metal cases, offering a dozen kinds of beef, a dozen kinds of pork . . . And I didn't want to try a place I had already eaten at. We walked about. I was getting ravenous. My assistant was losing her patience. Finally, we made it to the Crispy Duck, a dive with dirty walls and floors, smoked tea duck hanging in the windows, and very low prices: perfect perhaps. And I was hungry and tired; I could not have walked another block. But you could smell acrid grease and soapy steam when you walked in.

We were ushered upstairs, to a small table against a wall with peeling paint; there was a hole in the tablecloth. The menu was enormous, and the more you looked at it the more expensive and complicated it got. But on the first few pages were set value meals, like one where you could get crispy duck, mixed vegetables, sweet and sour pork and prawns in black bean sauce for £11.50. I had given up eating sweet and sour pork when I was twenty years old, but who was I to argue against crispy duck with pancakes, mixed vegetables, and prawns for £11.50? My research assistant dissented. She wanted to try the à la carte. There were all kinds of things we could try. 'No!' I insisted, thinking about my budget and my hunger, and reduced at this point to early stages of a tantrum. The £11.50 was dancing in my head like characters in a Technicolor cartoon. £11.50. Crispy duck. £11.50. Crispy duck.

Most of the food, when it arrived, was pretty bad. (It is not judgemental to say that: the food was bad the way the weather outside is either good or bad.) The duck was passable but stale; the vegetables were overcooked, soggy and tasteless; the pork was as unsavoury as one might expect it to be, deep-fried meat pieces swimming in artificially coloured, gloppy sweet sauce, cheek by jowl with stray onions and peppers. Only the prawns were really decent. Meanwhile, at the table next to us, a pair of posh young Chinese women had ordered à la carte. The food came on what looked like better dishes. A handsome pork dish, with the pork slices fanned over a dark and steaming sauce, came first, followed by a plate of dark green Chinese broccoli, sprinkled with what looked like flecks of garlic and ginger. In fact, the women called the waiter over, and got into a heated discussion (in Chinese) with him about the broccoli. Look at this, they were apparently saying, it's too . . . soggy probably. Eventually, after extensive negotiation, the waiter picked up the plate and took it back to the kitchen. About five minutes later he returned with another dish of broccoli, which this time indeed looked a bit brighter and crisper. He also brought the women a plate of fish slices, lightly sautéed and served with a pale, translucent sauce. The women dug in: the pork, the fish, the greens. Meanwhile I was getting a bellyache, forcing myself to consume our glop, trying to put on a good show for my assistant, who had only picked at her food, and was finding solace in the crisp white wine we had ordered.

I had made the most fundamental and common mistake of gastronomic tourism, the kind of mistake no food critic, or for that matter social geographer, should ever make. I had ordered the food devised for the ignorant. I had let my hunger and impatience and greed get the better of me. But I could not have been the first of my kind to make such a mistake. No, there must be a thousand cases like mine: restaurant critics, upon whom so much depends, the prosperity of restaurateurs, the happiness of diners, ordering the wrong thing. Only they never tell you that. No. They tell you that the restaurant was wrong. Or else, more likely, they keep silent about the experience entirely. Never once have I read a restaurant review which includes such details as finding oneself humiliated in front of one's dinner companions, beside the example of true savoir faire expressed by diners at the next table over. No restaurant critics I know of have ever (by their own accounts) spilled the wine, bickered with their guests, got sick and run to the bathroom or, as I did, found themselves forced to consume soggy cabbage and deep-fried sugar-candy pork in a desperate attempt to redeem their dignity. No, the restaurant is always wrong, and the only real thing in question is whether it is a little bit wrong or very wrong indeed.

Embedded in this critical practice is a common assumption that the customer is always right. Only the provider can get it wrong. But as our experience at the Crispy Duck attested, that is clearly incorrect. Customers can get it wrong too. And embedded in the practice as well is the assumption that critics can never get it wrong either. No: critics are *always* right. I am not suggesting that every critic is Anton Ego, the nasty narcissist in the animated film *Ratatouille*, but the genre of the restaurant requires diffidence or dissimulation about personal matters coupled with a never-to-be-compromised confidence. Critics never get cramps at the table; they never insult their guests or cower in front of an imperious waiter; they are never worried about their debts and the depletion of their expense accounts; they never spill the soup; they are never too drunk to remember what they are doing, or not drunk enough to enjoy themselves; they are never grieving the loss of a loved one; they are never allergic to peanuts or chocolate or lamb; and they never order the wrong thing. And in addition, they are never wrong in what they write about what they have ordered. Let down your shield, express your doubts, open yourselves to criticism, communicate to the world that after all, in your heart of hearts, you are only a poor, bare, forked animal . . . and you are no longer a critic. Instead, you are one of us.

But the Chinatown fiasco was only the first of many experiences high and low for bare, forked Marion and me. For the next four days and nights we were diligent, looking and eating. It is perhaps important to point out that London is the kind of place where it is possible to make an investigation like this, and to do it mainly by foot, examining the restaurant in the context of what has been called the 'phenomenology of the street'.[8] (You couldn't do this in Columbus, where you would need a car.) In central London, on the commercial streets, phenomenologically (and really, too) there are restaurants everywhere you go. But it is also important to point out that perambulating in London will not take you past many places like Le Gavroche or Sketch; in fact we saw neither, and very few other places of the kind. What you see everywhere are places like Pret A Manger, the cafe where the main food, the sandwich, is wrapped in cardboard boxes with cellophane windows, and grabbed from a cooler, along with EAT. The Real Food Company (sic), a similar chain with similar sandwiches, the former with 149 locations in Greater London, the latter ('a small company dedicated to Quality Food') with 80. A Pizza Hut and a Nando's and a Pizza Express are usually hard by too. Most of these establishments are fairly new, or else newly decorated, with thick plate-glass windows from floor to ceiling, colourful laminate tables, solid chairs, clean tile floors, nicely arranged floor plans and warm and even lighting. This gives the city, as you walk along, an air of prosperity, a demeanour of comfort and swank. Many of them, in addition, have the air of being what is called 'trendy'; this gives the city an air of artiness, of up-to-datedness. But the preponderance of them also gives the city a kind of claustrophobic homogeneity. Everywhere you go – if you are wandering about as I was wandering, having a look with no particular destination – there are all kinds of choices, but they are almost always the same choices. Everywhere you go you are enclosed by the logic of the multiple, a continuity-in-variety imposed by the spread of corporate entities whose nature it is to reproduce themselves and grow – here there and everywhere, the old octopus of corporate capitalism having stretched its tentacles into every lane of foot traffic where commerce is allowed. Pizza Hut and Nando's. Pizza Hut and Nando's. EAT. EAT. EAT. This is not a circumstance unique to London. But it is inescapable in London, as is the fact that London expresses this logic of the multiple in its own way – relatively posh, arty and cool, comfortable and swank, driven by High Concepts like organic 'Real Food' and French-pretend 'Ready to Eat', but all the same expressive of nothing so much as homogeneity.

The mistake the buzz makes, the buzz that tells us that London is one of the food capitals of the world, is that it is only concerned with a fraction of what is actually happening in London, and it pretends that the fraction is equal to the whole. To be sure, there are the zones of exception I have mentioned, Soho above all, along with Chinatown and Theatreland and parts of Mayfair and Marylebone and several districts in the East End. These are the 'go to' areas. But even the 'go to' areas are under pressure from the multiples – yes, there are chain restaurants in Soho, a Wagamama, a Pizza Hut, a TGI Friday's, a Nando's, a Café Rouge – and, in keeping with the logic of multiplication, some establishments that start in the 'go to' areas end up being multiplied outward toward the more residential areas, so that they make themselves into multiples too. The buzz is all about singularity. But the reality is continuity-in-variety. The reality is the continuity-in-variety caused by corporate multiplicity, by a general programme of high-end McDonaldization, with a few exceptions of variety by a more random source of energy thrown in.

The dining scene, it turns out, operates on at least six levels. I am not going to say which is the 'top' level, which is the 'bottom', because that implies the fixture of a hierarchy which is not universally recognized or even understood. But at one level come the fast food joints, which themselves can be divided between national or multinational chains and local joints, the former mainly involving hamburgers, pizza and fried chicken and a large dining hall, the latter mainly involving fish and chips or kebabs and a couple of bar stools by the window.[9] On another level comes the posh or high concept fast food, where the food is served slightly more slowly, and may even be brought to the table by a server, and the customers are expected to spend a little more money and take slightly more time over their meals – Nando's and Pizza Hut are the most prominent examples, but the sandwich cafes like Pret A Manger probably ought to be placed in this category, however 'organic' and 'free trade' and 'sensibly sourced' their espresso coffee and their 'pole and line-caught tuna on multi-grain bread' may be. On still another level come the pubs, though some pubs aspire toward being restaurant quality 'gastropubs' and some don't aspire at all: there are several levels within this level. And on yet another come the 'mid-range' restaurants, beloved by *Time Out*, and often based on an ethnic theme. 'Italian' restaurants often belong to this category, like the Strada and the Caffè Uno I encountered when I left my hotel in Kensington. So does the Giraffe I encountered there, with its global ethnic theme (at one and the same time missing the point of being 'global' and that of being 'ethnic') as well as the trendier places like Wagamama and, at the high end of the category, more 'Italian' restaurants like Prezzo, Zizzi and Pizza Express (distinguished by the quality of ingredients, the care of the cooking and even by a certain professionalism of service), and other themed restaurants ('themed' rather than authentically ethnic, because of their corporate structure and lack of ethno-geographic focus) like Yo! Sushi (founded by an English TV personality) and Gourmet Burger Kitchen (brought to the shores of the UK, offering American food, by way of New Zealand).

We tried three of these 'mid-range' themed places, full of high hopes, since this is where a large part of the future seems to lie, but I have to say we were disappointed in them all:

- A Wagamama, which was pitiful: mushy noodles – overcooked semi-instant noodles, not much different if at all from the kind you get in a Styrofoam cup and add boiling water to – a 'yasai chilli men', drowning in condiments, prepared by cooks, as Marion put it in her log of the evening, who had seen pictures of Asian noodle dishes but 'had no idea how they were supposed to taste'.
- A Canteen, a small upscale British-theme chain, a winner of design awards in the business district, which was just starting out and still only has four outlets, and which provided us with an irritating afternoon: having arrived at 12.15 for lunch to this wide open sleek blond wood and aluminium space in the recently remade and expanded Old Spitalfields Market, and being told, coldly, that an hour and fifteen minutes after being seated we would have to vacate our table for a party that had reserved it, we then sat down on uncomfortable bench seats (popular in these mid-range theme restaurants in London, as if your back needs to suffer in order that the rest of you may

deserve the relatively low prices) in an extremely noisy room – the wood and aluminium serving to amplify rather than baffle the sound – and being served, peremptorily by a harried waiter from Italy, a burnt platter of macaroni cheese and a run-of-the-mill dish of posh fish and chips.

- A Yo! Sushi where, after we sampled a few items from the conveyor belt, we realized that apart from a number of variations (often cooked, even fried, not raw) on tuna, salmon, crab and shrimp, you aren't going to get any of the real stuff – the *hamachi*, the *hirame*, the *hokkigai*. The food was freshly made and not untasty (I liked the seaweed salad), and the service was good, but the food lacked depth, mystery, life. Eating Japanese food there was like going to a Gothic cathedral, sticking your head through the door, and leaving before visiting any of the cathedral's treasures. Yo! Sushi, we found (which has now spread its tentacles into Dublin, Moscow, the United Arab Emirates and Kuala Lampur) is to a real kaiten sushi bar what Wagamama is to a real Japanese noodle house.

But the most important thing to take note of with regard to these mid-range and even some of the posh fast food places, it seems to me, has to do with what kind of person you are made to be when you dine there. You are treated civilly. The food (at least in some of the places) is healthful and tasty: this is not *junk* food. But in the end the restaurant hollows you out. You get recruited into participation into a corporate food machine, its *brand* (you betcha', the MBAs get involved), its *economy*, and though you are trying to do your best, and the staff (almost always very young, not to mention Continental) are doing their very best (*staff morale* is taken very seriously by corporations), and in any case youth springs eternal), and though your needs as a consumer therefore are being competently addressed, your deeper needs as a human being are altogether ignored. That applies both to the individual experience you have when you are inside one of these establishments, giving your order and dining, and to the multiplicity of experiences the multiplicity of outlets imposes upon you. Every Pret A Manger is another Pret A Manger. Every Pizza Express is another Pizza Express. Each one thereby becomes, in the phrase again of anthropologist Marc Augé, a 'non-place', and so you too, when you are dining there, become placeless. *Homo sacer*, as Giorgio Agamben puts it in another context: you are treated not as a full human being with the dignity of an identity but as a bundle of bare human life, placeless and stateless, a creature with needs and open orifices, requiring a way-station where you may park your butt and fill your holes. Only you are not a destitute and stateless migrant, a *homo sacer* in the classic sense; you are a middle income office worker and tax-paying citizen, with money to spend and an eye to fashion: *homo sucker*. The trick of the places is to make you think that what they normally give you – the 'line-caught' tuna sandwich, the limp noodles in a spicy sauce, the reheated macaroni cheese, the tiny rolls of cold *tekka maki* on a plastic plate, delivered to you by a machine – are ALREADY giving you surplus pleasure, already giving you IT. And so you want more and don't pay attention to the fact that you really haven't had anything yet.

It was different with the next two categories, the traditional restaurant and the palace of haute cuisine. I knew that I was in an establishment that could be called, in the first case, simply, a traditional restaurant, when dining there made it possible to imagine what the name, restaurant, says: that one was actually being restored, as a person, as one dined there. The place did not have to be expensive – The Crispy Duck, after all, *almost* made it for me, and certainly did perform as required for the two ladies at the next table over. Nor did it have to serve any particular kind of cuisine, although the service would generally be in the original French tradition. But it had to be human. In other words, it had to speak to me. It had to be *for* me, even if it wasn't (as a majestic consumer might mistake it to be) for me in particular.

Two places of this kind really spoke to Marion and me during the week, Acorn House and Sardo. The former is a socially experimental, ecologically oriented, non-profit 'training' restaurant in King's Cross, presenting what it calls Italian food by way of a strictly seasonal and mainly locally sourced menu. We had a fine meal there of soup, fish from the Thames (some kind of bass, from way upstream, we were assured), guinea fowl and platters of mixed lukewarm 'salad' vegetables, though the meal wasn't really Italian, more like Italian cooking techniques and sensibilities applied to modern British food, and we had the impression that forty years since the founding of Chez Panisse in Berkeley the institution may have been working a little too hard to reinvent the wheel. But we heard what the restaurant was saying to us: we are trying to do something different; we are trying to do something moral and social, good for the planet, good for the animals, good for society; but as for you, enjoy! Try this beetroot and cardamom soup. It's going to taste of beetroot and cardamom, only better. And so it did. Try this salsify with your fowl, a local root vegetable with a taste somewhere between celery, parsnip and asparagus. I'll bet you never had that before. No we hadn't, but the next time we find it on a menu we will order it again.

We felt ourselves being spoken to at Sardo as well, the Sardinian restaurant in Fitzrovia, to which we brought a guest, Andrew. We had spaghetti bottariga, made with mullet roe, a veal chop with beans, grilled swordfish, asparagus salad and sautéed mixed vegetables, washed down with a couple of bottles of Vermentino Funtana, a full-bodied but very drinkable Sardinian white. Here there was no agenda, no didacticism, no turning of the customer into a pupil, only a commitment to bringing simple but rare and careful Sardinian things to a sophisticated London crowd, and to having a good time doing it. This was the only restaurant we visited that week where we were made to feel (even by a very blonde, British waitress) that it was good clean fun to enjoy ourselves, or even to push ourselves a little beyond enjoyment (that second bottle of Vermentino). The more fun we had, the more fun the restaurant had. Though the place was mainly filled with suits, in the middle of a work day, we felt relaxed there; everyone felt relaxed there. Or rather, not relaxed but intoxicated. Sardo delivers an Italian speciality: the use of care and artistry to enhance rather than challenge the intense, intoxicating leisureliness of the meal and the anonymous good fellowship of a dining room. Other restaurants in London will make you feel that, if you must, it is okay to eat, it is okay to indulge the little machine of need and desire within you, making a virtue out of necessity. After all, you have to eat, and may as well have fun. And if you do it right, it may be harmless to the planet. You may even be doing some tribal Thames fisherman a favour. But at Sardo we were made to feel that it is a shame that it is sometimes not okay to eat; we were made to feel that it is tragic that eventually our machineries of need and desire would shut down, and we would have to stop eating and drinking and leave the premises. At Sardo the servers and the cooks say 'this is *you*' and '*this* was you', in your essence. And it was here, at the dining table, having had your identity established as a person who eats, you were convinced, that the good meaning of life was always to be found. The prices weren't bad either.

But there is one level more, the level of restaurant that aspires not to fine but to exceptional dining: haute cuisine if you are French, and if you are anything else there is really no word for it, which says something about the nature of the experience. It was this level of dining which was supposed to have so triumphed in London as of late, making it a world capital, home of some of 'the best restaurants in the world'. Now as I mentioned before, I had eaten in some pretty good places in America and France, but I had never dined in a palace of traditional haute cuisine anywhere, and suddenly there were all these places in London boasting – what? Boasting Michelin stars. Now if you want to know how the Michelin system works you will have to turn to books that have not been translated into English, such as Pascal Remy's *L'inspecteur se met à table* (2004), Jean-François Mesplède's *Trois étoiles au Michelin* (2004) and François Simon's deliciously cynical *Pique assiette* (2008).[10] These are not scholarly books; they are meant for the general public and they make all kinds of concessions in order to be readable, including in Simon's case an affectation for earthy French slang that can make reading it rough going for the non-native speaker. Each in its own way emphasizes the Gallocentric view of fine dining that animates the Michelin project, a view which (as Remy shows) causes 'ethnic' restaurants in France to be marginalized, and which (as Simon protests) is being diluted and squandered as Michelin star-type restaurants proliferate in places like Abu Dhabi, Las Vegas and London. The Michelin institution encourages this proliferation, Simon shows, as the Michelin Guides come to cover more and more areas in the world (New York, San Francisco, Tokyo, Hong Kong, Austria . . .), and hence come to impose more and more of its *standard* around the world. (Simon is not, however, xenophobic: his problem with the multiplication of restaurants by very French Michelin-rated chefs like Alain Ducasse or Joël Robuchon is that multiplication stifles creativity and locality and compromises quality. Las Vegas ought to have *Las Vegas* restaurants, not clones of French ones. And you can't be *creative,* Simon adds, if you are busy *duplicating* what you have already done.)

But apart from understanding how the system works from the accounts of people intimate with it from the inside, in order to know what a Michelin-recommended restaurant actually is you have to try one. You have find out for yourself not only what it is like, but what you become as a subject when you find out what one is like. Who and what does a Michelin-recommended restaurant require you to be? In a restaurant like this, what is your *identity*? For the purposes of this book I have actually tried a number of Michelin-recommended establishments (and some of them, by the way, were absolutely fab). But it was during this London visit that I tried for the first time one of the more exalted Michelin nominees. Admittedly, it had only two stars, and one of the stars was newly awarded. But it was trying for three. And it was in London. In fact, going through the guidebooks and the blogs I saw that, if you don't think you can afford or get into one of the three-stars, and if you are looking for a good deal for lunch, this was the place to go.

It was called Petrus at the time, sometimes spelled the French way with an acute accent, *Pétrus.* It was run by a celebrity chef, Marcus Wareing, a protégé of Gordon Ramsay. (It is still run by him, but now the restaurant is called Marcus Wareing at the Berkeley, and Ramsay has given the name Petrus or Pétrus to a new establishment run by a different chef down the road.) All of the guidebooks suggested that this was one of the premier places to eat in London. We studied pictures of the dining room and were impressed. Situated in the Berkeley Hotel in Knightsbridge (where single rooms start at £259 a night), it looked comfortable and chic, a nouveau art nouveau establishment with dark wood and velvet-clothed walls, high windows, brass fittings, claret-coloured furnishings and white linen tablecloths. It had an enormous wine list, somewhat smugly featuring the red wines of Chateau Pétrus (though the food has no connection to the region, the terroir or the people who work at the chateau), and a complex tasting menu. (This was therefore a *theme* restaurant, in spite of itself.) It also had a special lunch menu, three courses featuring either a pork or a beef dish, for £30 a person, which was about as much as we could afford. And as I guessed, correctly, among the most prominent restaurants of London, during this boom year of 2007, it was one of the easiest to secure a reservation for. Marion and I nervously phoned in, and requested a time slot we thought would most likely be available, two o'clock on a Wednesday afternoon. Our request was accepted, though only on condition that we leave a credit card deposit and agree to the restaurant's dress code, and not wear jeans, tennis shoes or other proletarian paraphernalia.

So we were going to eat in a Michelin two-star in one of the swankest parts of London, on the ground floor of one of its most expensive hotels, with a suitably snooty clientele, in a dining room overseen by a renowned chef. For us it would be the culinary equivalent of visiting the Eiffel Tower the first time; only, since it was only a two-star, not a three, and since we were going to order the bargain lunch, it would be like going to see the Eiffel Tower but not taking the lift to the top.

Just getting there was something, though. Marion and I were uninitiated in the ways of the world we were about to visit, and felt it. Needing to arrive by appointment to an elaborate midday dinner, we got a little anxious; we suffered from stage fright. We spent a lot of time grooming ourselves that morning, picking out our clothes and, once dressed, worrying whether we were dressed appropriately. We spent the morning wandering about the streets of London involved in other research, looking at food markets, but with our minds distracted and our hearts in our mouths. Would we make it on time? Would our clothes be mussed by the time we got there? Would we make a good entrance? Would we, as we partook of our sybaritic pleasures, as it were, remember our lines? By one o'clock in the afternoon we were frantic with expectation. The day was nearly wasted because we could think of nothing else and by the time of our arrival – we were five minutes late, since we had turned left rather than right as we neared our destination, ended up in the wrong neighbourhood and were forced to rush about looking for a cab – I was in a sweat. But we were welcomed, with easy graciousness, by a young woman at the door, who seemed to have had it held open for us by yet an invisible genie, and then by the maître d' standing front and centre, a smiling young Frenchman with slicked-back hair, and, at our table, by a relieved, serious and heavy-lidded waiter, all of them greeting us as if we had come home from a hard day in the fields oppressing the natives, or short-selling government bonds, and everyone was glad at our safe return.

The restaurant, it turned out, was excellent. We were seated at a large square table that stood as if an island within a broad archipelago of table-islands, with the spacious sea of the thick wine-red carpet all about us. Whatever else I enjoyed that afternoon, I can safely say that, in a public restaurant, I have never been given so much room to eat in before. Only about ten of about twenty tables were occupied, populated by very well-dressed couples and trios, who every now and then raised their eyes from their own tables and gave fellow diners mischievous looks, across the wine-red expanse, of guilty self-satisfaction, as if they had been caught dallying with the ladies (and/or the eunuchs) in someone else's harem. A private room behind us was occupied by about a dozen young revellers: some kind of guilt-ridden office party, it seemed. The food was delicious, if not surprising, with only two slight disappointments: an *amuse-bouche* of salt cod puree (in other words, a *brandade de morue*, though the restaurant eschewed French terms when it could), which was placed on our table as we arrived and that was a bit bland as *brandades* go; and a *tarte tatin* (there's no English equivalent) for two, which was very brown and bubbly but neither particularly sweet, nor succulent, nor sour, nor fruity, nor crusty, nor rich. But for the rest, all was very fine. In order, this is what we had:

- For both of us, a glass of mushroom-shallot soup, topped by truffle foam and resembling a glass of sweet mocha with cream on top, but tasting savoury only.
- For her, a smoked trout ravioli in a seafood cream, which tasted (she claimed) like sex.
- For him, a crab bisque served in a small sauce boat and then drizzled over a pyramid of shredded crab meat and ribbons of drizzled sauces in a white soup bowl.
- For her, aged, hung, lovingly reared Angus Aberdeen rump steak, served au jus on a mound of tiny crinkly root vegetables, the medium rare beef so fat and juicy one almost didn't need to chew it.

- For him, twenty-four-hour wine-braised belly pork, also served with its juices and baby vegetables, the meat again very tender and in this case intensively flavoured, as if wine and pork and vegetables had been combined and sublimated into a new essence.
- For both, a palate cleanser served in oversized shot glasses, with layers of apple sorbet, *sauce anglaise* and apple jelly.
- For both, a cheese plate, chosen from an impressive cheese board, their selections including an Epoisse and an Ami de Chambertin (both soft, rinded cow's milk cheeses from Burgundy, to go with the wine from Burgundy we had chosen) which were unctuous and earthy, one milky-tasting and the other one cheesy and salty.
- For both, but ordered by her, the fatal *tarte tatin*, served with a boat of clotted cream and a scoop of banana ice cream.
- For both, coffee and bon-bons, the bon-bons with the sweetness and crackle of cookies from the cookie jar, taken on the sly, but better, and in a great quantity.
- For both, inebriation and surfeit.

We didn't get all of this for our £30 each, it must be added. The cheese course was extra. And we found ourselves encouraged to drink a bit more than we expected, and more extravagantly, which added substantially to the cost.

As we sat down, after the *amuse-bouche* appeared on the table, a Champagne trolley was wheeled in front of us, smelling of ice and bubbles. It was hard to say no when we were asked if we would care for a glass of Champagne. We were given three choices from already open bottles in a silver tub. We chose the first, without quite understanding what the waiter had said. Enjoying what turned out to be a good but unexceptional Ayala Brut Majeur, we found out when the menu came that our little acquiescence to bubbles and ice had already cost us an extra £24. If we had chosen the third Champagne offered, a vintage something or other, it would have cost us £70.

As our order was taken, we found ourselves both having fish for a first course and meat for a second, and as we thought it silly, having come this far, and having already been soaked for the Champagne, not to enjoy each course to its full, with proper accoutrements, we decided to take a little splurge on the wine. (The French call this 'going all the way'.) So we ordered half a bottle of white Jean-Max Roger 2005 Sancerre for the fish course, and to go with the meat and the rest a full bottle of red burgundy, a 1998 Pernand-Vergelesses, indeed a Premier Cru Laleure-Piot 'Vergelesses', which, though I (to my shame) had never heard of either the winemaker or the appellation before, seemed a bargain at only £59, since it was the only impressive-sounding wine more than a few years old available at less than £70. (Unlike Marion, however, who raved about it, I was a bit disappointed by the results, finding the wine to be too thin and overly fruity. It was still perhaps a little young.)

In any case, the total bill came to £221, far more than I had ever paid for lunch or dinner before. I pretended not to be shocked. I pretended that it was worth it. Perhaps it was. I paid the bill and walked out on my own two feet as if I were accustomed to spending two hundred quid for lunch, with smiles and thanks to the servers all around, the fine captain who supervised our meal and the assistant waiter who brought the main courses and the assistant assistant waiter who brought the secondary items and the assistant assistant assistant waiter who filled our wine and water glasses if someone higher up wasn't around and who brushed the crumbs off the tablecloth, and along with them the sommelier, his sidekick the evil demon tending the champagne trolley, the receptionist at the front who had had the genie open the front door for us and showed up by the table every now and then, swaying her hips, and above all the slick, smiling, joking, friendly, helpful and altogether artificial maître d'. I walked out with Marion on my arm, out through a bar and an informal, cheaper dining facility, out through the marble-floored hotel lobby, and out into the cool bracing air of a late London afternoon. Did we hail a taxi to get back to our hotel, which wasn't that far down the road? I don't remember. But I remember the two of us getting back to the room and collapsing, overwhelmed by the amount of food and drink we had squeezed into our bodies, uncomfortable, bloated, exhausted. We threw our clothes off and went to sleep, dreaming the uncomfortable dreams of the overstuffed, and woke up in the dark, still a bit bibulous and full. We weren't able to eat another thing for the next 24 hours.

Paris

City of Light. I never performed a single-minded calamity-ridden Cartesian meditation on the food culture in Paris, as I did in London, but I made a number of visits while researching an entirely unrelated subject, and busied myself with the same kind of meditations whenever I could. And so, with the aid of a modest expense account – a *very* modest expense account, insufficient by itself to pay for almost any meal for two for dinner at a Parisian restaurant, but enough to encourage us to try – Marion and I sampled some of the wares the city had to offer.

Phenomenologically, Paris presents a very different experience, of course. London is a city in which one can and does walk, sometimes very pleasantly. Paris is a city which is made for walking. And when you walk, even in the twenty-first century, everywhere you go there is not only a commercial establishment with food for sale, but an establishment that tempts you, beckons you, all but commands you to interrupt the walking and come in and *avoir à manger* or *avoir à boire*.

Everywhere you go, just about: for continuity-in-variety has a different texture in Paris. It is not without its corporate and multinational intrusions – McDonald's and Pizza Hut again, and Starbucks and Subway ('Préparés sous vos yeux!'), along with KFC ('C'est différent!') and the Belgian chain Quick ('Nous, c'est le goût'). It is not without its own homegrown chains either; Restaurant Clément, for example, with twelve locations, and Indiana Café with ten, most of them at major *carrefours* (Bastille, Montparnasse, etc.) and therefore hard to miss. And let me say, having tried the chains for research purposes, that you may as well stay in London or Columbus as come to Paris and eat in any one of them. The old-restaurant-style Clément serves boil-in-the-bag food, though with a bit of perfunctory French panache (adding insult to injury). The large handsome brasserie-style Indiana serves Tex-Mex treats, burritos and enchiladas, prepared and served by happy young Gauls who have never been to either Tex or Mex and who wouldn't seem to know a jalapeño from a sombrero, or at least from a habeñero. (The happy workers are only following orders.) And yet the old texture of the city, for the *gourmand-flâneur*,

168

stays intact. It is only in the *banlieues* and the ex-urban zones of France's cities that the multinational hordes have obstructed the fabric of life, dumping garish freestanding structures along roadways unsuited to pedestrian traffic, as if some cosmic being, in a fit of hilarity, were taking giant shits on the outskirts of France's towns, and daring the citizens to get in their cars, drive up and brave the smell.

Inside Paris all the same there is still that texture – the cobblestones, the lampposts, the awnings, the outdoor tables and chairs, the sinuous curves of the porticoes, the rush of the traffic, the flow of the walkers passing by, the women in coats and boots, the men in suits and broughams, the open-air markets – that makes your heart beat, that sets you in a rhythm. London presents the pedestrian with a newly revised streetscape, freshly provisioned for the new *homo restauranticus*, or at least the new *homo sucker*, for whom the old pubs are inadequate. Paris presents the pedestrian with the same streetscape as ever, already designed with the needs of the modern consumer in mind – or rather, designed to fashion a certain sort of consumer, designed to entice the *homo sapiens* into a form of life constituted by a rhythm of movement and rest, of production and consumption Paris-style.

British visitors to Paris in the nineteenth century were already struck by that. One Lady Morgan, in a very popular book on the subject, remarked how the 'street-population of Paris', lacking the ruffians and drunkards commonly seen prowling through London (as far as she was concerned) could be

characterised by great temperance, mildness, gaiety, and activity, and to be peculiarly governed by a spirit of innocent, though luxurious enjoyment, evidently influenced by their climate. They are perpetually buying or selling fruit and flowers . . . Lemonades and *eau-de groseille* are measured out at every corner of every street, from fantastic vessels, jingling with bells, to thirsty tradesmen or wearied messengers. Cakes are baking, soup is bubbling, sweetmeats are vending in every quarter, in the open streets, over little stoves, and under temporary sheds.

Buskers abounded, singing and dancing in the street. Families and friends gathered in the parks and the cafes and cafe-restaurants, in the open air. And on the whole – though it should be borne in mind that Lady Morgan was visiting in the summer – the Parisians were inclined to gather out of doors rather than in. The inside-outside distinction that was typical of English life was turned inside out in Paris, she thought: 'Most of the domestic life of England, is passed at the fireside; most of the domestic life of France, is enjoyed in the open air . . .'[11]

In 1819 a rejoinder by an English diplomat was published, claiming that Lady Morgan had a too superficial a view of France, given the limited time she stayed there. But on the subject of street life in Paris the author was in agreement with her, especially with regard to cafes. 'Paris is literally crowded with coffee-houses, particularly in the public streets and the boulevards.' (It should be understood that many of these coffee-houses were also either taverns or restaurants and in fair weather put tables and chairs on the pavement outside.)

> It is impossible to conceive either their number, variety, or elegance, without having seen them. In no other city is there any thing of a description resembling them; they are every way adapted for convenience and amusement . . . Many are crowded to excess, and almost all are well frequented . . . There are certain classes of Parisians, and many strangers, that pass nearly the whole of the day in coffee-houses, of which there are at least two thousand, and which are frequented from nine in the morning till twelve at night . . . In Paris, all is a mixture; people converse with each other, though strangers; and ladies, as well as gentlemen, partake of what refreshments they want.[12]

The restaurant scene was in itself a striking phenomenon for British visitors. In *Paris As It Was and As It Is* (1803) the prolific Francis W. Blagdon describes the scene at the Grande Taverne de Londres, or, more simply, Beauvilliers, a restaurant which Grimod quietly admired and which Brillat-Savarin, in *The Physiology of Taste*, would go on to celebrate as the best there ever was. Antoine Beauvilliers, formerly the chef to the Prince of Condé, had founded the establishment in 1782 on the rue de Richelieu, the first *grand* restaurant of Paris. Blagdon the Englishman had visited the restaurant before the Revolution, and came back to find, to his delight, that the restaurant was still flourishing. He describes the place as 'a suite of apartments, decorated with arabesques, and mirrors of large dimensions, in a style no less elegant than splendid, where tables are completely arranged for large or small parties'. The rooms 'are capable of accommodating from two hundred and fifty to three hundred persons', and were often full. The restaurant was no quiet temple of fine dining, though fine dining was certainly on offer. Blagdon describes a busy, boisterous place, presided over by Beauvilliers himself, who visits with the clientele and supervises operations, along with Madame Beauvilliers, the owner's wife, who was to be found seated on 'a sort of throne, not unlike the estrado in the grand audience-chamber of a Spanish viceroy. This throne is encircled by a barrier to keep intruders at a respectful distance.' The 'lady' there, 'who, from her majestic gravity and dignified bulk, you might naturally suppose to be an empress', is responsible for collecting money from the waiters, who seem to be rushing about helter-skelter at all times, but who are actually very much in control of things. By six o'clock 'there will scarcely be a vacant seat at any of the tables. *"Garçon, la carte!"* – *"La voilà, devant vous, Monsieur".'*

The menu is enormous. It comes 'as a printed sheet of double folio, of the size of an English newspaper. It will require half an hour at least to con over this important catalogue. Let us see. Soups, thirteen sorts. *Hors-d'oeuvres*, twenty-two species. Beef, dressed in eleven different ways . . .'. Blagdon is not exaggerating; he reproduces the menu, which goes on, for example, from *boeuf au naturel* to *langue de boeuf glacée aux épinards*, and then on to an even greater number of veal dishes, along with 23 different preparations of fish. As for how the restaurant was organized, Blagdon goes on to say this about its operations:

> Each cook has a distinct branch to attend to in the kitchen, and the call of a particular waiter to answer, as each waiter has a distinct number of tables, and the orders of particular guests to obey in the dining rooms. In spite of the confused

noise arising from the gabble of so many tongues, there being probably eighty or hundred persons calling for different articles, many of whom are hasty and impatient, such is the habitual good order observed, that seldom does any mistake occur; the louder the vociferations of the hungry guests, the greater the diligence of the alert waiters. Should any article, when served, happen not to suit your taste, it is taken back and changed without the slightest murmur.[13]

One of the most striking things about this account is the picture it draws of the theatricality of the restaurant, with the waiters taking centre stage. The picture is reinforced by the later reminiscences (based on sources I have not been able to find) recorded by Scottish journalist Abraham Hayward, in *The Art of Dining; Or, Gastronomy and Gastronomers* (1852). Hayward writes about Grimod's favourite haunt, the Rocher de Cancale:

> If unable to make a party, or compelled to improvise a dinner, connoisseurs were in the habit of asking the *garçon* to specify the luxuries of the day; and it was amusing to witness the quiet self-possessed manner, the *con amore* intelligent air, with which he dictated his instructions, invariably concluding with the same phrase, uttered in an exulting self-gratulatory tone – *Bien, Monsieur, vous avez-là un excellent diner!* Never, too, shall we forget the dignity with which he once corrected a blunder made in a *menu* by a tyro of the party, who had interpolated a *salmi* between the *bisque* and the *turbot à la crême et au gratin.* 'Messieurs,' said he, as he brought in the turbot according to the pre-ordained order of things, '*le poisson est naturellement le relevé du potage.*' The whole establishment was instinct with the same zeal.[14]

All of this 'theatre' adds up to the performance of what I have been calling 'formularity' – an invention of form, and of form for the sake of form, as a ceremony of everyday life. It is what performance sociologists from Erving Goffman to Randall Collins have been talking about, going back to the idea that 'all the world is a stage' as well as to the social criticism of George Orwell and Jean-Paul Sartre, and amounting to the idea that all social interaction (for better or worse) involves an element of ritualization. Only I am emphasizing that in this case the 'formulary' ritual involves creative input. The performance of the French waiters requires ad hoc enforcement; sometimes some of the participants, that is some of the customers, have to be told what to do. The performance also requires a spirit of improvization, by way of what Hayward calls self-possession, *con amore* and 'zeal'. A formularity can be become *formulaic*, when participants simply go through the motions, when the spirit of improvisation and zeal has been replaced by mechanical routine. It will especially become formulaic in cases where a situation has been wholly compromised by bad faith, where no one really believes in what they are doing – neither the staff members nor the customers – but they do it all the same, and they lie to themselves in order to do it. That is the real bane of the chain restaurant, in Columbus, London and Paris alike: the de-skilling of labour and the commodifying of experience, the reduction of all interaction into commercial and phony formality, that leads to bad faith all around, from the careless cook and the incompetent waiter to the impatient diner. But formularity, when it works, as it certainly seems to have worked at the Grande Taverne de Londres and the Rocher de Cancale, involves a daily performance that is at once ritualized and improvised, reiterated and recreated.

And the main point here is that this formularity had already, by the mid-nineteenth century, become embedded in the social life of Paris. It had found its way into the fabric of the streetscape and routines of its inhabitants, in the habits of production and consumption it promoted. And it is still there today, though perhaps more fragilely than before, given such things as the 24/7 work week of the global economy, generational shifts, the growth of virtual communities (where a 'cafe' even for the French need only be the avatar of a cafe) and the inclination of multinational firms (including French multinational firms) to deposit their *ordure* everywhere they can. Paris today is at once modern, postmodern and hypermodern, with the old modernity forming the foundation, and later developments juxtaposed upon it.

That does not mean that most restaurants in Paris are lively, zealous, interesting or even good. On the contrary, there is a problem with restaurants in Paris, as many commentators have noted. 'When I returned to Paris', says one, '. . . after an absence of twelve years, I noticed a serious decline in the quality of the restaurants . . . The decline, I later learned, had been going on even [before] . . .'. Says another commentator, 'How is it that French restaurant cooking has so notably, so sadly, deteriorated during the past two or three decades?' A third commentator notes that 'a lot of people who live in France are worried about French cooking, and so are a lot of people who don't.' He notes that 'the word *crise* in connection with cooking' has appeared even in *Le Monde*, and he says that 'the fear – first unspoken, then whispered, then cautiously enunciated, and now loudly insisted on by certain competitors – is that the muse of cooking has migrated across the ocean to a spot in Berkeley, with occasional trips to New York and, of all places, Great Britain'. A fourth commentator writes that the France memorialized by great gastronomic writers seems to be 'dying' and that something needs to be done to get 'French cooking out of its slump'. Now, the first remark was from A. J. Liebling, writing about the 1920s and '30s. The second was from Elizabeth David, writing about the 1950s and '60s. The third was from Adam Gopnik, writing about the 1980s and '90s, and the fourth was from Michael Steinberger, in a book published in 2009.[15]

Everyone agrees that the 1970s, when *nouvelle cuisine* was born, was a great decade for French food, including Paris. But apart from the 1970s, it seems that French food, including Parisian food, is always in decline. And so in decline it often seemed to me as I revisited France over the past decade.

Not that I ever imagined myself in possession of enough facts to agree or disagree with the experts. I could not occupy the authoritative position of an ideal consumer from which they delivered their pronouncements. I wandered through the streets of Paris as a visitor, with a limited understanding of what was going on around me, and though I was motivated in part by my desire for the consumer's perfect moments, I had other interests as well, sightseeing and business engagements and something like self-education, the pursuit of travel for the sake of travel, among them. It was sometimes difficult for Marion and I to accommodate all our interests at once, to see what we wanted to see and feel whatever our movement inspired us to feel and learn what we found we needed to learn and also to eat and drink all we could, the best we could, and have those perfect moments together. Of course, it was and is impossible to do it all. But in any case, I was also interested, philosophically, in the difficulty itself.

> But the true voyagers are only those who leave
> Just to be leaving; hearts light, like balloons,
> They never turn aside from their fatality
> And without knowing why they always say: 'Let's go!'
>   Charles Baudelaire, 'The Voyage'[16]

One of the pitfalls is how alluring so many establishments can be. In America or Great Britain, if you wander about on a restaurant walk, the decor of a restaurant, inside and out, is a good key to the kind of meal you are likely to have. What you look for is mainly an establishment that, whatever the cuisine it serves, resembles a French restaurant. In America and Britain alike that is almost always a good sign. It shows that the restaurateur is thinking, and possibly even knows a thing or two. But you can't use that as a guide in France, because all kinds of places look like French restaurants, with a menu out front, small, tightly spaced and nicely laid tables inside, wooden chairs, gauze curtains, tile floors, waiters in jackets . . . and they are in fact French restaurants.

Another pitfall is how many of these restaurants there are. When you march down a main street of London or New York you are probably going to pass a number of chain cafes and fast food joints (Dunkin' Donuts, anyone?) before you pass by a nice little establishment with gauze curtains and a selection of wines by the glass. In Paris the multiples recede from vision, and instead you espy one place after another with the allure of a decent place to eat, some expensive, some cheap, some elegant, some dingy, some cavernous, some cramped, but street after street of them. If you don't know what you're doing you may be taken in by some of the clutches of restaurants which hold out their gaudy Gallic arms to tourists, especially in zones like the rue de la Harpe, near Notre Dame, and be served 'French food', or better yet 'Italian-style' pizza. Or you can wander into the student dining area in the Latin Quarter, by rue Mouffetard, which has in large part been overtaken by restaurateurs from Savoy with a predilection for melted cheese, who have to cut corners to keep prices low enough for students. Inside and out the places seem like, well, French restaurants. But not too many of them actually serve the real deal.

You can be bedazzled by time and space, and betrayed by your own footfalls, like the time when we went to the famous Le Petit Zinc. It was on a Monday evening when we found ourselves in Saint Germain. As it was a Monday many of the restaurants in the area were closed; those few we saw that looked interesting were full, or else just too damn expensive. I led Marion on a march in search of a seafood restaurant I remembered, somewhere just around the corner of the Place de l'Odéon, just below it, I thought, or maybe just to the right, or maybe . . . Eventually I began hearing something about somebody being in high heels. This was about the same time as, having left the Place de l'Odéon well behind us, we were coming upon the Boulevard and the Church of Saint Germain-des-Prés, at a corner of the area I didn't know that well because it had always seemed too tourist-chic or just plain chic to me. There was the Café de Flore; there was the Café Les Deux Magots. I wasn't sure if either of them served dinner and I couldn't remember which of the two persons of fashion was supposed to avoid and which they were supposed to patronize. So we marched on, one of us wearing comfortable shoes and the other one of us testy but gorgeous and both of us getting a little wet as it had started to rain. Ahead, I saw, was Le Petit Zinc. I remember having heard about it – it had been quite renowned in its time. I remembered passing it by on an earlier trip and thinking that it might be worth a visit. I remembered having seen it mentioned in a guidebook, though I couldn't remember what the guidebook had said.

We went in, stepping past a modest facade before which, on the sidewalk, an impressive seafood counter was arranged with a multi-tiered display of grey oysters, bright red crabs and any number of dark ovular creatures in shells, and in a moment found ourselves welcomed graciously at the door and quickly swept into a scene that looked like a Hollywood movie set trying to portray a fantasy version of an elegant turn-of-the century French restaurant, only this was in fact an elegant turn-of-the-century French restaurant, lovingly restored, arranged on several levels, all art nouveau and all curves and dark sculpted wood and marble and, of course, zinc, with a sweeping dramatic staircase running through it. There was nothing 'petit' about this place except the bar. Yet the room was crowded – crowded with French people, I might add, not foreign visitors. We were ushered to a comfortable table on the lower recessed floor and handed menus. And there we sat and waited. And waited some more. The menu itself was boring. There were few choices (no 23 sorts of veal here, but only one kind of this and one kind of that) and there was nothing on it that we hadn't seen time and again – simple preparations of a piece of meat or fish with potatoes, mainly, with glances toward traditional garnishes that sounded some-how better than they were: a 'gateau de pommes de terre' or a 'lit de poireaux' – that is to say, a ladleful of mashed potatoes or leeks, though arranged like a 'cake' or a 'bed'. When our handsome young waiter in a stiff jacket finally returned and we had our order taken, I went for a house speciality, the seafood platter (not the deluxe, the regular). It looked impressive when it came. But two of the items on the multi-tiered salver, the whelks and the mussels, were absolutely ex-hausted from having stayed out the night before, and another item, the oysters, though alert, were rather small and only moderately entertain-ing. Marion had roast chicken with sage, which was overcooked, a bit dry and under-seasoned. We picked at our food gamely but dispiritedly. Our handsome young waiter continued to play hide and seek with us and eventually won the game altogether: he disappeared, and we had to flag down another waiter to finish our meal and get the bill.

It was only later that I realized that Le Petit Zinc, glorious and original though it was inside, was owned and operated by a corpora-tion, Le Groupe Frères Blanc, located in suburban Saint Denis, who have bought up and renovated eleven other famous great restaurants and brasseries in Paris, and who also own and operate Chez Clément. I once had an extremely entertaining meal at one of their other famous establishments, Au Pied de Cochon, where I had an old-fashioned breadcrumb-encrusted pig's foot (Marion's kidneys, by contrast, were not so wonderful). And I had once had a mediocre meal, albeit with a fantastic aperitif (an absinthe served from an absinthe fountain) at still another outlet of the empire, Le Procope, the oldest restaur-ant in Paris. I had also twice found myself ordering something boiled in the bag from Chez Clément. But what is really remarkable about all this is the fact that, though I have spent only a limited time in Paris over the past few years, I have managed, unknowingly, in a city of several thousand restaurants, to visit four locations owned by a single corporation, which owns only a total of 24 of them inside the city limits.

It would be tedious to fulminate over the McDonaldization of so many of Paris's glorious eateries; but the fact that I unknowingly managed to land, marooned, in four of them in so short a time says something about the restaurant economics and tourism and, in general, the production of consumption. The Groupe Frères Blanc had managed to find the points of transaction where someone like me will likely find himself at the point of need. Wander where you will, if you're someone in my situation, and you will encounter the Frères Blanc. If you're lost, you will nevertheless be found. If you are resourceful, one of your guidebooks, or a copy of the weekly *Pariscope* (which doesn't hesitate to recommend its advertisers), will help you along. Go here! Go here! Go in! The Frères have done nothing less than commandeer French culinary history, and they have not only packaged it for you, but dispersed it around the major arteries of the city like lodestones to find the iron in your wandering, hungry blood.

What the Frères Blanc cannot provide, despite the magnetism of their establishments, is good food or good service or, really, the *amor fati* of *homo restauranticus*. The main reason is their corporate approach, which makes every one of the establishments, whatever their historical differences and personal specialities, into an expression of a central mind, as if one of James Bond's master villains is manipulating the controls from a secret hideaway underground. I do not know to what extent they employ the notorious trick of cooking food for several restaurants off premises in a central kitchen. I do know that once you are inside one of their restaurants, apart from being very graciously welcomed and seated, you are not entertained by a great deal of zeal, either from the kitchen staff or the people front of house. The employees may be well trained, they may even be trying to do their best, but you know that they are only employees when you encounter them; you know that they are only doing their jobs, and they are evidently operating in a condition of alienated labour. The restaurant is not theirs, the customers are not theirs, the food is not theirs;

only the labour they devote to it is theirs and, once they give up their labour, that isn't theirs either. The profit of it belongs to the executives at the Groupe Frères Blanc, not to mention, even more important, the group's *investors*. The group was taken over (or bailed out with strings attached) a few years ago by a venture capital agency controlled by the French government, CDC Entreprises ('Small and medium size firms have a major role to play in the adaptation of the French economy to the new worldwide conditions', says their president on their Internet site). In other words, what the group has eliminated from the equation of their 24 restaurants and counting (they own several more outside the city, and even a simulated Au Pied de Cochon in Mexico City) is the petit bourgeois, the old stakeholders of French cuisine. Now it's all about the suburban suits, the new grand bourgeois de banlieue who pull the strings, and the new urban proletariat labouring at the end of the strings. Well yes, I've seen some happy employees at these establishments ('our employees', says the president of the Groupe, Jean-Michel Texier, 'are very proud of their being a part not only of the image of the group, but also of the magnificent brands they represent') but not many. A central mind is in charge, and who knows what the central mind really wants from you? Who knows what its *ultimate mission* is? And who knows what it really has in store for you, while it goes about pursuing, if this is its ultimate mission, world domination? The few happy employees we did encounter, it seems to me, were waiters who perked themselves up trying to flirt with my wife – not that either of us minded, but the situation seemed gratuitous and unfair. It doesn't take a great deal of creativity to make eyes at Marion.

But what then are these restaurants really offering, and what are the throngs of customers really looking for? An easy answer would be, history, or at least the simulacra of history. But what is history, in this case? An easy answer, again, would be the history that would satisfy the cravings of nostalgia – the days when Le Petit Zinc was really something, when it was the site of a genuine formularity, and everybody, from the waiters shouting instructions to the customers shouting back, and there were 23 kinds of veal to choose from, actually believed in what they were doing. But there is also something elemental which restaurants like these partially satisfy, and that is a certain need to eat in a certain kind of way, which is to say the traditional French-restaurant way. The French-restaurant way with bread and wine, several courses, good tableware, religious attentiveness, an accommodating server and a cuisine which is eternally *reminiscent*, a *passéiste* cuisine, as Roland Barthes once put it – that is what the Groupe Frères Blanc still caters to. That is what just about every French restaurant everywhere in Paris begins by trying to provide.

If you choose your restaurant with a little more care, or less desperation, you will find that it is not so hard to avoid being gripped by the extended tentacle of the corporate octopus, and you will even find that Paris offers an untold number of opportunities to eat decently in the French way, and at all price levels. You wander into a small unheard-of brasserie in the Marais that looks bright and happy, Au Bouquet Saint Paul, and you get exuberant service, a view of the street, the company of locals, a dish and a thick juicy porterhouse steak with bone marrow, perfectly cooked, and a carafe of wine, for €20. You do your homework and you reserve a place at Mon Viel Ami, operated by a star chef from Alsace, Antoine Westermann, and you find yourself in a very smart crowded room with cramped tables off a main drag of the Ile Saint Louis that actually specializes in vegetables – though not vegetarian fare, as the main seasoning for half the vegetables is pork. Spending €40 now, or €50 or more, because there are wines to splurge on too, you're getting something exciting. And so on. You can do all right for €15 sometimes, especially at lunch. A favourite haunt of mine was Café de Sully, a family-run establishment across from the Bibliothèque de l'Arsenal, a traditional cafe restaurant with offerings at three different price levels – bar, terrace and dining room – and everything is honest and good, beginning with a home-made *foie gras*, served in a *salade gourmande* for €12, accompanied (on recommendation) by a glass of Faugères, an underappreciated red with lots of structure from the Languedoc.

These places aren't exceptions, in the way a good moderately priced restaurant in London is an exception. Marion and I made all kinds of discoveries during our wanderings, sometimes by accident, such as the Le Pavé, a chef-owned 'Bistrot de Terroir' on the rue des Lombards, with a mirrored ceiling, serving the cuisine of the Auvergne. That occasion was another case of our finding ourselves perplexed and needing a place to sit down, and this time, at under €20 each, striking it rich. In the summer we had fresh gaspacho and a seafood salad; in the winter, returning there on purpose, we had dark, meaty braised hare in a traditional blood and wine sauce. And then there was the time we got caught in the rain near Place Pigalle, and dove into a hole in the wall frequented by local clerical workers, ageing divas and alcoholics, bringing in their dogs, stopping in for a coffee or a glass of wine from an interesting selection or sitting down at one of the handful of tables for a simple dinner, Le Colibri. We were served a fine meal of calves head with sauce *griboche*, a condiment similar to tartare sauce, and (for timid Marion) a nice bit of roast beef with *pommes soufflés*. In fact, the calves head and the beef were the only two things on the menu that day for lunch, which is as it should be when there is only one server and one cook – the former a cordial fellow who also tended the bar and discussed with us the unknown wines of Orange, north of Avignon, the latter a portly old guy who came out afterwards in a tee-shirt and bloodstained apron for a drink and a chat with the customers at the counter.

What we didn't find, however, was something our American and British backgrounds had led us to expect, a cuisine that surprised you, a cuisine that went out of its way to startle your senses and reawaken your awareness of food. We were like the American in London at first. We wanted to make discoveries; we wanted to experience something we could never have at home; we wanted the exotic. And wasn't that what the food revolutions in America and Britain had been teaching us to desire? The love of ethnic restaurants I had acquired in San Francisco, and could have acquired in several other American cities, a love of new spices and systems of preparation, of new ethnic regions and agricultural *terroir* – not just Chinese but *Hakka*, not just North African but *Eritrean* or *West Moroccan*, and indeed not just French but *Provençal* or better yet *Marseillaise* – was part of a general reorientation of the senses away from the *old* and onto the *new*. Living most of her life in the north of England, Marion had fewer exotica to choose from, but for her too, if it was only just to a Sicilian pizzeria or a standard Thai restaurant serving international Thai dishes, the logic was the same. Out of the old world of the senses, the 'American' and the 'British', one could venture into a new territory. And so, when we started eating regularly in France, we kept looking for that next new excitement.

We found that excitement to some extent by travelling about, having *ttoro* in Saint Jean-de-Luz, bouillabaisse in Marseille and *cotriade* in Brittany – but then, we were travelling about, we were manufacturing our own experiences of the new. For us, these old ways of making a fish stew were new. In Paris, however, the restaurants are stunningly regimented, with limited menus, again and again offering the same old dishes. You could order the *soupe à l'oignon* before you got there, because even before you got there you knew that the *soupe à l'oignon* would be there. Even the regional restaurants seem regimented. (Guess what, the south-western restaurant serves *cassoulet*!) And if we weren't looking for anything besides French food most of the time, we were at least looking for something original, for what the French themselves call *cuisine inventive*. Come on, come on, we kept on hoping in vain, surprise me!

Well, said Roland Barthes long ago, 'French food is never supposed to innovate except for rediscovering lost secrets.' French food is *not* supposed to surprise you. It is supposed to *remind* you of something. If you are French, it is supposed to establish for you 'a certain continuity of the nation: food, through a thousand detours permits [you] to become implanted in [your] past on a daily basis'.[17] Apparently, one of the things it is supposed to remind you of is that food used to be better. But another thing it is supposed to remind you of, more positively, is *hey, you're French!* And if you are only a visitor, still the cuisine still has something to say to you too. *Hey, you're a guest of the French! Don't let the bastards grind you down!*

On one trip to Paris Marion and I found ourselves particularly irked by the food we were being served. Not only was excitement missing, but even knowhow and integrity. How many places had we gone to, ordering such simple dishes as steak-frites or omelettes and frites, and, though the steak or the eggs might be okay, the chips had clearly been cooked from frozen? Marion is an expert in such things. 'Frozen', she would say as the chips came to the table. 'Frozen', she would repeat as she took a bite into one of them. I tried to make excuses for them. These places we were eating at were *not* expensive. Some of them not only had only one cook, but only one person working in the kitchen altogether. Once he had finished cooking, the cook had to wash the dishes. And anyway, the food was served on time, with graciousness, and the meat or the eggs were good, and after all the fries weren't bad, they might just be fresh after all, or only bought from suppliers cut and oiled and radiated for pasteurization in advance. 'Frozen', Marion said.

It was a working trip for me and we could visit only so many places together, and I still hadn't learned that instead of being delighted by restaurant food I was supposed to be reminded of something, and presumably of something more interesting than my childhood in New York and Cleveland or my adolescence in Chicago. Our last day, a little desperate, with a plane to catch in the evening, we went out of our way to try Aux Lyonnais. The well known restaurant was out of our way because, though it is in the centre of the city, a few blocks from the Bourse, it does not seem to be near much of anything. And it was a bit of a queer fish, for us, a kind of institution to which I was both attracted in principle and repelled. The restaurant dates back to 1890, or 1914, depending on how you look at it, a casual *bouchon* in the Lyonnais style, serving Lyonnais food, or something of that sort – its history is actually rather complicated. In any case, in 2002 it was taken over by the Monte Carlo-based Groupe Alain Ducasse. Yes, a 'groupe', with some twenty restaurants worldwide, and over €60 million in annual revenues, though in this case a 'groupe' run by a famous chef.[18] I was attracted because one of my guidebooks said that the place was cheap but excellent. I was attracted because I wanted to know more about the ethic of a famous chef – yes, a chef with Michelin stars, with restaurants commonly elected to be among the 'best in the world' – and how a famous chef would treat *cuisine bourgeoise*, or something even humbler, the food of the *bouchon*. I was attracted too because I had not been to Lyon yet, and didn't know much about Lyonnais food. The *bouchon* I went to in Le Havre, it will be remembered, was serving Norman food along with wines from Beaujolais. But I was repelled because I didn't want to patronize any more corporate restaurants, even if Alain Ducasse was the CEO; because it seemed to me that if I were going to sample proper Lyonnais food, if I couldn't eat it in Lyon at least I ought to have been able to eat it cooked by a chef from Lyon, in a restaurant owned by a family from Lyon; because I was tired of simulacra. I wanted the real thing.

My interest was nevertheless piqued by research I did about the restaurant over the Internet. The chef, Fréderic Thévenet, reports the following: 'While respecting tradition and conserving the associations of tastes, we wish to reinterpret Lyonnaise cuisine while adding a touch of modernity, to make it lighter, more accessible, and still more flavourful.' What more could one ask: to be at once reminded of the past and delighted by the present. But meanwhile, looking at the little blogs at Zagat.com I found that Aux Lyonnais, for the Zagat cognoscenti, was repeatedly problematic. The place was given a high rating, and well known to readers of the *New York Times*, yet the Zagatarians weren't always happy. They didn't always get what they were expecting. Often they didn't even seem to get what other people in the restaurant were getting. I quote:

> A victim of its own success, this place is too popular. Having a reservation does not guarantee you a table. Having a reservation simply means that the maitre d' will put you on the waiting list and send you to cool your heels in the upstairs holding pen. The food has slipped and it is no longer worth the hassle.

> This place is far too full of itself to be charming or interesting. Service is practically hostile and totally indifferent to individual interests. For example, the fixed price menu included two dessert choices on our visit, cheese and a baked pear dessert. The cheese was soft, served with a spoon. When my spoon was placed, I realized I would not care for the cheese and asked to change to the pear dessert. The waitress said it was 'too late' and . . .

> Resting on the laurels of the chef. A major disappointment! Small portions and surly servers. They are very impressed with themselves. Alain Ducasse is doing to Paris what George Bush has done to the US's reputation.

I recently attempted to eat at Aux Lyonnais with my wife and children. We arrived fifteen minutes late and the manager, Eric Mercier, met our taxi at the door waving his finger while telling us not to bother getting out of the car because he had given away our table. After arguing for a few minutes, we called for a taxi. While waiting to be picked up, we saw a party of seven Parisians arrive, who told me they did not have a reservation, seated at a table.

Dashed expectations. One of the worst meals I've had in Paris with surly service.

Soup was served lukewarm.

Prix fixe menu of 30 euros is pretty skimpy. The specials are by and large good (with the exception of a dull pig's foot in brioche appetizer). Excellent sauteed fresh cepes, roasted skate on the bone, and *pintadeau* were well prepared and attractively presented. The small front room decor was disappointing, as was the mix of patrons, mostly Americans and Japanese. Tired and unhelpful waitstaff seemed only interested in our hasty departure.

No English language menus and little help for Americans. Food, once terrific, is just ok   many better places to choose from.

Wheelchair accessible. I love Lyonnais cooking, but not this place. I am perplexed at what Ducasse has to do with this place or why it gets all the good press.

Actually, only about half of the entries are like this. The other entries use words like 'outstanding' and 'great' and 'fun', although some who liked it also added, a bit preposterously, that the food was 'too flavoursome' or 'too rich'. So I was intrigued.

Of course, the confrontation between Americans in Paris and Paris itself that the blogs document is all about majestic consumption and the 'dream' of expectations that the consumers bring to the experience. It is also an old story. But I wanted to find out for myself. I wanted to find out even though I had misgivings about doing so, since I saw that if one read between the lines the restaurant wasn't really all that cheap, and I would be coming to the experience not just as a social scientist doing field work but also as one of the hungry, as one of the disappointed and hungry, as one of the desperate and disappointed and hungry, and with little money to rectify the situation.

When we arrived, we were surprised at how small the restaurant was, even with its very high ceiling, as if it had been built in an age of Lilliputians. We were also surprised at how coldly garish the facilities were, inside and out, with all its bright white tile work and curlicues and mirrors, as if the meeting hall of a fancy metro station. It wasn't so much belle époque as white French industrial Victorian. It was not nearly so comfortable as Le Petit Zinc or that simulacrum of a *bouchon* in Le Havre, Le Bistrot des Halles – though it was not without charm either. We were also surprised, upon being greeted at the door at about twelve thirty in the afternoon, that in place of the imposing Frenchman who had made American tourists tremble was a kid in his early twenties who was somewhat unskilful and lacking in confidence, working in tandem with a young woman who was equally unskilful and lacking in confidence.

We were seated at a good table near the tall windows, overlooking the ugly modern office building across the street, next to a pair of businessmen going about the business of lunch. The waitress was also young, unskilful and lacking in confidence, the third of her kind so far, and she wasn't French. But we managed to get our orders placed and have our food brought to us in good time. Marion and I both ordered the same thing, from the fixed price menu of a little under €30 (what wasn't cheap was the wine): dandelion green salad, followed by *quenelles de brochet*, served with foamy double-coloured *nantua* sauce and crayfish tails. I will make a long story short and say that the salad, which came with a mysteriously sweet and toothsome boiled potato and a melt-in-your mouth square of belly pork topped by crisp bitter greens, was one of the best salads I have had in my life, and the quenelles were by far the best quenelles I have ever had period. They were exquisite, the sauce at once rich and light, the quenelles at once so fluffy and dense that it was like both a soufflé and a ravioli, lovingly merged into one. It wasn't even a little bit slimy. The dessert – a praline tart topped with an *île flotante* – was exquisite too. We ate very happily and we walked away very happy. At last, we had had a meal worth travelling to Paris for.

And the problem was, it wasn't supposed to be like that. Damn it all! I thought. And damn that Alain Ducasse! Outsmarted me, he had. It wasn't from my idealized *peuple français* that my meal had appeared before me; it wasn't from a family of restaurateurs, or an independent owner-operator; it wasn't even from someone from Lyon. It was from the mind of a celebrity chef, and the corporation he controlled, among whom there were evidently not a few employees suffering from alienation. I'd been totally outsmarted by that fellow. I could imagine him grinning, counting out his coins. And what I wanted to know, indignantly, was this: who the hell did Alain Ducasse think I was?

At the end of *Down and Out in Paris and London*, Orwell says that his time being 'hard up' in the two cities hasn't really taught him much, only a thing or two about the world and the attitude he should bring to it. 'I shall never again think that all tramps are drunken scoundrels', for example. And oh yes, he shall never again 'enjoy a meal at a smart restaurant'.[19] But those were the 1930s. And Paris and London have changed. The needs of the people who eat in them have changed, and so have the needs of the people who feed them. I've got a clear and distinct, if not a satisfactory, idea about that now.

six

The Production of Production: Novelists and Cooks

Up till now most of the emphasis of this book has been on consumption. The restaurant has been analysed as a site of consumption. It has also been placed in the context of the advent of the consumer society, a society that operates as a system for the production of consumption. Here, however, I want to take a look at another part of the equation: the production of production.

The idea of a 'consumer society', in the hands of most social theorists, is fatalistic. We are condemned, the idea goes, to live as consumers. We are condemned to live alienated from our own productive capacities, since after all we do not produce what we consume . . . and still, we consume. Most of our lives all we ever do is consume. Going shopping, getting dressed, putting on a new pair of socks, sitting at home with the television on, driving in our cars with the stereo on, having a snack at our desks, drinking a coffee in the lounge, struggling to win a video game on our PS3 or scrolling though text messages on our iPhone, travelling in a plane en route to a holiday in Spain, watching a football game at the local stadium, brushing our teeth, grabbing a sandwich at EAT., getting a haircut – all we ever seem to do is consume. It is not impossible to see the most intimate moments of our lives, including lovemaking, as part of an overall pattern of virtually uninterrupted consumption. At work itself we continue consuming – that snack at one's desk, the designer suits one wears to mark one's position in the workplace hierarchy or make an impression on potential sexual partners, the YouTube clip on one's computer. And at most, since work does not seem to have much of a social meaning any more, when we are really working, the snack finished, the video off – when we are working but not consuming, we are, above all else, endeavouring to produce for ourselves more opportunities for consumption. We are condemned to all this, the idea goes, and ultimately there is no escape from it. Even in an economic downturn, like the one I am writing in now, the real tragedy, so far as the media and politicians discuss it, seems to be that people losing their credit, their savings, their homes or their jobs are being deprived of their habitual opportunities for consumption – and there is no way out of this tragedy except to restore the economy back to itself, to return to 'growth', and get us all back into consuming again. We will have 'recovered' when we have returned to normal levels of consumption. For all we will ever be able to do is consume, or lamentably fail to consume, and all consumption in the modern consumer society – this being the key to how it operates – is therefore condemned to be alike. No matter what it is, a pair of socks, a university education or a lifestyle, we have commodified it, we have put a price on it, we want it and we must consume it. We must consume it in order to consume: or, as Baudrillard put it, in a consumer society the aim of life is the consumption of consumption.

It seems to me that one of the functions of the restaurant in modern life, however, is to provide an alternative, or at least an idea of an alternative, to this de-personalized form of consumer society consumption. The phone in my hand was made I don't know where; it came to me in a box; I ordered it online. The same thing can even be said sometimes of the pizza in my oven. But in a restaurant, before I touch my plate someone else has touched and held it first. Before the plate has been set before me I have made contact, whether in only a glance or in the signal of slight inclination of my shoulder or a wrinkle in my brow, with the person who has brought it to me. Before the server took hold of the plate, someone else had taken hold of it, taking a steak off a grill or a tong-full of vegetables from a steamer and arranging it on top with the tips of his fingers, and the cook had known, if not who I was, that at least *someone* was there – some other human being was going to receive what the cook had prepared for him or her.

The steps backward from my first touch of my own plate of food to the server and the cook can continue to the suppliers of the raw ingredients, and these later steps may well go back to corporate wholesalers, factories, factory farms and the migrant workers who labour in the fields. Alternatively, they may go back to a more idyllic kind of food production – tribal fishermen on the Thames. But either way, the steps back from the plate of food set before us on the table at the restaurant will send us inevitably to the economic system responsible for production in the consumer society. Even the idyllic organic family farm will depend upon state subsidies today, and those subsidies will come from a system of production, governance and taxation that involves bankers, lawyers and engineers every bit as much as farmhands, honeybees and cows.[1] In the consumer society the simple life is never simple. Sustainability-minded Acorn House in London, which refuses to serve bottled water because of the ecological costs, and therefore only serves water, filtered, from a tap, relies on the vast infrastructure established for providing fresh water around the nation, including reservoirs and filtration plants, sewers and pumps, and miles and miles of plumbing. Acorn House can no more make the simple life simple than any other institution can.

But still, in the restaurant a form of direct human contact intervenes between consumers and consumption. The diners know it; the servers know it; the cooks know it. The restaurant itself may be an outlet of an impersonal corporation, and belong to 'investors'. The menu may have been devised in a central 'kitchen' in suburban Saint Denis, home of the Groupe Frères Blanc, or it may have been devised rather in a 'kitchen' in Maryville, Tennessee, home of Ruby Tuesday, which offers 'Simple Fresh American Food' ('Where Else Can You Get Mac 'n Cheese To Go With Your Lobster?') at about 770 locations throughout the United States. The operation may be overseen by a professional manager along with a district manager, and a regional manager and their assistants, not to mention corporate headquarter functionaries in accounting, purchasing, human resources, property management and so forth, up to a Board of Directors that includes retired executives from Saks, Inc. and Brain Works Ventures (I am not making this up). But in the restaurant itself, humans come into contact with one another, by touch and by glance, by intention and reception, hand to hand and eye to eye. They even speak to one another. And they know that. They know that they have entered into a compact with one another, even if they have entered into it in bad faith, or with regret, or because of the imposition of necessity.

And the compact is not just humanizing from the point of view of the consumer, who has taken the spotlight in most of this study. It is humanizing from the point of view of the producers. In fact, though restaurant work can be just a job, something that one does because one has to do *something* and one *can* do *this*, restaurant work must always also enter into a relation with a certain (humanizing) ideal. At the far end of this ideal lies the notion of art, and art for the sake of art; at the near end of it lies the concept of hospitality, of generosity for the sake of generosity. And through it all comes the process (inspired by Deleuze and Guattari, and their landmark book *Anti-Oedipus*, as well as by Baudrillard's opposite notion of the consumption of consumption) that I call the production of production. When you speak to a restaurateur today – I'm not talking about members of the Board of Directors at Ruby Tuesday or P. F. Chang's, but the humbler individual who may have opened an establishment or two – what you will hear is that the reason why the restaurateur does what he does is for the sake of doing it. People want to start restaurants, or work in them, because that is what it seems to them that they want to *do*. Instead of *doing something else*, like driving a bus, sweeping floors, arguing cases of law, inputting data, fixing plumbing, healing the sick, teaching chemistry, building cars, shoplifting or trading stock options they want – maybe – to do this: to produce the experience of the restaurant. 'Expressive entrepreneurialism', sociologist Gary Fine calls it. They may end up being disappointed, or they may end up fabulously successful. But first comes a two-step process of reflection. Step one: I have to do something in order to live. Step two: what I want to do is start a restaurant, or at least work in one. I want to be involved in *creating* something, and the restaurant is what I want to help create.

Our otherwise understandable focus on consumption may distract us from this basic truth. People do *not* only want to consume. They also want to *produce*. And the restaurant is an appealing site of production, even if the work is hard and the pay is not so great.

When the corporations and their boards of directors are in control, to be sure, *homo restauranticus* is ever and always *homo sucker*, and the humanization of production and consumption is never a primary objective. From the point of view of global commerce, as taught in business schools all over the world, the human being is a consuming machine; and the goal must ever and always be to *catch* that machine at an opportunity for engaging it in consumption, and indeed to manipulate that sucker-machine into falling into the consumption trap you have laid for him. Go to a major train station or airport anywhere in Europe today and you will see how that works. Your objective is to go from A to B – already probably a form of consumption for you. But to get from A to B, first you have to get to your seat on the train or the plane, and to get to your seat you have to pass by so much junk, you have to *work* your way past so many kiosks, so many coffee stands, sandwich shops, perfume counters and gadgetry emporia that it is very hard to *get anywhere*. The suits have tried to make getting trapped into consumption a habit of yours. When you go to catch a train or a plane, it shall become a habit of yours to find that what you are also doing is being delayed in the station, having a doughnut, sipping a Coke and buying a tie – producing consumption. The moment you get to the check-in hall, your glands have begun salivating and the veins in your head have begun to throb, you feel your hand on your wallet. You are going to go in there and *delay and eat and drink and purchase some commodities.*

In the restaurant, however – which is not to say that restaurants aren't also chock-a-block in the train stations, airports and malls of Europe – the diner may entertain the idea that he or she is not consuming commodities but having a relationship. Whether that idea is in any way illusory is a point worth considering, but for the people involved the relationship is in any case tangible, literally tangible, communicated from hand to hand, from cook to server to customer. The restaurateur and the restaurant worker, whatever else they may be, *cannot* simply be out to catch the consumption of a consuming machine; the agency of the process puts limits on the trickery. The restaurateur and the restaurant worker are *in production*, and what they are producing involves a tangible, humanizing connection with the consumer. Moreover, as they make their approaches to the customer, the personnel of the restaurant are at the same time producing *themselves* as subjects of humanization. To work anywhere, in any trade, involves an initiating project of self-invention. And here is what restaurateurs and workers are ever initiating and fashioning: themselves as agents of service, feeding people, themselves being people.

Even the franchisee of a fast food outlet and the gang of transitory workers he or she has engaged for the purpose are involved in such a humanizing transaction. There may be something irreparably defective in that transaction. The handoff of the paper-wrapped food in a paper bag or on a paper-lined plastic tray from the order taker to the customer may be too controlled and mechanical, too quick and abrupt, and for that and other reasons too humiliating both to the order-taker and the customer to be enjoyed on either side. The whole process can *defeat* humanization even in the process of making one last gesture in the direction of the humanization. Personally, I find it sad and painful, and I avoid fast food restaurants as much as I can in order to avoid entering into this compact of humiliation with the order-taker. It's not the food that gets me down so much – although there is a great deal to be said about the poor quality of what is offered at most fast food joints (the Whopper excepted, in my view) – but the depersonalization that I am being made to contribute to. Given the basic ingredients of what George Ritzer calls the 'McDonaldization' of production in any fast food restaurant – efficiency, calculability and predictability, as I have already mentioned, along with 'control through nonhuman technology' – it would seem that a compact of humiliation and depersonalization would be the inevitable outcome of any transaction there, and one can only wonder why more people don't therefore avoid it.[2] Nevertheless, the personnel of a fast food restaurant are also contributing their humanity to the process. Indeed, they are trying to fashion their own humanity while sliding your fries into a red cardboard cornet, and slapping it onto your advertisement-lined plastic tray. It is the system that fails them, not their humanity.

There is a special relation to production and self-production that restaurant work entails. It is not only hand to hand, at least so far as a 'non-human technology' has taken control of it; it is hand to hand in the expression of a kind of freedom. Perhaps it is relevant to remember that the word 'freedom' in English originally means not liberty from constraints – the 'freedom from' that Isaiah Berlin discussed – but a power to accomplish objectives on behalf of others – Berlin's 'freedom to' or 'freedom for'. This freedom may never be absolute; in the restaurant it can be compromised and belittled. Bad faith can intervene at all levels; so, for that matter, can alienation. Sartre might fault the production of production in a restaurant because it lacks spontaneity and seldom really crosses over from the aesthetic to the ethical. But in the restaurant freedom may nevertheless be available in two related ways, because in the restaurant it is possible to parti-cipate in the production of something like a work of art, and at the same time to contribute to the practice of hospitality. The restaurant produces art and hospitality, and restaurant owners and workers produce themselves as subjects of art and hospitality.

Everyone knows this. Even the suits in headquarters know this. There is something special about our restaurants. That is why we love them. But it is very hard to come to terms with this today. The special problem of fast food aside, it has been hard to come to terms with artistry and hospitality even with regard to the most comfortable establishments. In fact, it has been hard to come to terms with it for well over a hundred years. How can restaurants, commercial establish-ments serving consumers, practise 'art'? How, since their objective is to make a profit, can they practise 'hospitality'? How can we even begin to *think* about restaurants as something other than what they are, commercial ventures? How can we imagine them as engines for a genuinely free and human production of production?

Let us restrict ourselves to the matter of literature. As we have seen, there has been a lot of writing about restaurants since the first edition of the *Almanach des Gourmands* came out in 1803. But most of it has been from the point of view of the consumer. Very few writers have attempted to imagine the restaurant from the point of view of its productivity. Restaurants do not have much of a *story* in modern literature, as I said at the outset, except as stopping points for protag-onists who enjoy their little trysts with dinner and then go on to do something else. Nor do restaurant *workers* have much of a story. They are usually at most part of the background against which the real protagonists of fiction try to be the heroes of their own lives.

Even in literature that has tried to make restaurant work part of its main narrative, the social and cultural productivity of the restaurant and restaurant work has been something of a problem. When Anthony

Bourdain's non-fictional memoir *Kitchen Confidential* came out in 2000, what was revealed in popular literature for virtually the first time, since fiction hadn't much bothered about it yet, was the narrative power of the figure of the cook: the cook revealed as the hero of his own life. The scene of that life was complex, a macho world of drug abuse, violence and brushes with poverty and crime as well as college idylls, prankish humour and a lust for literature, loud music and luxurious French food, and all of that combined with a Hemingway-esque dedication to the hardness and purity of form. Bourdain's culinary/ literary life is spent in the man's world of manly writers like Hemingway, Norman Mailer and Henry Miller, a world of complicity and guilt as well as defiance, anger and love. 'This business', says Bourdain, 'grows assholes: it's our principal export. I'm an asshole. You should probably be an asshole too.' This is Hem, Mailer and Miller *redivivus*. But so is the sequel: 'I love heating duck confit', Bourdain goes on to say, 'saucisson de canard, confit gizzard, saucisson de Toulouse, poitrine and duck fat with those wonderful tarbais beans, spooning it into an earthernware crock and sprinkling it with bread-crumbs. I love making those little mountains of chive-mashed potatoes, wild mushrooms, ris de veau . . . I enjoy the look on the face of my boss when I do a pot-au-feu special . . . I love that look . . . it's the gaze of wonder . . .'.[3] This combination of anger and love, of com-petitiveness and camaraderie, of cynicism and reverence, of anarchy and art – that was not what people had come to expect from the hid-den world of chefs. Nor were the many tensions Bourdain expresses between cooks and their customers, or between cooks and their bosses, or between cooks among themselves – tensions that are related directly to class conflict, as well as to egotism, passion, job pressure (the long hours, the low pay, the heat), depression and the violent rivalries of masculine identity. This revelation, said the refined, Harvard-educated food critic Jeffrey Steingarten, had 'foodies fuming'.[4] It has Steingarten fuming a bit too. After all, 'Bourdain has never worked in any of the city's top kitchens, or even at the level just below . . . Until recently, Bourdain has worked in only one restaurant worthy of a star from the *Times* . . . [F]unny as this book can be, it misrepresents what goes on in the kitchen of a really good restaurant.' No, the masculine drama in restaurants that were not 'really good' was not what Steingarten and his foodies wanted to hear about, nor the class conflict behind the scenes, or the class oppression under which most cooks suffer, eating away as it does at their masculine self-esteem and making them, among other things, angry. Foodies did not want to hear that their beloved eateries 'grow assholes'. And yet Bourdain's view of the kitchen world is more or less confirmed by the only major sociological study of restaurant workers, *Kitchens: The Culture of Restaurant Work* by Gary Alan Fine (although Fine's cooks in Minnesota are much more *polite* than Bourdain's New Yorkers).[5] It is confirmed again by journalist Bill Buford, visiting the New York kitchen of a 'really good' contemporary restaurant in *Heat*.[6]

What kitchens actually are, what restaurants actually are, from the point of view of their owners and workers, are sites of production. And is not the site of production the real horror that modern society has continually turned its gaze away from? Isn't the site of production the real asshole, the shit-making machine (and sexual destination) at which no one can bear to gaze? Here is the contradiction: on the one hand, the restaurant has been one of the few sites of production in the modern world to which people know they can turn in order to remain in contact with what is human in themselves and others; on the other hand, it is precisely *not* as a site of production that they want to turn to it, lest they be horrified at what they see. Or rather, they both do and do not want to turn their attention to the restaurant and its kitchen in this way. Jeffrey Steingarten is also a regular judge on the American TV version of *Iron Chef*. It's okay when TV is involved, when the asshole is placed under lights and the struggle to survive has been sublimated into a game show, and the labourers compete not to survive but merely to receive a small prize, as awarded by His Majesty the Critic. As for the novelists, when they get into the act, rare though that is, they may be willing to make cooks into heroes; only, they cannot seem to correlate the hero-cook with the institution he works for. Either the institution is absent, or the heroism is. For it is not easy to practise the ethics of art and hospitality that the production of production in a restaurant requires. It may even be impossible. The nature of the restaurant, the nature of people and the nature of art and hospitality all seem to militate against the possibility of making the work in a restaurant a project of freedom. Restaurants are the human face of a form of production – capitalism – that, as far as the modern novel is concerned, is inherently slavish and horrid.

I've chosen four works of fiction to illustrate the point, and I will discuss them one by one: William Morris's *News from Nowhere* (1890); Isak Dinesen's 'Babette's Feast' (1958); Anne Tyler's *Dinner at the Homesick Restaurant* (1982); and Monica Ali's *In the Kitchen* (2009). Not all of these works are masterpieces, and I could have chosen other books. But looking at them, chronologically and one by one, we see a pattern emerge: the production of production in the restaurant as inevitably cheapened, contradictory, impossible or oppressive, or perhaps all four at once. These stories are full of good ideas and observations about the world of the restaurant. But they are also full of reservations about it, as if afraid of what they see.

News from Nowhere

In *News from Nowhere*, the socialist designer, poet and political organizer William Morris imagines what it would be like to go else-where and actually arrive at the world his socialist agitation has been agitating for. The encounter, as is usually the case in utopian fantasy, is double: on the one hand, the world is encountered from the point of view of a stranger, in this case one William Guest of Hammersmith, who has been mysteriously transported over one hundred years into the future, and cannot quite understand everything he sees; on the other hand, the world is lived and explained from the point of view of the people who inhabit it, who cannot communicate with the stranger. This double encounter, and the gap of understanding it creates, generates the 'space of play' of the utopian text.[7] We should be cautious about reading any utopian fantasy naturalistically, not only because the fantasy is a fantasy, but also because the text is about the play between reality and fantasy, and the text itself is play.

In any case, William Guest finds himself arrived in an England transformed into a communist democracy. There is no such thing as private property, there is no inequality, and there is no want. In fact, everybody seems to have *more* of what they need and desire than people of William's Victorian England did – everybody, that is, except for the rich, who do not exist any more. People are better dressed and housed and better fed; they look better – there's no huddling there – and they are certainly healthier, living much longer than Victorians ever did. They are apparently sexier too. But people also work. Without pay, and without being coerced, they find things to do. They find things that need doing – bridge repair, clothing manufacture, boat piloting, shopkeeping – and they find things that they enjoy doing. The principle is Marxist: to each according to his needs, from each according to his abilities. In fact, the people are inclined to switch the work they do regularly, one day piloting a barge, the next day harvesting wheat, printing a book or blowing glass. The England of the future answers to much of Marx's slightly whimsical vision of life in communist society, 'where nobody has one exclusive sphere of activity' and where 'society regulates production and thus makes it possible for me to do one thing today and another tomorrow, to hunt in the morning, fish in the afternoon, rear cattle in the evening, criticize after dinner, just as I have a mind to, without ever becoming a hunter, fisherman, shepherd or critic'.[8]

It turns out that yes, the England of the future has something like restaurants. You don't have to pay to eat at them, but there they are. The first is simply called 'the Guest House'. It occupies, in what used to be Morris's and William Guest's Hammersmith, 'a longish building with its gable ends turned away from the road, and long traceried windows coming rather low down set in the wall that faced us. It was very handsomely built of red brick with a lead roof . . .'. Inside is 'a hall with a floor of marble mosaic and open timber roof', a 'pleasant place' where the narrator finds 'three young women . . . flitting to and fro'.[9] As the narrator and two fellow travellers, Dick and Robert, men of the future, walk in, we are told the ladies 'came up to us at once merrily and without the least affectation of shyness, and all three shook hands with me as if I were a friend newly come back from a long journey'. After 'a word or two from Robert', the women 'bustled about on our behoof, and presently came and took us by the hands and led us to a table in the pleasantest corner of the hall, where our breakfast was spread out for us'. About the meal itself the narrator has only a little to say: it 'was simple enough, but most delicately cooked, and set on the table with much daintiness. The bread was particularly good'. Along with a 'farmhouse bread', Piedmont-style bread sticks and a platter of freshly picked wild strawberries, the men are served we do not know what.[10] But we do find out that the society of the future encourages convivial drinking, and we see that the women running the Guest House take part in the conversations of the guests when it is suitable to do so.

The second restaurant, in Bloomsbury, next to what used to be the British Museum, occupies the neighbourhood's market hall. Now accompanied by Dick, Dick's girlfriend Clara and Clara's grandfather, William finds himself led to 'a richly moulded and carved doorway, where a very pretty dark-haired young girl gave us each a beautiful bunch of summer flowers, and we entered a hall much bigger than that of the Hammersmith Guest House, more elaborate in its architecture and perhaps more beautiful'. Soon after William and his party are seated, 'the pretty waitresses came to us smiling, and chattering sweetly like reed warblers by the river-side, and fell to giving us our dinner'. Again the narrator says little about what he actually ate, but he is full of praise for it: 'as at our breakfast, everything was cooked and served with a daintiness which showed that those who had prepared it were interested in it; but there was no excess either of quantity or of gourmandize; everything was simple, though excellent in its kind; and it was made clear to us that this was no feast, only an ordinary meal. The glass, crockery, and plate were very beautiful to my eyes . . .'. In its equipment and furnishings the dining hall is medievalist in spirit, as Morris's own interior designs and aesthetic values tended to be. He goes on to say that although 'there was a total lack of what the nineteenth century calls "comfort" – that is, stuffy inconvenience . . . I had never eaten my dinner so pleasantly before'. After dinner, William and the grandfather continue to sit and talk about history, revolution and utopia over 'a bottle of very good Bordeaux wine'.[11]

It is unforgivable that Morris never takes us behind the scenes of the restaurant of the future, never shows us the food being cooked, and never shows us exactly what his people of the future eat. Morris will not look at that, or have his readers look at it. Perhaps it wouldn't have been pretty enough. It is also unforgivable that he would never be able to explain, within the context of his romance, how it was that a communist democracy in England was able to serve a very good Bordeaux from France. Among other things, there is no account in his romance about world trade (in fact, at one point it says that the 'world trade' of the Victorians has long since been abolished), or about how non-Anglophone societies have gone about organizing themselves in the ideal future, much less how or why the latter would continue fabricating and exporting something so precious as quality Bordeaux to a country without money. Some readers will also find it unforgivable that Morris always has beautiful women running these establishments. But Morris thinks beauty is a good thing, and flirtatiousness divine, and he sees no reason why women should not be more attracted to working in restaurants than men. 'I saw at the Guest House', says William Guest to the grandfather, before they move on to the market hall, 'that the women were waiting on the men: that seems a little like reaction, doesn't it?' 'Does it?' replies his interlocutor; 'perhaps you think housekeeping an unimportant occupation . . . Come now, my friend, [quoth he], don't you know that it is a great pleasure for a clever woman to manage a house skilfully?'[12]

Today's readers may still wish to take issue with what appears to be a sexist assumption, as they will with the Bordeaux and the failure to look into the kitchen. But Morris is trying to imagine both a different set of values and a different system of political economy to control it. In that system, there no longer seems to be a difference between household management and public service. The 'restaurant' is actually a 'guest house' or a community hall, and in managing it these women are providing not a commodity but a combination of household maintenance and hospitality. In the England of the future, everyone practises what might be called Big H Hospitality, or giving for the sake of giving, where what is mine – including my household – is also yours, no matter who you are. So what is private to me is also public, and it is at your service. The only reason I *have* it is so that I will be able to give it away. At the same time, restaurant workers, like all the other workers in the England of the future, are very happy in their work, happy in that the work itself is pleasurable and in that the work provides them with a sense of accomplishment. That is one of the reasons why the narrator notes that 'those who had prepared' the meal showed signs that they 'were interested in it'.

In Morris's non-alienating utopia, '*all* work is now pleasurable', William is told; 'either because of the hope of gain in honour and wealth with which the work is done, which causes pleasurable excitement, even when the actual work is not pleasant; or else because it has grown into a pleasurable *habit*, as in the case with what you may call mechanical work; and lastly (and most of our work is of this kind) because there is conscious sensuous pleasure in the work itself; it is done, that is, by artists'.[13] The restaurant workers of the future are 'interested' in what they do because it is honorific and wealth-generating; they are interested in it because it is an enjoyable task to prepare food and dispense hospitality; and they are interested in it because it is artistic.

In fact, Morris was part of a general movement, with its origins in the Romantics and John Ruskin, that challenged the distinction between 'fine art' and 'craftsmanship'. If there was a difference between an epic poem and a hand-carved knife, or between an opera and a plate of *ris de veau à la financière*, what was *common* to all of them was nevertheless more important than their differences, and what was common to them was on the one hand the freedom with which they were engaged in the process and on the other the aesthetic intentionality of the objects they produced. So, in Morris's utopia, the cook is *free* and the cook is *an artist*. He will therefore be 'interested' in what he produces, and interested in the promotion of the process itself, the production of production that it entails. In *Heat*, author Bill Buford discusses a famous Tuscan butcher under whom he apprenticed, Dario Cecchini, a man who apart from his preference for post-medieval form still speaks the language of William Morris and the arts and crafts movement: 'I am repelled by marketing', says Dario. 'I am an artisan. I work with my hands. My model is from the Renaissance. The bodega. The artist workshop. Giotto. Raphael. Michelangelo. These are my inspirations.'[14] Buford has his doubts about the analogy: for him, fine art is fine art, and craftsmanship something else; but that is a distinction that, in the spirit of cultural democracy, William Morris along with Dario Cecchini thinks it unimportant, or even vitiating, to draw. What is important is the freedom of creation, which in an ideal world is accessible to all. And what is also important is the spirit of the gift with which artefacts and services are created, the Big H Hospitality with which the work of art is given away to the public.

On an economic level, Morris's argument (following Marx to some extent, and Ruskin to some extent as well) is that modern capitalism is responsible for severing the worker from his freedom and his generosity. Of course, before capitalism there was plenty of oppression. But capitalism devised a new kind of oppression, the systemic oppression of humanity by its own means of production. (It is this ascendency of the machinery of men over men themselves that makes it so hard for men to take a look at their machines for what they are.) Capitalism requires the continued generation of commodities and their surplus values for the sake of the continued growth of capital. 'Once set a-going', as the grandfather puts it, the capitalist system of the world market forced labourers 'to make more and more of these wares, whether they needed them or not. So that while (of course) they could not free themselves from the toil of making real necessaries, they created a never-ending series of sham or artificial necessaries.' At a certain point they could not stop themselves, heaping one sham necessity upon another. 'By all this they burdened themselves with a prodigious mass of work merely for the sake of keeping their wretched system going.' This burden to create more and more brought about a 'cheapening of production'.[15] Not only were labourers made to suffer so that capitalists could prosper, but the activity of work itself was cheapened, cut off from creativity and generosity, and made into something onerous.

The old man thus notes an important difference between the past and present with regard to food. He can't help laughing, he says, 'at the silly nineteenth-century fashion, current amongst rich so-called cultivated people, of ignoring all the steps by which their daily dinner was reached, as matters too low for their lofty intelligence. Useless idiots! Come, now, I am a "literary man" as we queer animals used to be called, yet I am a pretty good cook myself.'[16] (Presumably it is *not* therefore only women who manage kitchens in utopia.) Another old man, later in the romance, talks with William Guest about the 'arts of life' which he understands were lost in the nineteenth century because of mechanization and the cheapening of production; 'not only was it impossible to find a carpenter or a smith in a village or a small country town, but . . . people in such places have even forgotten how to bake bread'.[17]

In 1890, therefore, William Morris was already analysing and critiquing the food alienation that we have seen so many examples of in the twenty-first century: the cheapening of production, whether in McDonald's, Pret A Manger, Ruby Tuesday or Le Petit Zinc; the cheapening therefore of goods, so that the present can very seldom seem to measure up to the past; the cheapening, as a result, of the meaning of labour, as servers and cooks are cut off from the pride, the intrinsic pleasantness and the free and generous artistry that Morris believes is necessary to happy labour; and the cheapened, estranged relationship of consumers with the production of the things they consume. A society that is accumulating more and more capital and producing more and more commodities and the needs that go along with them will nevertheless see its members cut off from the basic energies and crafts of civilized life, including baking and cooking, which may well come to seem horrid – things to be avoided, things to be neither looked at or touched.

Morris has a solution: the restaurant of the future. That would be a restaurant, however, that would seem to have escaped everything we know about restaurants as they are today. It would not be run for profit. It could probably not differentiate itself according to the categories we take for granted – high and low, near and far, and so forth. Or could it? There are differentiations in the world of the future, but they are not *our* differentiations, and neither we nor William Guest have direct access to them. At the end of the story, our hero is coming upon yet another communal feast, this one being arranged in an old and otherwise disused church, and held in honour of the wheat harvest to which everyone has been contributing. But he finds his own presence in the church slipping away from the scene. His friend Dick, he finds, 'was looking round the company with an air of proprietorship in them' an odd thing to observe, I think, in a world without private property, but a shrewd thing too: this world *belongs* to the people who inhabit it. Meanwhile, the other people with whom he has come to the church dinner (beautiful women, of course) are not paying attention to him any more; they hardly seem to see him. In the end, William turns to his special beautiful female friend, Ellen. 'I turned to Ellen, and she *did* seem to recognise me for an instant; but her bright face turned sad directly, and she shook her head with a mournful look, and the next moment all consciousness of my presence had faded from her face.'[18] All William can do is turn around and leave 'lonely and sick at heart'. He doesn't belong to the world of the future, and the world of the future doesn't belong to him. In an instant he finds himself back in the present of 1890. And then he wakes up, back into the world of cheapened production, and the horror of production.

'Babette's Feast'

Isak Dinesen's 'Babette's Feast' (1958) takes us from a Victorian fantasy of a twenty-first century utopia to a mid-twentieth century recollection of the grim realities of the Victorian era. I am referring here and throughout only to Dinesen's story, included in the collection of stories called *Anecdotes of Destiny*, not to the much-admired film based upon it, directed by Gabriel Axel. The film, made in 1987, has a utopian appeal, not unlike William Morris's romance. People who deeply care about food cannot help but be satisfied by the vision it provides of the rare feast as an occasion of transcendence, a momentary solution to the ills and disappointments of life that is spiritual as well as sensual. But as Priscilla Ferguson has observed, the original 'Babette's Feast' is a much more political work than the movie, punctuated as its story is by the memory of the tragedy of the French Commune of 1870–71, in which the title character and her family have fatally participated.[19] It is also an unhappier work – and that unhappiness is key to what it is actually saying about the contradictions of production in capitalist society.

Babette, the cook, is everything we may want a cook to be. 'I am a great artist!' she cries out to her two mistresses, Martine and Phillipa.[20] And the dinner she prepares for her guests, along with the testimony of only one among them who has experience in these things, General Loewenhielm, confirms it. But she is a great artist, a restaurant chef, in a small Norwegian town. The town, called Berlevaag, does not have any restaurants; few of its residents have ever even eaten at a restaurant, and most have no understanding of gastronomy, and are antipathetic to what they imagine it stands for. Her mistresses are prominent figures in an ageing sectarian community that is suspicious, if not downright contemptuous, of the temptations of the flesh, and they do not know anything about food. This situation is important from a narratological and mythological point of view. In order to make the cook into the hero of a story, the writer removes her from her natural habitat. In the restaurant, she is just a cook, having a successful career.[21] Torn away from the restaurant by political events, thrown into a society without restaurants, she can now be the hero of a story. And she can be that hero precisely *because* she cooks. The story of exile is one thing, already lending itself to narration; the story of a chef in exile is another, lending itself to an 'anecdote of destiny'.

Among the consequences of Babette's being removed from her Parisian restaurant and placed among puritanical sectarians in provincial Norway is that, as was the case in Morris's utopia, her preparing and serving a restaurant-like feast can become an act of Big H Hospitality. The completeness of the hospitality is emphasized by one of the bitter ironies of the story. Babette can give her feast because she has won ten thousand francs in the French national lottery, a lot of money. She spends all of it on the feast. And when her mistresses express astonishment at the expenditure, Babette assures them that 'a dinner for twelve at the Café Anglais', the famed establishment whose head chef she used to be, 'would cost ten thousand francs'. The bitter irony comes in the logic of equivalence and non-equivalence that Babette's expenditure entails.[22] Martine and Phillipa assume that with ten thousand francs Babette now is 'rich', and will likely return to Paris and live comfortably there. Babette shows them that the wealth that interests her is not the wealth through which one can consume what one wants, but the wealth through which one can give what one wants. Yet this great wealth, however one reckons it, is only equal to the cost of a single dinner for twelve at a restaurant in Paris.

So, with bitter irony, Babette's feast exemplifies a kind of utter Big H Hospitality, along with the structural contradiction it must entail. This is not a chef working for pay or for any other reward apart from the satisfaction of what she is doing; nor is it a servant paying back her mistresses for the charity they have shown her. There is no *exchange* entailed, as far as Babette is concerned. There is only giving. And that is as it should be, as far as the chef is concerned, for she equates hospitality with the freedom of art. 'I shall never be poor', Babette tells her mistresses, even after she has expended all of her winnings. 'I told you that I am a great artist. A great artist, Mesdames, is never poor. We have something, Mesdames, of which other people know nothing.'[23] The great artist makes great art, and in making that art she gives without asking for anything in return, since there is nothing equivalent to her art which could be returned in exchange for it. That is not to say that the artist does not require material opportunity; on the contrary, material opportunity is essential, as all of Babette's story testifies. The artist needs patronage. But the opportunity provided by patronage, the opportunity Babette craves, is for the expenditure of giving. Babette quotes what she heard from another artist, an opera singer. 'Through all the world there goes one long cry from the heart of the artist. Give me leave to do my utmost!'[24]

No doubt Dinesen is making an oblique comment about her own condition as an artist living in benighted Denmark, where her work was far less appreciated than it was abroad. She is similarly making a comment about her own frustrating attempts to earn money writing for the commercial fiction market in the United States.[25] Babette living among a people who do not know anything about haute cuisine is like a modern fiction writer living among a people who do not know anything about modern fiction. Neither the one people nor the other understand that the artist, qua artist, does not want anything in return except for the opportunity to be an artist and do her 'utmost'. One of the principle pitfalls of living among philistines is that even when one does one's utmost, and one gives the gift of art to them, they will misinterpret it: even when they enjoy it they are likely to fall into misprision. Babette's guests (save one) simply do not understand what they have received from her – the 'Blinis Demidoff', the turtle soup, the Veuve Clicquot 1860 – although they walk away delighted and moved. Even the one guest who does know what he has received, General Loewenhielm, misconstrues the dinner. As Ferguson observes, instead of inquiring into the miraculous kitchen where this unfathomably excellent Parisian meal has been concocted (that shit-hole-kitchen where Babette has been slaughtering creatures and even turning a dish of quail into a gruesome image of death, a *caille en sarcophage* which the diners have to plunder in order to feed themselves, and from which the champagne of *widow* Clicquot issues forth) – instead of looking for himself to find out how such a meal was prepared for him, the general, remaining in the dining room, thinks that he has been benefited from an act of 'Grace', or at least a lesson in the work of Grace. 'See! that which we have chosen is given us, and that which we have refused is, also and at the same time, granted us. Aye, that which we have rejected is poured upon us abundantly.'[26] A number of commentators have walked away from the story and the film (sometimes not making a clear distinction between the two) with the impression that the tale is a parable about divine grace and the sacraments – this in spite of the fact that Dinesen is known to have been hostile to organized religion, and that 'Babette's Feast' appears alongside several other 'anecdotes of destiny', all of which deal with the theme of art, the artist and the misinterpretation of his or her works.[27] There is a pearl diver, an artist of the sea, whom no one understands but everyone admires from a distance. There is an actress who mistakes reality for art, and then whose behaviour, whose *artistic* behaviour, is fatally misconstrued by a whole town. What do we get in return for living the life of an artist?, the actress asks her mentor, an old man of the theatre. 'In return', the mentor says, 'we get the world's distrust – and our dire loneliness. And nothing else.'[28]

This is the unhappiness of the artist-cook and the artist in general. The artist, if she is a real artist or a great one, can only give, can only strive to give her utmost. But on the one hand, she can only give her utmost if she is provided with a material opportunity for it. And on the other, even when the opportunity comes, and the performance is given or the work created, the artist receives nothing in return, and normally can receive nothing in return, apart from misprision and distrust. The great irony in all this stems from the essential difference between cookery and other forms of art and crafts, the fact that what cookery produces must be gobbled up and assimilated into the body of another. That difference is what has caused philosophers from Plato to Hannah Arendt to dismiss cookery as a non-art, to imagine it merely as an activity that caters to an ephemeral private need rather than as a productivity that serves a permanent public interest.[29] Babette and her author, at least for the purposes of Babette's story, refuse to allow that distinction, much like Dario the butcher. 'I am a great artist!' But unlike the cooks in Morris's *News from Nowhere*, Babette has found that serving the public interest is in complete conflict with the demands of great cookery.

Babette, we have known all along, was a Communard, and in exile because of it. Her husband and son have both been shot, and she herself was arrested as an arsonist. She does not regret it. 'Thanks be to God, I was a Communard!' The members of the ruling class against which she fought 'were evil and cruel. They let the people of Paris starve; they oppressed and wronged the poor. Thanks be to God, I stood upon a barricade; I loaded the gun for my menfolk!'[30] But the very people she fought against, who let the people of Paris starve, were the people for whom she cooked at the Café Anglais. They were the people for whom she cooked gladly, whom she knew by name, whose names she can still fondly recite, up to and including the general who had had her arrested as an arsonist. As far as she was concerned, the rich aristocrats for whom she cooked were the ideal audience for her art, the ideal diners to whom she could offer her utmost. For that reason, although her customers paid and Babette served, and although her customers were elite members of the ruling class and Babette was a woman of the oppressed people, Babette took a proprietary interest in them, and remembers them with regret. 'Those people belonged to me, they were mine', she tells Martine and Phillipa. 'They had been brought up and trained, with greater expense than you, my little ladies, could ever imagine or believe, to understand what a great artist I am. I could make them happy. When I did my very best I could make them perfectly happy.'[31]

Surely the aristocrats did not *deserve* what Babette used to do for them. What they deserved was to be shot from the barricades, or to have their mansions burnt down, and their own wives made into widows. It was the aristocrat who deserved to be cooked alive and entombed in a *sarcophage*, not a quail. But the unworthiness of her customers was what made them valuable to Babette; for it is only to the unworthy that the artist is really able to give without obligation. Religious interpreters of the story – a tenacious lot – may see in Babette a Christ-like figure, giving to the unworthy, dispensing grace, so that even 'that which we have rejected is poured upon us abundantly'. But surely, Dinesen is either actually poking fun at Christianity or at most appropriating its imagery. For 'Babette's Feast' is a parable about the conflict between the artist and society, a conflict amplified when the artist imagines herself as a 'great' creator of the gift of art, for which no reward can be exchanged, and further amplified when the artist is a chef, and when only the undeserving rich can figure as the recipients of the gift of food she offers.

As we saw in the case of the Self-Taught Man and Roquentin in the Maison Bottanet, as well as the utopia of William Morris, hospitality is inherently asymmetrical and incommensurate. The host gives without asking for anything in return, or at least imagines that that is what he is doing, and he gives not what the guest actually needs and desires but rather what Babette would call one's 'utmost'. As I put it before, the host says to his guest, 'I will spare you nothing, I will make you this gift, which you cannot repay, which you can only enjoy, and in order to do so I will force you to desire what I desire you to desire.' This is the logic of what anthropologists call the potlatch, naming it after the practices of the peoples of the Pacific Northwest.[32] In principle a 'symbolic exchange' is established between the giver of the gift and the recipient, since the giver received prestige and obligation in return for the display and expenditure of giving and what amounts to the squandering of wealth. We saw precisely such a symbolic exchange being attempted by the Self-Taught Man with his impositions of oysters and *coq au vin* on a guest who desired neither. But it is in the nature of that kind of exchange that the exchange cannot be openly acknowledged by either side. And now, in 'Babette's Feast', this logic of the potlatch is being equated with the logic of art, including the art of cookery, which in itself (since cooking means both making an object of art and giving it away to be consumed) already combines both the logic of the potlatch and the logic of art. The problem is that when cookery is a 'great art', it may well find the cook doing her utmost for the elite, and making them 'happy', even while letting the multitude go on starving. The core bitterness of Dinesen's unhappy celebration of the art of the cook, according to Babette's own logic, consists in this: that when the cook works *for* the rich she is working *against* the poor; for when she works for the benefit of the former she is working on behalf of the system that oppresses the latter, and when she *gives* to the rich she is apparently *taking away* from the poor. It is perhaps in a realization of the consequences of this logic that Babette stands before her two mistresses 'immovable', 'like a marble monument', stalwart in defiance – 'agonistic', as Mauss would have said.

She will not go back to Paris, and she will not ask for thanks from the people of Berlevaag. She will not even cook any restaurant meals for them again, because her money is exhausted and because, in any case, Berlevaag is a town without restaurants, and apparently it doesn't need them. She will merely assert her identity as a great artist in need of nothing because she has her art. However, as she has no one *for whom* she can produce this art any more, and there isn't even any *material opportunity* for her to be able to make it, there is no reason *why* she will ever get involved in it again. The production of production comes to a halt in the face of the immovable pride of the chef who must also be an artist, practising the big H Hospitality that is also the Big A Art, entirely without a public. It comes to a halt because it doesn't have a public, and it doesn't have a public precisely because of the inherent contradiction of the production of production that the art of cookery entails.

Dinner at the Homesick Restaurant

The Homesick Restaurant of the title of the book belongs to a man who, well into his forties, continues to live at home with his mother. That is the kind of irony one finds in the minimalist world of Anne Tyler and her fictional Baltimore. Ezra Tull inherited the restaurant by default from the woman restaurateur whose second-in-command he came to be. It was a glamorous Continental restaurant for years, Scarlatti's, with waiters in tuxedos, serving only the best of its kind, the food made from fresh and served with pride. But Ezra had another idea. If the restaurant were his alone, he had considered, he would make some changes. For example, he wouldn't serve tomatoes in the winter. 'People would ask for tomatoes, and I'd say, "what can you be thinking of, this is not the season." I'd give them something better.' That is not all, he goes on to say. 'I'd put up a blackboard, write on it every day just two or three good dishes. Of course! In France, they do it all the time. Or I'd offer no choice at all; examine people and say, "You look a little tired. I'll bring you an oxtail stew."'[33]

Ezra's ideas – the year is about 1960 – anticipate the American food revolution that historians like to begin a little later, punctuated with the founding of Chez Panisse in Berkeley in 1971. For once an

American restaurant – readers should note that the novel assumes, and rightly, that there was already a vibrant restaurant culture in America at the time – would stop trying to proliferate choices and focus on offering just a few good things.[34] For once a restaurant would even dare to nullify choice: instead of asking you to choose, it would tell you what is good and *give* it to you; it would even tell you what is good *for* you and give you that. Ezra's establishment would follow a French model in this – the same model as the little Restaurant Colibri above the Place Pigalle. But at the same time it would tear away at the pretensions of the 'Continental' restaurant that had dominated fine dining for so long. It would literally tear away at it, as Ezra would tear away at the structure of Scarlatti's, trying to strip it down into something more essential. 'He tore down the wall between the restaurant kitchen and the dining room.' 'He raced around the windows and dragged down the stiff brocade draperies; he peeled up the carpeting and persuaded a brigade of workmen to sand and polish the floorboards.' 'The wallpaper in the back hall was too cluttered and he ripped it off the wall. He tore away the ornate gilt sconces beside the telephone. He yanked the old-fashioned silhouettes from the restroom doors.'[35]

Next to go were the waiters and the cooks. They leave by attrition and in protest at what Ezra is doing to the restaurant. Ezra replaces them with 'motherly' women. The waitresses do a better job at making the customers understand what is available to them, and making them feel good about it. 'Try the gizzard soup', one of them would say. 'It's really hot and garlicky and it's made with love.'[36] When the cooks leave, Ezra mans the kitchen himself, as it were, but 'with the help of a woman from New Orleans and a Mexican', both of whom introduce their own recipes into the repertoire of the restaurant; eventually he hires a 'country cook' from the South, who introduces classic southern food to the menu.[37]

Down comes 'the old black and gilt sign' in front of the restaurant that says 'Scarlatti's'.[38] In its place comes a sign saying 'Homesick Restaurant', the name for a venue designed to serve its customers the food they are homesick for, even if they don't already know it. In Ezra's establishment the restaurant has been deconstructed: the barrier between the kitchen and the dining room has been eliminated, the ceremonies of the dining room discarded, motherly waitresses have replaced the manly waiters, the decorations have been taken away, the floors stripped to the boards, the exotic 'continental' cuisine has been replaced with something more American and earthy, and the very idea of a regular menu has been exchanged for an unpredictable offering of daily specials, whatever has 'popped into the heads' of the cooks that day. What results is a restaurant that is trying not to be a restaurant. It has became a simulation of home, a staged and living monument to the nostalgia for home. For Ezra, to be sure, the Homesick Restaurant is a kind of sublimation of the restaurant experience. 'This is something more', he says about a pot roast he is serving, which one customer has rejected, leaving, because he can get food like that at home. 'This something more. I mean, pot roast is really not the right name; it's more like . . . what you long for when you're sad and everyone's been wearing you down.'[39] What Ezra is trying to do is to overcome the kinds of contradictions that Morris and Dinesen had pointed out. He wants to de-commodify the restaurant. He wants to undermine the traditional balances and imbalances, the deference and antipathy, between the producer and the consumer. He wants to turn the restaurant into a sublime substitute for the home, and the restaurateur and his staffs into sublime substitutes for parents. And he believes that he can achieve that; he believes that what he is producing in the restaurant is not just a substitute for something missing but, somehow, the biggest IT of them all.

Anne Tyler is poking fun at Ezra and his restaurant. The running gag of the novel is that when this homesick adult living at home with his mother tries to organize dinners for the whole of his family at the Homesick Restaurant, including a brother and a sister and eventually a long-lost father, the dinner always gets broken off. The family reunion always turns into a disaster. There are too many unresolved tensions in this family. So Tyler creates the idea of a homesick restaurant in large part to mock it; she uses the idea to argue, in effect, that a simulation of the home can never provide a substitute for home, and a restaurant can never really be anything but a restaurant. But Tyler is also careful to show that the dysfunction of the family that Ezra continually wants to reunite is never strictly a psychological or moral problem. For what has broken this family apart is the way of the world.

The new mobility of American society in the age of twentieth-century capitalism has torn the family apart.

We needn't go into the details. We need only say that they are convincingly laid out, beginning with the story of a father who is a travelling salesman, constantly moving the family from one town to another until finally he abandons them in Baltimore, and leaves an unstable wife and three young children to their own devices. Ezra is homesick for a home he never really had. The situation could therefore be framed by way of the classic Baudrillardian analysis: Ezra's restaurant is a 'simulacrum' precisely in the sense that it actually preceded the thing it is supposed to be remembering and signifying. First comes the Homesick Restaurant. Then comes the home and the sickness for home. However, Tyler also shows that however displaced or artificial Ezra's ideas are, the sickness was actually real: if there was never any real home to be sick about, there was plenty to be sick about all the same.[40]

What bears remarking is that Tyler introduces some very profound ideas about the nature of restaurants in late modern America. She introduces, in the first place, a new dimension to the perennial ambiguity of familiarity and strangeness that is a part of the restaurant as such, the dimension of time, of memory and nostalgia. Familiarity and strangeness are not just functions of space and place, statically conceived; they are functions of the *having been there then* and the *going there now.* It will be recalled that Roland Barthes asserted that, for the French, eating is always about memory. Now we find that memory can play a major role in American dining too. One anthropologist has recently remarked how the 'family restaurant' in America – of which there are thousands all across the land, most of them owned by a handful of corporations – involves a contrived familiarity, down to the bric-a-brac on the walls, which almost always refer, nostalgically, to local and American history.[41] What Tyler adds to this picture is the perception that the nostalgic familiarity of the 'family' restaurant in America is based on a bad memory, in both senses of the term: a faulty memory and a traumatized one. For America is simply not a country with a secure past, or with the secure anchoring in the past it thinks it has.

Another idea that Tyler introduces, or rather re-introduces, is the asymmetry of hospitality. Neither Scarlatti's nor its offspring, the

Homesick Restaurant, operate according to the principle that the customer is always right, or that the point is always to give the customer what he or she wants. Both restaurants, as it were, *know better* than their customers. They offer a vision of what customers *ought* to be looking for, and then they give their customers, without cutting corners, what the restaurant has determined or will determine what they ought to have. Scarlatti's does this in a conventional way. It provides for the staging of a formularity into which the customer enters as into a new world, or at least a new kind of social space, in which the customer is only one among several actors, all of them playing the rules of a game determined in advance by the restaurateur. 'Used to be', the disgruntled old customer tells Ezra, 'this place had class . . . Used to be there was fine French cuisine, flamed at the table and all . . . And chandeliers. And a hat-check girl. And waiters in black tie.'[42] Ezra has deconstructed this, but he has retained the idea of productive hospitality that animated the original. Or rather, he has tried to bring this productive hospitality to its logical conclusion: a restaurant that not only determines in advance what the customer can do, but even gives orders, telling the customer *what* to do. This is homelike and nostalgic because, in Ezra's hands, the dictation to the customer by the restaurant mimics the assertive nurturing of the child by the mother. The restaurant, like the mother, gives its customers what is good for them. In fact, the restaurant will have recourse to disciplining its customers if necessary. 'You might not get what you asked for' at the Homesick Restaurant. '"The Smithfield ham", you'd say, and up would come the okra stew. "With that cough of yours, I know this will suit you better", Ezra would explain.'[43] Seduction is better; the Homesick Restaurant tries to seduce the customers into wanting what the restaurant wants to give them. But it does not shy away from putting down its foot. And in this it resembles not only the mothers it imitates, but also any number of great chefs.

Journalist Joseph Wechsberg relates the story of his first encounter, in the early 1950s, with the famous French chef Fernand Point at the latter's three-star restaurant, the Restaurant de la Pyramide in Vienne, south of Lyon. Wechsberg had already been forewarned. 'It's not a question of whether or not you will *go*', a friend tells him. 'The question is, will Monsieur Point let you eat at his place? He has thrown out American millionaires and French ex-ministers when he didn't feel like serving them.'[44] Getting an introduction and recommendation, Wechsberg finds himself graciously received by the great Point, but he is soon educated as to who is actually in charge. '*La grande cuisine* doesn't wait for the client', Point tells him. 'It is the client who must wait for *la grande cuisine*.' All the time he visits the restaurant Wechsberg has the 'feeling of being in a home'.[45] As for what Wechsberg will eat, he leaves it entirely up to Point. And in fact, Point will have it no other way. 'Let us think about what you will eat', Point says on several occasions, though it is Point who is doing all the thinking about this; Wechsberg, like a pupil, must passively accept what Point is going to teach him, and, like a child, must contentedly consume what Point is going to feed him. Wechsberg is delighted, of course; the food at Le Pyramide is probably the best he's ever eaten.

So Ezra's deconstruction of the restaurant only reiterates, in a homesick American version, the asymmetrical ethic of *grande cuisine*. But Tyler has to introduce one more idea, which makes Ezra's interventions possible. This is the (unnamed) idea of *resistance*. A chef like Fernand Point, at the height of his fame, can presume to speak for an entire nation, on behalf of its national culture of gastronomy. But Ezra can no more do that than Babette could. For such a national culture (in Ezra Tull's America) does not exist. On the contrary, national culture is a kind of enemy; for national culture is what has destroyed the home life (with its regional specialities) that the restaurant is trying to defend. So Ezra's deconstruction will also be the reconstruction of an institution of resistance, a kind of barricade against certain dominant trends in American life. In the name of nostalgia, Ezra is actually doing something unprecedented. In the name of healing his customers, he is actually defying them to lose the name of consumer, and adopt instead the identity of a comrade, pupil and child. It is just such a dream – the typical American dream of reinventing one's identity, but also the peculiar dream of the 1960s, of exhorting the people en masse to transform their identities in order to transform the world, and bring down 'The System' – that animated any number of alternative restaurants that were founded in America in the 1960s and '70s. Some of them were health food restaurants. Some of them, like Chez Panisse, started out as exercises in consciousness-raising, even if they also promoted fine dining in the European style. *Dinner at the Homesick Restaurant* celebrates that impulse of resistance and reinvention, and underscores the *need* for it. But it also challenges the restaurant's authenticity. The restaurant of the book is after all a simulacrum of the home it is supposed to either express or replace, and as far as the wounded lives of its main charac- ters are concerned, though it may serve a good meal, the restaurant changes nothing. In the end, Tyler imagines how the deconstruction of the restaurant for purposes of resistance must deconstruct itself. No family can actually eat in this family restaurant without becoming a parody of itself.

In the Kitchen

Monica Ali's recent novel *In the Kitchen* is not without faults, but it is very valuable to anyone who wants to study the culture of the restaurant today. The novel fails to convince us that it has captured the realities of the main object of its drama, the tremulous inner life of its main character, an aspiring yet ageing chef at a posh if dowdy hotel in central London. But the novel is revealing because Ali erects a compelling picture of the social world of the elite English restaurant. One might think of it as an analysis of the London food world according to the world view of the world-weary left-wing *Guardian* reader. Now, after the days of William Guest in utopia and chef Babette in Norway, after the 1960s radicalism of characters like Ezra Tull, and after London has come to be celebrated as a capital of world cuisine and its status has been entirely mediatized, *this* is where we have arrived, Ali argues. We have arrived at a world founded on exploitation and cynicism; and there is nothing to be done about it.[46]

Ali places her main character not just in a London restaurant, but also in the framework of a literary convention. Gabriel Lightfoot, the chef, comes from a working-class family in post-industrial Lancashire, and his life follows in the footsteps of any number of prominent London chefs in the real world, including the Lancashireman Marcus Wareing, the London chef at the (undowdy) Berkeley today.[47] (Monica Ali hails from provincial Lancashire too.[48]) Intelligent and driven but estranged from his immediate milieu (in Britain the figure is almost always a 'he'), full of curiosity about the world but uninterested or unskilled in academics, the young man finds a calling in the kitchen, and from an early age he starts on a journey through the 'food world', including apprenticeships and special schooling, until he gets a name for himself and lands a job as a head chef or even an executive chef (as Gabriel's position turns out to be) in the midst of the food world, art world, media world, business world and political world of the capital. But apart from his background in the northern English working class, Gabriel is also a character out of modern American fiction, and especially modern Jewish-American fiction (though granted, this tradition of fiction is rooted in the nineteenth-century work of writers like Balzac and Dickens). Like Isaac Bashevis Singer's *The Magician of Lublin* or any number of Saul Bellow's main characters, Gabriel Lightfoot is a man who has risen in the world but not risen all the way. He aspires to rise higher. (For Gabriel, it is a matter of opening his own restaurant, a posh French restaurant in Pimlico along with a couple of media-world, business-world, political-world partners.) But something intervenes: a chance encounter, an interruption of plans and routines, the appearance of something from the world outside of one's own day-dreams and preoccupations that shakes up the dreams, and undermines the preoccupations. This chance encounter (for Gabriel, an encounter with a young woman from Belarus, who had been illegally employed as a porter in his restaurant, and who has served time, she claims, as a prostitute in thrall to a trafficker) causes an unravelling of the main character's life: moral crises, physical crises, a nervous break-down. The ruined self is then free to rise again, in a new form, though the new form (in this convention) is usually something less, rather than more, than the self with which the story began. This pattern of tragicomic unravelling serves to ennoble the main character. It makes him a witness to the tragedy of being human. It ends in the character's coming to know himself, even if what he knows is something reduced, a disappointment, and it ends therefore in the character's coming to stand as a pathetic if not altogether un-ironic or unlovable representative of us all.[49]

Ali places her chef in precisely this framework of literary development, but she doesn't really believe in it. As reviewers have noted, she simply cannot get inside the moral universe of her main character, or make us care about it. 'Gabriel is a small man on a big stage', complains William Grimes. 'Gabe's disintegration never quite engages the reader, who is left feeling better informed but oddly unaffected', writes Stephanie Merritt. And though the fault can be assigned to Ali's artistry, the fault must also, I believe, be attributed to the novelist's attitude toward her subject. For if Ali finds that the food world of London is founded on cynicism and exploitation, her own attitude toward it is itself awash in cynicism – philosophical cynicism, the cynicism of the social critic with no solutions, combined with literary cynicism, the cynicism of black comedy and anger.

Ali's double cynicism, providing a cynical view of a cynical society, is what is interesting in the current context. For though Ali's novel fails as the novel of a man whose life unravels, it succeeds in producing a sadly convincing view of the 'state-of-the-nation' (as Christopher Tayler puts it). For once, in this national state, the restaurant and its production of production are centre stage. This is a novel where what happens in a restaurant stands for what happens in the nation as a whole. But this representative institution of cultural and economic production itself is so cynical, Ali shows, that the only possible response to it may well be the revenge of philosophic and literary cynicism.

You can see the institutional cynicism represented in the novel in moral lives of the men who finance the restaurant: either absent corporate investors, like the ones who own the Hotel Imperial over whose expensive but mediocre restaurant Gabriel presides as executive chef; or hands-on scoundrels like the businessman and the Labour MP (the latter named Fairweather, of course) who have arranged to finance two-thirds of the small French restaurant Gabriel is planning to open. You can see that in the men who manage the restaurant: the slimy hotel manager who is Gabriel's supervisor, a Machiavel who understands himself to be inhabiting a universe of Machiavels; the equally slimy restaurant maître d', involved in an unseemly scam to exploit migrant workers. Gabriel himself is not much different, for he doesn't really believe in the hotel restaurant where he is working, and he is pretty much indifferent to the people who work for him, unless they can serve his turn; his only motive at this point is to get ahead in the restaurant world, and his only desire is to leave the hotel restaurant for a place of his own. But you can see the cynicism of the restaurant business even in the workers of the restaurant. A few show themselves to be honourable types, even tragically honourable men and women, victims of political turmoil who have managed, in the belly of London, to hold on to their dignity. But most of them are self-centred and greedy; some of them are violent. This 'United Nations' of a restaurant staff is very much like the similar staff in Bourdain's *Kitchen Confidential* (which Ali credits as a source of inspiration in her acknowledgements), although it is a United Nations mainly of Eastern Europe and a few outposts of the old British Empire, and it appears to be both more pathetic and more dangerous. While some of the people are comic and likeable, and some of them earn our pity, few of them are worthy of our admiration.

So, the world of the restaurant is cynical. And again, Ali's treatment of that world is cynical – critical of it in a dog-like way, a Diogenes-the-Cynic-like way. ('I am looking for a man', Diogenes is supposed to have said, when walking in the daylight through the city with a lighted candle in his hand.) If Ali cannot quite get us into the head of a real-life Gabriel Lightfoot, she can show us a sad but believable context for the existence of people like Gabriel Lightfoot, and she can set her character on symbolically resonant, if emotionally unconvincing narrative journey through the byways of the restaurant world.

The journey is supposed to be like the proverbial journey of the celebrity chef or any novelistic man on the make – the journey from the provinces to the capital, from modest circumstances to wealth, from obscurity to fame. Most people in the novel, Gabriel included, seem to know that this is supposed to be Gabriel's trajectory. The myth of success precedes his success. But the journey is also supposed to follow along an axis of meaning that could have been adopted from anthropologist Mary Douglas, the axis of purity and danger, or purity and pollution.[50] Gabriel is supposed to be journeying from one site of purity, his hometown working-class culture, to another site of purity, the French restaurant of his dreams, where he will be the chef and the artist and the food will be (as he says) 'clean' and 'precise' yet 'modern'. The danger and the pollution are what Gabriel is supposed to be travelling through as he learns the trade, works for others and earns the right to open a place of his own – this danger and pollution symbolized above all by the Hotel Imperial where he has landed, whose perils he has to master before he moves on. The problem is that just as the myth of success is obviously a myth, so the trajectory between the purity of the Lightfoot home in Lancashire and the purity of Lightfoot the restaurant in Pimlico is a myth: it is myth both because the endpoints of the journey are not so pure and because the danger and pollution in between cannot provide a valid means of growth and escape.

That the corporate-owned Imperial Hotel and its Restaurant Jacques comprise a space of danger and pollution the novel makes clear from the outset. As the novel opens, in the dingy cellar of the restaurant a porter from the Ukraine – formerly an engineer, but now just an alcoholic porter in exile who actually lives (illegally) in the cellar, saving his money to send to his daughters back home – has accidentally died, smashing his skull in a drunken fall. Upstairs from the cellar, to go from the tragic to the ridiculous, but to round out the picture, the restaurant is putting artificial flowers on the tables instead of the real flowers a restaurant with its ambitions ought to have. After the death, a failure to celebrate the living. 'Great restaurants, like great hotels, delivered coherent design and consistent standards', Gabriel reflects. But the artificial flowers, not plastic but silk, as if the dead silk were the living, and as if silk flowers were really what a classy restaurant named Jacques was all about, 'gave the game away', as far as Gabriel was concerned. 'If the Imperial were a person, thought Gabe, you would say here is someone who does not know show she is.'[51] Identity in this novel is another kind of purity – unless it is impure identity, such as it turns out that most of the characters and institutions are afflicted with, beginning with the Restaurant Jacques in the Hotel Imperial. The kitchen, meanwhile, with the dead man still below as the police inspect the premises, is a place of heat, ethnic conflict, violence and incompetence, all of which Gabriel can just barely keep under control. The hotel owners are not 'expecting miracles. We're not talking Michelin and all that crap. Just some food you can eat without gagging.' But only one member of the kitchen staff besides Gabe is said to show 'any interest in food'.[52] A menu for an important banquet the restaurant was about to put on included 'Canapés: spring rolls, smoked salmon, quiche squares, guacamole, vol-au-vents (prawn), mini choc mousses'.[53] Gabriel finds this hodgepodge of convenience snacks from three continents depressing, but he feels powerless to change it. One of the cooks is still using frozen chips, although Gabriel has banned them. And Gabriel himself is compromised. 'He was not here because he wanted to be, but only to prove himself. Show us, said the would-be backers for his restaurant, manage a kitchen on that scale and we'll put up the money.'[54] In fact, Gabriel has taken the job promising to stay on for years, knowing that he is only going to stay for at most twelve months, and thinking, as he shakes hands on the deal with his new employer, in what he and the employer both knew to be an 'empty gesture', how his father had once told him, 'Never, ever, shake hands with a man and then go back on your word'.[55]

So the restaurant is impure and treacherous in all kinds of ways. Yet the imagined forms of purity from which and to which Gabriel has been headed are shown to be polluted as well. Gabriel's hometown, to which he makes visits to see his ailing father, is a post-industrial wasteland, clinging to imaginary past glory and the high-minded ethics of moribund working-class culture, even as it is being repopulated with post-industrial immigrants and afflicted with the reactionary racism that arises in response to the influx of foreigners. The zone of purity toward which Gabriel is headed is the French restaurant he wants to open: as he says in full, 'Traditional French cuisine – precisely executed classics with a clean, modern interpretation.'[56] The novel makes clear, however, that though 'traditional French' is an ideal Gabriel respects, and possibly a product he is capable of producing, Gabriel has little genuine background in it, and not much a spontaneous taste for it either. Certainly he was never exposed to it at home, in Lancashire. Even his apprenticeship in France was brief, and largely unrewarding. Moreover, the few times the reader finds Gabriel cooking – he doesn't do much actual cooking while on the job, since he acts as the executive chef, but occasionally he spontaneously cooks for the love of it – Gabriel starts messing around with chillies and other spices and other non-French ideas. But not even his flirtation with non-Western foods is successful. In fact, twice while he starts cooking with chillies and other spices, trying to express himself, Gabriel can't finish the job. 'Sorry', he has to say to a girlfriend on one of those occasions, after he has gotten so lost in thoughts of nostalgia and gloom that he hasn't been able to continue with the ingredients he has set out to make a meal for her in her kitchen: 'couscous, garlic, root ginger, coriander, a jar of harissa sauce, a tin of chickpeas, and lamb chops'. 'Look at me', he says to her. 'Useless. I haven't done a thing.' They have to settle for one of the five takeaways the girlfriend has on her speed dial.[57] In fact, every time Gabriel tries to do something with food in this novel, every time he takes up a body of ingredients and tries to make dinner, he ends up failing. He is not, at bottom, all that much of a cook any more, if ever he was.

So, in this world of mythical ideals and factual incompetence, there is no real going forward. But forward the protagonist must nevertheless go. Gabriel must have his one-sided affair with Lena, and lose his girlfriend and a good part of his sanity because of it. He must begin to unravel too because he finds out that his father, back in Lancashire, is dying – and because the Lancashire of his youth is already dead. He must also go off on a journey. As his sanity unravels, Gabriel finds himself getting carted off to a farm in a bus full of migrant labourers, and then put to work picking vegetables. This is his journey into the heart of darkness – although it is actually only flat and rural Essex. He discovers the literal filth and injustice, the nearly slave-like conditions of labour, through which London's fine restaurants acquire the raw materials for fine French cooking, even in Essex. Then, once rescued from the farm – or rather booted out, when he tries to protest against an injustice there – he returns to the hotel only to come face to face with the absolute tawdriness of the men who are supposed to be financing Lightfoot. He comes face to face with it at a charity ball, upstairs from the restaurant, where the elite raise funds for the poor by bidding at auction for goods like celebrity underwear. Gabriel loses control, attacks the MP, gets tossed out, loses his job, loses his restaurant, loses the money he had already invested in it along with his partners . . .

Since this is a comic novel, having lost everything, there is hope that Gabriel will eventually re-emerge as another kind of person. At the end there is even some hope expressed that Gabriel's girlfriend will take him back. But clearly, if Gabriel is to find his way it will not be through his dream of 'traditional French cuisine – precisely executed classics with a clean, modern interpretation'. As far as the novel is concerned, you can light as many candles on the culinary scene in

London as you want; but in the kitchen, at least, that violent scene of the production of production, it is unlikely that one will find there anyone whom one can confidently call a man. For there is dirt beneath, dirt above and dirt within, and the kitchen – and the whole apparatus of production it is a part of – has already un-manned the producer of production.

I am not going to try to draw conclusions from this foray into the fictional production of production. I want to leave that in the hands of the reader. But I do want to emphasize how all these works of fiction lift a veil from our sight of reality. They show us how much is really at stake in this transaction of restaurant work. And they remind us of how little, as majestic consumers, we are likely to take that into account. *Our* interests as the people who pay and eat and digest is usually quite different from the interests of restaurateurs, cooks and servers – unless we're eating in a restaurant for the rest of us, or maybe in a guest house in William Morris's Nowhere.

seven

Culture, Civilization and Resistance

Cultural democracy: as I have gone in search of the restaurant experience, I have gone again and again in search of the experience *for us*. Not the experience *of* us, although I have had to try to account for that too, but the experience *for* us, we members of the species *homo restauranticus*, we members of the *dēmos* of restaurant-goers. And I have searched again and again for the experience *for* us not as consumers, or majestic consumers, but as consumers without consumerism, consumers who have a stake in the restaurant world, consumers who participate in the world alongside and in cooperation with its producers, consumers who along with producers participate, or rather *strive* to participate (since doing so is not always easy: there are all kinds of obstacles in the way) in a democracy of restaurant-going. A crazy idea, no doubt. As funny as ordering shit in a French restaurant. Up till now, as I said at the beginning, no one has ever thought of 'the people' as 'the people who eat out'. But since eating out is what all of us in the developed world are doing, that is who we are. Among other things, of course.

Economic democracy is a long way off. In most developed countries in the past thirty years, and especially since the 1990s, economic inequality has grown, not shrunk. The recent recession, the Great Recession as some are calling it, has exacerbated the situation, especially in cold-hearted America, which lacks an adequate safety net. And as economic inequality has become worse, the distribution of restaurant-going has become worse: with a decline in economic democracy, there has also come a decline in cultural democracy. Junk food for the poor, 'Big Mouth® Bites' for the middling masses, and *ris de veau* (sometimes, on special occasions) for the lucky few and *ris de veau* or whatever as often as you like for the very lucky few. Of course, the distribution of restaurant experience is a function of what Bourdieu called 'cultural capital' as well as of 'real capital'. It is not just the rich who eat better, it is also the well-educated who eat better. (I am myself one of the lucky few almost entirely because of my cultural capital – and I have the lack of economic capital to prove it.) But take the two things together, cultural capital and economic capital, and you can see that the 'food revolution' so vaunted by foodies in places like America and Britain, which has led to the opening of so many good restaurants everywhere, has come *precisely at the same time* as the explosion of restaurant culture everywhere, at all levels of dining. The food revolution is part of a larger revolution in the organization of society and the means by which members of society have come to feed themselves. It takes no great leap of imagination to see that the proliferation of good restaurants in urban centres around the world is a symptom of the growth of inequality around the world. As Baudrillard argued long ago, we think of modern capitalism as a wealth-generating engine that enhances life opportunities for all, and so we think that the prevalence of inequality over the years is just a blip, an accident that the system itself, if it is properly run, will eventually balance out. But in fact, modern capitalism is really a system for *creating* inequality. That's what it does, and that's what it does best. And that's what the growth of explosion of restaurants around the world, the good, the bad and the ugly, by and large *expresses*. It expresses inequality.

Can the restaurant experience nevertheless contribute, however modestly, to cultural democracy? Let us begin by considering a few basics, and start at the top, at the so-called world leaders in restaurant culture. Or rather, let us begin by disburdening ourselves of some understandable but counterproductive assumptions that derive from the existence of a presumably top-down model of cultural development.

In order to contribute to cultural democracy, an institution has to be open to all – or, at least, it has to be productive of certain cultural effects that are open to all. But the problem, then, is obvious. There is nothing less open to us today than a three Michelin-star restaurant, apart from those gated communities and resorts of the rich which are not only closed to the rest of us because we don't have the money but also because they are literally shut off to us, self-enclosed, remotely located and, of course, walled-in and gated. The three Michelin-star will be a public-private commercial institution, granted, open to anyone who can afford it, and that is important; it isn't protected by walls and gates. But except for a small portion of the population, the cost is prohibitive, and the venue is, by definition as by fact, very rare. In all of New York City there are only four of them, about the same as the number of opera companies. In Los Angeles there are none. So, 'the best' – though they do not actually exist outside of the practice that makes of them 'the best'; outside of that practice the idea is meaningless – are in effect closed to the public. They have nothing to do with the rest of us directly. They aren't *for* us.

What about indirectly, then? Do elite restaurants have a productive and positive impact on the general culinary culture? The answer is yes and no. The temples of haute cuisine train cooks as apprentices and journeymen and keep up standards; they develop styles and set fashions; they advance the art of cookery, using new techniques or combinations of ingredients or inventing new dishes and modes of service, and promoting an ethic of artistry for its own sake; they provide unique and induplicatable opportunities for experimentation and discovery. In all those ways elite restaurants have an impact on the general culture, and may be thought to contribute to the development and experience of cultural democracy. That is how those older famous temples, like Fernand Point's Le Pyramide, came to be regarded by the connoisseurs of France, and that is how any number of aspiring chefs and restaurant critics look up to them still. But the fact is, if this is what they are supposed to do as contributors to culture, and if this is what they are still trying to do, they are not doing it very well. On the one hand, gastronomes today can discuss a 'food world' much as art connoisseurs can discuss an 'art world' – a subculture of the high end, dominated by famous chefs and wealthy, fashionable patrons, to which both producers and consumers can aspire to belong. Individuals with ambitions to cook or eat will have a world of accomplishment to seek out.[1] But on the other, this new 'food world' co-exists, in the developed countries, with a dominant mode of production which depends on a cheapening of production and the exploitation of consumers; it depends on 'Big Mouth® Bites', and haute cuisine has really nothing to say to it. The majority culture, the culture of the masses, is systemically resistant to the values and practices of haute cuisine. To imagine that haute cuisine is really a leading force in culinary culture and contributing to cultural democracy is to surrender to an illusion – in fact, it is to surrender to an ideology whose real value isn't democracy, the rule of the many, but plutocracy, the rule of the rich.

It may even help spread a downright lie. While the food world puts on a face of generating cultural capital, distributing fine dining to the far-flung reaches of the world – or at least to the far-flung capitals of the concentration of wealth in the world, like Las Vegas and Dubai – it is actually contributing to inequality. I am not saying, as Babette might have done, that eating a £200 meal of select Persian Gulf seafood at the Al Mahara at the Burj Al Arab Hotel in Dubai (where the dark and glitzy dining room surrounds an opulent aquarium, with big white sharks) is going to cause a herdsmen in Yemen, on the other side of the Arabian peninsula, to go without his yoghurt. Economic activity generates more economic activity, as far as the activity extends, and it is unlikely to have much effect in places to which it does not extend. But eating that meal contributes to the balance of inequality anyway. And we all know that; even aspiring young chefs, working for a minimum wage to get the experience of apprenticing at great restaurants, know this. The wealth that elite restaurants participate in generating is distributed with obscene unevenness, and the culture of elite restaurants contributes in that way and others to the erection of obscene boundaries between the wealthy and the non-wealthy wherever they are found. To invert an Aristotelian idea, the food world as it is constituted today produces distributive injustice – both in the flows of money and capital that the industry generates and in the parcelling-out of culinary experience. If there are a handful or so of posh restaurants in Dubai with their own aquariums, or that are merely supervised by respected chefs from France and Britain, among them Gordon Ramsay and Pierre Gagnaire – who presumably 'own' the class of investment bankers and energy brokers they serve the same way Babette 'owned' the aristocrats of the Second Empire – there are twelve Burger Kings, eleven Hardees, 27 Kentucky Fried Chickens and sixteen Subways. Meanwhile in Yemen, there aren't any outlets of haute cuisine at all, apparently . . . and there are hardly any multinational fast food joints either. On the one hand, Yemen hasn't yet benefited from the spread of global capital as Dubai has, and it doesn't have the restaurants that go along with it. On the other, Dubai hasn't suffered from the McDonaldization of popular food culture that goes along with the spread of global capital either.[2]

The model of the 'food world', where the 'best restaurants in the world' are supposed to promote artistry, set the trends, train the chefs, educate the diners and disseminate fine dining through the other reaches of society, is a trickle-down model of cultural value and economic production. It works to some extent. Fine dining might well be lost without it. We need this system, for the pursuit of excellence belongs to *everybody*, and the pursuit of excellence requires its own mechanisms, hierarchies, training grounds and competitions for prestige. But the system doesn't work very well. When I was partaking of a fine crab bisque at Marcus Wareing at the Berkeley Hotel, almost all the rest of London was eating a sandwich.[3] And they were the lucky ones. They could have ordered the chicken tikka at a pub, or the eggs Benedict at Euston Station; if they were down in Canary Wharf, they could even have dined in a Chili's and had themselves a few 'Big Mouth® Bites'. The finest restaurants have some effect of trickling down their artistry to the general public. But in an age that has seen the most exacerbated inequality of income since the Second World War, the fine restaurants serving the fine diners of England have an even greater effect in erecting boundaries between themselves and the general public; they help *deprive* the general public of access to culinary excellence, absorbing the energies of culinary excellence into the compounds of the few, and spreading out, on the other side of the fence, culinary junk for the many.

For the rest of us some other model has to be put in use. In fact, some other model is already in use, though not as widely as it ought to be. I have already mentioned a few of the places I know of that subscribe to that alternative model, from San Francisco to Collioure; I have even mentioned a couple in London; I could have mentioned a thousand, if I had but world and time enough to do so. Readers of this book can mention thousands more, not discounting establishments in Dubai, or Sana'a, the capital of Yemen, or even Columbus, Ohio (though I have my doubts). These will not be the ideal establishments of William Morris's utopia, for they have to survive in a non-ideal world and make a profit. They will seldom be Homesick Restaurants, for few restaurateurs could succeed at being as presumptuous as Ezra Tull (though some might do so); there will usually have to be compromises between giving the public what is good for them and giving them what they think they want. In addition, real restaurants for the rest of us will almost never be part of a chain, for the food at a restaurant for the rest of us has to made, not manufactured. It has to be *food*, something that *sustains* us, not a simulation of food with its own trademark, and it has to be served in a spirit of hospitality, not dispatched to the table under orders from absentee investors.[4] But the alternatives will be restaurants where the people at work in them can believe in what they are doing and where it is clear that they are *really doing it*, offering a measure of art and hospitality to *homo restauranticus,* whomever he or she may be. The restaurant for the rest of us is open to the rest of us. It is not trying to squeeze money out of our wallets by impressing us with how rare and costly and exquisitely ingenious it is, although it may well serve something that is ingenious, costly and rare. (There is no getting away from the fact that not everything in the culinary world will ever be equal, for some things really are more ingenious, costly, rare and worthwhile than others.) And the restaurant for the rest of us is not trying to sucker us into settling for mediocrity, although even some examples of this kind of restaurant are not always going to be successful at rising above the level of mediocrity. But it is trying to serve us something good, which the workers responsible believe to be good or even know to be good – a rare thing in itself. It is trying to serve something good, and it is trying to serve *us*.

But who are 'we', the subjects of this 'us'? The 'we' I have been appealing to is not without its own inclusions and exclusions. But this 'we' is a lot more inclusive than one might at first imagine, for *homo restauranticus* can be found all over the world, at many different levels of income, status and class. The species can be found wherever modernity has triumphed. It can be found in abundance especially where modernity has shaded into the conditions of postmodernity and hypermodernity, and life has become more mobile, more 'liquid' as Zygmunt Bauman likes to put it, and older conventions of dining (based on the family meal, or the boarding-house table) have become dissolved into a larger mix of eating habits.

Let us talk about 'us', then.

For I am not going to conclude this book by telling restaurateurs and cooks and servers what they ought to do. I am not even going to conclude this book by criticizing those restaurateurs or corporate suits who are guilty of putting profit ahead of other objectives. It would be presumptuous of me to do so. It would also be stupid. We cannot blame people for wanting to make money, or for desiring more comfortable or prestigious employment, and we cannot expect a certain class of individuals – talented chefs, for example – to be different from everybody else in their society and defy the values according to which they have been raised. We can only *desire* them to be different. We can only *wish* them somehow not to have given in, selling themselves out, and surrendering to the ideology of plutocracy.

But what about our desires and wishes, then? Let us talk about 'us' and our desires and wishes. And let us talk about ourselves not sociologically, as an aggregate of individuals whose needs and aspirations can be assessed with statistical objectivity – even if we wanted to do, such an objectivity, in my view, is entirely a delusion – but philosophically, as subjects who are capable of thinking critically about the practices of everyday life, and capable of theorizing our own values and desires.

What is our theory of the restaurant for the rest of us? From where do the values of our restaurant-going stem? And where do we think our values ought to lead us?

Let me begin, on the level of micro-theory, with an anecdote and its sequel. On a warm sunny afternoon, I was sitting with Marion and Sara on the outdoor terrace of a restaurant outside Mont-Saint-Michel in Normandy, eating fish. Because of the angles and spacing of the tables I had a good view of what was going on at two other tables, but I was at a safe enough distance away that my observing could not itself be observed. At one table sat a large party of French people of three or four generations, maybe ten or twelve people in all, and almost all of them were eating the same thing, *moules frites*, and filling their glasses from carafes of white wine distributed at intervals around the table. At a smaller table sat a party of four, a couple in their twenties along with a couple in their late fifties, the latter probably the parents of one of the young people. They were either British or Australian – from a distance, I couldn't quite make out their accents exactly, although I could tell that they were speaking non-American English. At this Anglophone table everyone seemed to be eating something different, servings of some kind of fish or meat with a garnish, each with a slightly different design and colouration. Each was drinking something different too. The older man was drinking a beer. The older woman was drinking a cup of tea. The younger sort each had a glass of wine.

I watched the French people. They were animated, smiling, laughing, and they were eating with joy, rhythmically digging into their mussels, using one shell to pry out the meat from another, clicking them together like castanets. Each of these people, I noticed, old and young, was sitting up at the table with a kind of enthusiastic uprightness, backs straight and heads erect, looking into one another in the eyes. When a Frenchman picked at his mussel, brought it to his mouth and chewed, he kept his head erect, he looked directly ahead of him toward the person sitting opposite, and grinned. As he worked his teeth and jaws with a properly closed mouth, and eventually swallowed, he kept looking straight ahead and kept grinning, and when he finished he allowed himself a split second of a pause, as if to congratulate himself for having completed a job well done. Then he fell to the next mussel, or else allowed himself a sip of wine or a sly bite of a *frite*.

I watched the Anglophones. They were not very animated. In fact, they ate in virtual silence. And as they ate I noticed something peculiar. Partaking with knives and forks, sawing into morsels of fish or meat, when they were ready to put the food into their mouths they bent their heads away from the others and leaned sideways. They opened their mouths, took in some food, and began to chew with their heads down and their eyes to the side. Then, as they arrived at the last stages of chewing they lifted and straightened their heads again.

The contrast could not have been more plain. When the Anglophones bent down to take in their food, they didn't just turn away from the plate in front of them; they turned away from each other, people on the right side of the table turning toward the right, people on the left side of the table turning toward the left. They ate glumly too. Maybe it was just a bad day. Maybe they were tired of one another's company. Who knows for how long they had been travelling together? But maybe also this was their custom – to eat in silence.

Back at home, I tried an experiment. I observed my own family members as they tucked into their dinners, and I had them observe me, and then I trained myself to observe myself. I found that we too, all three of us Anglophones, turned our heads to the side as we ate. For my own part, I found that when I put knife and fork to my mouth, I was looking at the table, I was looking at the bottom of my wine glass, I was looking at the salt shaker, I was looking anywhere but at the people I was eating with. Moreover, when I put my food into my mouth in that way, I was putting the food into the side of my mouth, toward the middle of my tongue – precisely the area, as I had been taught at a wine museum in Sancerre, where the tongue has the fewest taste buds. I was not only being sideways with others as I ate, but I was even being sideways with my taste buds, and eating in a way to minimize rather than maximize my sensations. I was getting the food as quickly as possible into the tracts of my molars, where there are no taste buds at all. Then, having made that discovery of my own eating habits, I did a little bit of observing around Lancaster. Same thing. Most people – but not all – turned to the side when they ate, and commonly put the food in sideways, to the dull middle of their tongues, and as quickly as possible into their back molars. Moreover, when one person ate in front of another, the person watching averted his or her eyes. The unspoken rule in Anglophone society would seem to be that it is impolite to watch another person chewing, and it is not polite to make one's chewing conspicuous either. Not even to oneself, apparently, is one supposed to make one's chewing conspicuous.

With all of this in mind, I went about making certain reforms. I trained myself to sit forward when I ate, and to look straight into the eyes of the person sitting opposite me, and put the food in the front of my mouth, on the front of my tongue, where the first acute taste buds are. As that person sitting opposite me was usually my wife, while I felt the sharp salty sensations of what I was putting into my mouth I also experienced, well, my wife, and the joy of the life we have together, concentrated into the moment of ingestion: I to thee, together we eat, and taste. When the person sitting opposite me was not my wife, the situation was not always so relaxed or joyous, but my new etiquette still worked; there was a happy recognition of mutuality between me and whoever I was eating opposite from. We smiled a little at one another while we ate; we smiled and tasted together. And I got more *flavour* out of my food too.

Was this the secret of the proverbial contrast between French and British attitudes and habits? If so, it was on the level of the tacit rather than the spoken. Even if remarks have ever been made in etiquette books about what to do with your head and your eyes when chewing, those books are no longer read by anyone. We learn those things tacitly. And if this tacit understanding of how to eat is the secret of the difference between the French and the British at table, it is a difference that comes at the level of *culture*. I italicize (*as usual*) because I want to emphasize a point. By *culture* in this instance I mean what anthropologists usually mean: a complex web of symbolic meanings and patterns of behaviour autonomically shared by the members of a social group; or, to put a different emphasis on it, a shared, meaningful and self-valorized system of biological adaptation and social interactivity. Eating is a *practice*; it involves a 'body technique', as Marcel Mauss once put it.[5] If this use of the head, the eyes, the mouth and the tongue in the context of communal eating that I observed was key, then the difference between French and British attitudes and habits was less about the history of haute cuisine or the development of court culture or the triumph of Protestantism and Puritanism in Britain – the usual kinds of causes entered for why the French are traditionally much more enthusiastic about the pleasures of the table than the British – than about the internalized codes of physical activity that people of either culture acquire from childhood on.

Casual observation continued to confirm the idea. I watched young people with their families at the table in both countries. I saw French kids sitting upright, tucking into calves' liver or *jambon persillé*, their eyes bright and clear and looking straight ahead, tasting their food, the kids *easy* with what they were doing. I saw English kids slumping and fidgeting in their chairs, their eyes downcast, picking at their chips and peas and ketchup, and it seemed to me that the English mothers (and fathers too) were *encouraging* their kids not to be social as they ate, encouraging them to retreat into themselves and to be picky while they ate. *Of course*, mothers and fathers acknowledged, sometimes kindly and sometimes not so kindly, *you don't like it and you don't even want to be here, you'd rather be off on your own, but sit still and eat it anyway, and close your mouth while you chew.*[6]

However, I made several other observations that challenged this view of differences in eating habits between the two nations. At high-end restaurants in London and elsewhere, when I saw people eating in groups in the course of animated conversation, under the influence of alcohol, and especially when the people I saw were not in family groups but assembled as colleagues, it was common for people to keep their heads erect while eating, and to gaze straight ahead and smile, just like the French. I observed people acting in the movies and on television too, who also ate with their heads erect and expressions of pleasure on their faces. I particularly well remember watching the divine Gwyneth Paltrow on a (mainly stupid) food programme host-ed by celebrity chef Mario Batali. Sitting outdoors at a restaurant in Spain, she was posed as forward and erect and elegant as any French woman I ever saw, looking into the camera as if into the eyes of a dinner date; she put the food in her mouth front and centre, where the taste buds were, and subtlety but seriously *tasted*, from the tip of her tongue to the back of it. Ah, I thought, either she has learned how to eat and taste during all the time she has spent as a rich person in Europe, or else, she has simply been taught how to eat in front of a camera, by directors or acting coaches. Or maybe she had been trained to eat that way as a child in urban Jewish America – but if that were the case, why hadn't I been similarly trained? In any event, whether in the matter of happy English businesspeople or a well-trained and glamorous American actress, it became clear that eating in what I took to be the French way, according to a deep and tacit cul-tural code, was not entirely a *secret*. It had only been a secret to me – to me and the rest of us who hadn't had a proper education in body technique and the manners of the senses.

Then came the day Marion and I found ourselves at a chic outdoor restaurant in Arcachon, a resort town by the Atlantic coast outside Bordeaux. We had a fantastic meal there, *gambas* (giant prawns) in a

Madeira sauce for Marion, oysters and sausages (a local speciality) for me. At the table next to us sat a party of about twelve people, French, having their Sunday afternoon lunch, two pairs of what looked like grandmothers and grandfathers, along with about five adults ranging in age from their twenties to their fifties, and three or four kids of various ages. This group was not as harmonious as the one we saw in Mont-Saint-Michel. The kids were getting impatient. Well before the dinner ended, two of the elder children, with permission, got up from the table and left. Nor were the adult members of the party uniformly cheerful, or comfortable in one another's company. It was hard to tell which of them were couples, or father and daughter, or uncle and nephew, and which were relative strangers: the conversation followed uneven paths. They weren't even, like the people in Mont-Saint-Michel, making a point of eating the same thing. Yet a general gaiety nevertheless prevailed under the Gascogne sun, a gaiety which allowed one of the older women to take the liberty of raising her voice and good-naturedly chiding Marion and me from across her table, as she overheard us, for turning down dessert when the server came to take our order for it. 'There is always room for dessert!' she insisted. 'Not today', I feebly protested. Seated to my right was an attractive dark-haired woman in her late twenties, who wasn't paying us any mind and wasn't paying much mind to the company at her own table either. She was seated across from an older fellow with greying hair and a bit of a paunch for a belly, and she was doing more listening than talking. This younger woman had ordered a very rare steak for lunch. It looked delicious. I could almost smell it. Although it seemed to me that ordering a steak at a seafood restaurant by the sea was bad form, I envied the young woman anyway. I still wasn't eating much meat that year, in spite of the sausages, which I had ordered in the interests of scientific research, but I was beginning to acquire a jealous appetite for it. In any case, as the young woman was not paying any attention to me, I was able to watch her and see how she ate. She cut a piece of meat and raised it to her mouth. As expected, she was turning to neither the right nor the left. She kept her head erect and kept her eyes staring straight ahead of her, and as she chewed, taking the meat from the front and centre of her mouth down along her tongue and palate, methodically ruminating, to the back of her throat, a beam of satisfaction came over her face. It was almost erotic. Maybe it *was* erotic. The feeling of joy at the taste of her thick rare steak seemed to reach from the back of her neck to her groin. But she wasn't looking *at* anybody. She was looking into space. She was looking into the space half a foot to the right of the man sitting opposite her, as if she were eating, elegantly, contentedly and voluptuously alone.

I have since been able to determine that this is a common practice among the French, this looking straight ahead and looking at no one. What I took to be something 'cultural', intimately habitual and symbolically communal, an eye-to-eye contact at the dinner table, was also something else, or had been allowed to become something else; it had become as it were a secondary practice, far less communitarian than the first but no less social. It was a happily distracted practice which I attribute not to *culture* but to its counterpart, *civilization*.

I began by talking about cultural and economic democracy, and I am still on that subject, but two new terms present themselves for consideration: culture and civilization. It is somewhere between the two that the restaurant for the rest of us must live – somewhere between the two along with the aid, I think it should be clear by now, of something like *resistance*. Cultural democracy is not just about 'culture', it is about 'civilization', and it is also about 'resistance'; it is about a certain striving against the many obstacles to culture, civility and democracy that we find obstructing us today.

Let me begin with culture, and then move on first to civilization and then to the subject of resistance.

Culture, then. It isn't only tacit. Culture also generates explicit rules, do's and don'ts, as well as myths and ideologies. The anthropological definition of culture, concerning webs of shared meanings and practices, shades off into the humanist definition, culture as the art, literature, dance and other self-aware products and practices in a society. For 'high culture' as we sometimes call it also involves the sharing of meanings and practices. In turn, the idea of 'high culture' shades off into the German idea discussed by historical sociologist Norbert Elias, *Kultur*, culture as a kind of ethic, rooted in the high culture of Western tradition, perhaps, but dedicated in its current form to modern ideas of sincerity, austerity, human dignity and the permanent rather than the merely fleeting meanings of life. These are three very different things – culture, high culture and *Kultur*, not to mention *popular culture*, which by and large intersects all the others while also taking on a life of its own – but they share, in opposition to the other concept I want to discuss, civilization, a dimension of immediacy. Culture in all its forms comes to us straight; if culture ever requires mediation to get from a source of it to a user or a recipient, it is culture itself – what the sociologist Émile Durkeim would have called an 'independent fact' – that does the mediation. So I may learn how to eat, more or less tacitly, from my parents. My lessons in eating may be supplemented by explicit oral directives from my parents and others, as well as from the general ideas and myths that circulate in my community. In a literate culture, my lessons may be further supplemented by writings about how to eat, whether actual etiquette books or by more indirect treatments of manners and mores. In a mediatized culture, such lessons can further be supplemented by fashion magazines, television shows, movies and the like. 'Popular culture' can spread all kinds of do's and don'ts, even when it is adopting airs of non-conformity, its wild and crazy disrespectfulness. But whatever the lessons, they come, under the guise of what we call 'culture', in an immediate form, a form that more or less goes without saying.

Now from the point of view of civilization, there is nothing seamless or natural about any of this. 'Culture' too, in any of its forms, is artificial, hybrid and mediated: the 'local' is generated by the non-local, the family by the state, and so forth. But I will get back to that. What I am concerned with here is, however the independent facts of culture find their independence, as we live in and through culture, and as we think about how eating and drinking is part of what we do in culture, we rely not just on certain facts but, emotionally as well as intellectually, on ideas that take shelter under the rubric of culture. I am concerned with the notion of the phenomenon of culture as a place where things like body techniques are learned and people do their eating and drinking; and I am equally concerned with what may be called the rhetoric of culture. For wherever you find advocates of traditional food identities and practices, there you will find a dependence on the idea of culture and its immediacy and the rhetoric to which it leads.

You will find this idea and its rhetoric, for example, permeating such sophisticated works as *Food is Culture* by the Italian historian Massimo Montanari and *The Italian Way* by sociologist Douglas Harper. Italy provides an especially pertinent pretext for the rhetoric of culture, it appears; but a general case can be made out of the example of Italy too. This then is what Montanari writes, summing up: 'The history of our food culture is a growing – not a shrinking – plant . . . The product is on the surface – visible, clear, and well-defined: that is us. The roots are underneath – generous, numerous, diffuse.'[7] The language is lovely even in translation. But the assumption underlying it entails an unfounded myth of organic continuity. Montanari knows as well as anyone how often history has been disrupted by war, natural disasters and social upheavals; but when it comes to food he holds onto this idea of a self-generating culture, a kind of second nature, which survives (even if only 'underneath') the ruptures of human time. The proverbial connection between the ideas of 'culture' and 'cultivation' is key to this: Montanari wants us to keep cultivating our gardens, to keep nurturing what is in any case a 'growing plant' even if history sometimes intervenes: we need to keep cultivating the culture of our cuisine.

And then there are the food-loving and highly traditional yet also highly educated citizens of Bologna interviewed by Harper in *The Italian Way*.[8] The interviewees are not so metaphorical as Montanari, and yet again and again, as they try to explain what it is they do at the dinner table, they say much the same thing. They insist that they do things the way they do them because . . . that is the way things are done, and have always been done. That is their 'culture'. And their culture is by and large non-negotiable. Such sentiments find an echo everywhere you go in Italy, Harper maintains. I am inclined to agree; and at the least I know for a fact that the same ideas often recur as well in the polemical writings of the influential activist Carlo Petrini, the leader of the Slow Food movement. There is a tradition, there is a culture, a 'slow' tradition and culture, according to Petrini; and that is what has to be nurtured; that is what we must not allow the 'fast' culture of global capitalism to snatch away from us.[9]

Whatever the integrity of this line of thought, there is a level of analysis at which it is perfectly true, and the rhetoric persuasive. Cuisine does require 'culture'. It requires an ensemble of traditional practices and attitudes, handed down tacitly and autonomically, as well as by supplementary means of discourse. It requires a system of body techniques and a non-negotiable set of values. It requires an agriculture and a conventional system of exploiting agricultural resources, including a practicum of food technologies and delivery systems in which users have been educated and trained. In sum, it requires what anthropologists call a 'foodway'. And no foodway can ever be entirely rationalized and divorced from the culture that produced it. A foodway can be modified, transplanted, hybridized or McDonaldized; it can be transformed (which is what happens in the case of 'Italian' restaurants outside Italy, and even a number of them in the tourist zones of Italy, not to mention 'French' restaurants outside France) into a theme: a systematic simulation of a foodway. But at the point where the foodway has been supplanted by a simulacrum something two-sided has happened to it. On the one hand, the foodway has been interfered with, compromised, 'deracinated' we might say; on the other hand, in order to keep the foodway operating in this instance, other cultural practices have been summoned to supplement it. Young workers from Poland or Lebanon have to be trained in London how to prepare and serve 'Italian' food in a British-managed chain restaurant like Pizza Express or Bella Italia. As they learn to do their jobs, they get training in 'the Italian way', so far as the British corporation has domesticated it; but the foreign workers will have also already brought their own cultures with them, the cultures of sociality, labour and food of their communities, and the adaptive culture of the guest worker that has developed among them over a number of years. The alert diner will have noticed this. For good or ill, it is quite apparent that even if the restaurant is serving good food and offering good service, something is absent, and something else is present in its place. This is not only a British phenomenon. Young workers from France have been trained in France to serve 'Mexican' food at Indiana Café in the centre of Montparnasse to visitors from around the world. Young Midwesterners, as memorably illustrated by Gary Alan Fine, have been trained in Minneapolis to prepare and serve 'French' food. In each case something is absent, and something else is present in its place. And the alert diner will have noticed this. The cooks and servers will probably be aware of this as well. (It is conventional today for ambitious cooks and would-be heads of house in America and Britain to go abroad – to France, Italy or the Far East – to get their 'real' training, to experience the culture of haute cuisine at first hand.)

In any event, it is clear that cooking and serving food demands culture. A strong culinary culture, based on a deep and sophisticated foodway, may lend itself to a strong restaurant culture, where generations sit together, smiling over their *moules frites*. A weak culinary culture, or culinary culture that has suffered disruptions, dislocations or an excess of McDonaldization may lead to a weak restaurant culture, where something not quite so happy is bound to transpire. If the customers themselves lack the tacit cultural competence for cultivating the experience of dining out in public, though their appetites may be quelled when they consume a meal in a restaurant, like those Anglophone diners at Mont-Saint-Michel, they may yet miss out on something larger, of which they have no knowledge: they don't even know they are missing it. As for restaurant workers, if the cooks and servers of a restaurant don't come from 'roots' of a culinary culture either, in the face of the triumph of consumer society and the demand for eating out, entrepreneurial or corporate capitalism may fill the gap with specially trained cooks and servers of their own, to simulate the missing system of life. Yet the rest of us will feel and know the difference. We will associate the restaurant rooted in a strong culinary culture with 'authenticity' and 'sincerity', with the dignity and the ecology of 'the indigenous' and 'the local', with the wisdom of 'regional tradition' and the excitement of 'immediacy'. But we will associate the restaurant where a strong culinary culture has been thematized and simulated rather than 'authentically' reproduced with a kind of institutional bad faith, an insincerity of means and ends, an outcome of deracination and displacement. And we will associate the worst cases of simulation, where restaurants have been superimposed willy-nilly upon a weak culinary culture, and Olive Gardens (an American 'Italian' chain) blossom in the middle of rural Kansas, and a Chili's sprouts in Canary Wharf, with 'artificiality' and 'phoniness', with the 'homogenization' and 'manipulativeness' of internationalization, Taylorization and McDonaldization.

Eating in a restaurant and cooking and serving in one all require culture, and success in the restaurant requires a strong culinary culture, rooted in the foodway of a people. Without culture, cooking is lost, hospitality is a sham, appreciation is shallow and gratitude is empty. Our rhetoric of culture is right to encourage the preservation of culture, for without it we are lost.

But that is not the whole story.

What shall we say about the case of the town of Lucca, Italy, putting a ban on 'ethnic' or 'foreign' restaurants in its city centre?[10] Some have called the ban a preventive measure taken for the sake of 'safeguarding our culture', or for preserving 'our culinary patrimony'. Others have called it 'gastronomic racism' and 'culinary ethnic cleansing'. Some have noted that the ban does not apparently include 'French' restaurants, and some have wondered whether the ban excludes Sicilian pizzerias as well as Turkish kebab shops and Chinese takeaways. But a proponent of the measure has said that it was designed to 'improve the image of the city' and that 'it targets McDonald's as much as kebab restaurants'. It is supposed to help 'protect' Tuscan products and benefit the tourism industry while preserving the historical character of the inner city.

Or consider another kind of case: a Japanese restaurant in Beaune, France, the capital of the Burgundy wine trade and a city dedicated to gastronomy. My 2009 Michelin Guide affectionately says, 'The Japanese born chef prepares traditional dishes from his country using French sourced produce.'[11] When I visited I saw that the restaurant was serving standard international Japanese food with standard ingredients, including sushi made with tuna and tempura made with tempura batter. It is only when one takes a second look that one notices that the restaurant sometimes utilizes ingredients like Bresse chicken and 'farmhouse' duck to make traditional international Japanese dishes, like skewers of grilled poultry teriyaki.

Or consider still another case. I refer to a moment reported by Alice Waters, a moment which she has in effect mythologized as the epiphany that gave rise to the birth of California cuisine. It was in rural Brittany, through which she was travelling with some French companions, and she had a meal in a restaurant there that her jaded French companions were united in praising. 'They applauded the chef and cried, "*C'est fantastique!*"', Waters writes.

I've remembered this dinner a thousand times: the old stone house, the stairs leading up to the small dining room, which seated no more than twelve at the pink cloth-covered tables and from which one could look through the windows to the stream running beside the house and the garden in back. The chef, a woman, announced the menu: cured ham and melon, trout with almonds, and raspberry tart. The trout had just come from the stream and the raspberries from the garden. It was this immediacy that made those dishes so special.[12]

All three of the cases are examples of *negotiation* in the realm of restaurant culture. The first entails negotiation through exclusion, the second negotiation through adaptation, the third (since Waters will use the model of the experience in Brittany to open a French-type single menu restaurant in Berkeley) negotiation through admiration and emulation. All three examples are common types of negotiation in these matters, and though many of us may be inclined to admire the second and third types of negotiation and be indignant about the first, even the first must be acknowledged to have its uses. For we would have reasons for objecting to the opening, in the middle of London's Chinatown, of an American TGI Friday's or a British Toby Carvery ('Tender cuts of freshly roasted meat, a healthy choice of fresh seasonal vegetables and a good old-fashioned British welcome every time . . .') even if we had no law to prevent it from happening, and were glad that we did not.[13]

My point, however, is that whether through exclusion, adaption, emulation or some other strategy, such negotiations *between* culinary cultures cannot take place *within* culinary culture. They take place in another kind of social space, with its own rhetoric, which I am calling civilization.

Civilization, then. This is the same 'civilization' that the French-woman in Arcachon inhabited, taking her pleasures in public and socially, but not taking them in the spirit of community, in direct communication with anybody. It is the same 'civilization' as is sometimes thought of as the space of 'cosmopolitanism', although frequently 'civilization' is also disparaged as a pretence for luxurious excess and exploitation.[14] In place of the indigenous immediacy we might experience of a local 'culture', this 'civilization', for good or ill, offers generalized mediations and utilizations. In the place of individual self-expression, the cook to the customer, the parent to the child, the husband to the wife, civilization offers transactions among a plurality of competing instances of self-expression and self-indulgence. In this 'civilization', in its positive aspects, people can eat with one another, and interact with one another, even take pleasure in one another, without being known to one another, and without even being members of the same community or possessors of the same culture. You pay for your food, after all, and so does everybody else. It is in the space of this 'civilization' that a Japanese restaurant serving Bresse chicken can thrive in the capital of Burgundy and that an American tourist can dine on raspberries from a Bretagne garden, and use the experience as the model for a single-menu French restaurant in Berkeley, California. We are all connected, after all; chickens are international and raspberries are international, even if varieties are sometimes local. Contexts – Tokyo, Burgundy, Brittany, Berkeley – are all connected too. It is even in this cosmopolitan space that kebab shops can find themselves debarred from doing business in a historic city centre – not out of ethnic hatred (though the possibility that ethnic hatred motivated some of the good burghers of Lucca is not to be dismissed out of hand), but out of respect for a kind of civility in the city centre, a preservation of bourgeois Italian-ness for the benefit of the tourism business. That too is a negotiation: the law in Lucca puts no restrictions on restaurants located outside its ancient walls.

The differences between 'culture' and 'civilization' can be schematized and elaborated at length. There is a long and honourable tradition of disparaging 'civilization' in favour of something more primary like 'culture' – Jean-Jacques Rousseau is a key figure in the tradition, as is Immanuel Kant.[15] If civilization advances the scale of what it takes to accomplish human progress, it does this at the expense of the world it is advancing upon, and it will not stop at harming an environment or a people in order to satisfy the demands of another people, inhabiting another environment. It may even encourage people to harm themselves in the pursuit of the benefits of pleasure or power or wealth. But the tradition of disparaging civility, the rhetoric, as it were (from Ovid and Rousseau to Walter Benjamin), of the barbarity underlying civilization, does not need to be accepted whole cloth, and in fact we are in trouble if we accept it at all. For if 'culture' is a necessary part of what we do and who we are, so is 'civilization'. We can (and should) think about what civilization amounts to, in relation to culture as in relation to other forms of association and practice and the languages we use; because otherwise we are not really thinking about ourselves. And though we cannot blind ourselves to what can be treacherous about civilization, or treacherously performed in the name of it, we have to think about what can be positive in it for us, who live within and by it. Wrote a near contemporary of Rousseau and Kant, 'For a nation to be barbarous, if we understand the term in a precise, philosophical sense, is simply for it to be ignorant of the things that are useful to it and how to attain them by readiest means and those most conducive to the happiness of each individual. For a nation to be civilized is for it to be acquainted with these things.'[16] Though the claims of 'culture' upon us are great, the claims of civilization are just as pressing.

An especially pertinent way of thinking about ourselves in this light can be found in the work of Belgian philosopher Jean-Marc Ferry. Ferry's thought is rooted in Jürgen Habermas's theory of communicative action. Ferry begins with the idea of civilization as the complex whole of material life, social organization and communication characteristic of advanced urbanized societies; and then he focuses on the 'civility' necessary to civilization as its code of public behaviour. Ferry is thinking of manners in the broadest sense, of how people live together outside the confines of immediate community, but below the level of political association. He is thinking of 'conviviality' – that's the word he uses – outside of familiar habitats, and so of interaction among strangers in cosmopolitan spaces. Civility allows modern society to subsist in 'a spirit of conviviality without immediacy', he writes. We live together; we live together peacefully and collaboratively, even if we are strangers, and even if we know ourselves by our differences from one another, because we are civil among ourselves.[17]

A main point of reference for Ferry is the postmodern city. Civility in the city is a form of mediation, allowing us to live together and pursue individual but common interests in an urban context, among fellow strangers. If you take it away, if you suffer a 'loss of civility', you take away both our ability to live together outside of our immediate communities and our connection to all those things that civility encourages: economic activity, political alliance, cultural production. Civility, moreover, has a value over and above its utility; for civility according to Ferry 'is a principle of socialization mediated by the recognition of individual differences, that is to say by a generalized form of respect'.[18] We have civility rather than some other form of sociality precisely because we live in a world of differences, and because, in a modern society of difference, we require from ourselves an ethos of 'respect'. I give way to the stranger on the pavement as he approaches on the right not because he is a member of my community, and holds a certain rank in it to which I defer, and not because it is the law of the state that I must give way, as it would be on a motorway, but because I am being civil. I am showing the passer-by not love, not solidarity, not political passion or legality, but respect. And so we live together.

Civilization is a web of material life and social organization that requires of its members this 'respect' for one another – not love, not community, not even direct communication, but respect. It is riddled with alienations and distractions – means from ends, intentions from effects, manners from morals. It cannot give you unconditional love. It is materialistic in its aims and its services demand payment. It is thoroughly artificial and in some ways arbitrary, creating zones of Chinese food in the old centre of imperial London, or of traditional Tuscan food in the centre of multicultural Lucca. But although, from the point of view of the rhetoric of culture, such disjunctions are deprivations, signalling a loss of meaning, integrity and authenticity, from the point of view of the idea or rhetoric of civilization these disjunctions can be enabling and productive. Cities are comprised of regulated zones of compartmentalized behaviour, for business, entertainment, residence and so forth; they are 'fantasy cities' to a large extent, cities as spectacles, and therefore false;[19] but it is in just such zones that civility and urbanity thrive, and people take their pleasures or do their business together. They *enable* economic and leisurely behaviour precisely through their organized disjunctions, and there is no getting away from them; for it is through them that disjoined practices and peoples – disjoined 'cultures' – are actually and productively conjoined.

The anecdote by Alice Waters can illustrate the point. For when Waters tells her story about dining out in Brittany, she tries to communicate a sense of 'culture' and ends up doing just the opposite. Waters appeals to the sanctity of the small scale, the ancient, the local and the picturesque, along with the priestly femininity of the chef and, finally, 'immediacy'. This was, in short, an un-alienated culinary scene, primitive in its purity. But the integrity of the scene begins to break down as soon as one takes a closer look at it. The party is served trout from the local stream, and raspberries from the garden. But where did the melon, the 'cured ham' and the almonds come from? The melon could be from anywhere, so far as the story is concerned. The ham, for its part, is most likely from a town like Bayonne or Parma, where ham made to be served with items like melon is cured. Far from being local and fresh, the ham has been transported from a great distance, and it has taken six months or more of ageing in order for it to be ready for consumption. As for the almonds, since they do not grow in wet and cool Brittany, they must have been brought in from southern France, or Spain, Italy or Morocco. Yet the trout from the local stream (itself no doubt under the jurisdiction of a national agency for the control of waterways) seems incomplete without the almonds from the Mediterranean.

I am not suggesting that the meal in Brittany was not a great experience worth emulating. I am suggesting that it didn't exist at the level of indigenous immediacy that Waters wants to celebrate. The diners themselves, the French companions with leisure and money and jaded palates, ready to applaud a work of culinary artistry well done, saying 'C'est fantastique!' – where did *they* come from? From the outset the scene in Brittany was actually an exchange between visitors and a commercial host, whose funds and resources derived from the national economy of France and the world economy in which France played a major role. The experience was *of* the local, but it was *through* the agency of global civilization. What happened at that restaurant in Brittany was that everyone treated one another with respect. They *negotiated* cultural and social differences. They negotiated them through the exercise of artistry and hospitality on one end and through enjoyment, appreciation and payment on the other. That *payment*, of course, is as key to the experience as anything else: for it is required to seal the conjunction of disjunctive agents, interests and processes.

Things are so simple in France, the main character of Hemingway's novel *The Sun Also Rises* asserts, talking about an experience he has had in a restaurant in Bayonne, in the southwest of the country. 'You can never tell whether a Spanish waiter will thank you.' Spain is a place of fierce but ephemeral loyalties as far as the narrator is concerned, a place of *afición*, where one has to continually prove oneself as a capable *aficionado*; in other words, where one has to continually prove one's standing with regard to the local representatives of *culture*. But in France, where these things operate on the level of something like civilization, you could receive the gratitude and appreciation of a waiter just by tipping him. Tipping in France will make the waiter happy, Jake Barnes, the narrator, says. 'Everything is on such a clear financial basis in France. It is the simplest country to live in. No one makes things complicated by becoming your friend for any obscure reason. If you want people to like you you have only to spend a little money. I spent a little money and the waiter liked me. He appreciated my valuable qualities. He would be glad to see me back. I would dine there again sometime and he would be glad to see me, and would want me at his table. It would be a sincere liking because it would have a sound basis.'[20]

Since Hemingway's time, the custom of tipping has changed, and by law in France a 15 per cent 'service charge' is tacked on to each and every bill, and servers do not by and large endeavour to extract any extra money from their guests. But the principle remains: a 'sincere liking' persists between a happy diner and a happy server precisely because of a business transaction, because of something apparently alien from 'sincerity' and 'liking', because of something artificial: the conventions of civilization.

Culture and civilization are both required today, even though they are in some ways incompatible. Culture gives us the space of autonomic meaning and tradition, of body techniques and community, of an immediacy of experience of self to self and a person eating to a dish being eaten. Civilization gives us a space of negotiation and innovation, of manners and civility, of transactional experiences where selves are pursuing, in concert with one another, individual interests and pleasures, in relation to products that are not only creatures of nature – flesh and fruit – but also commodities of commerce: *ris de veau à la financière*, or a Double Whopper with Cheese. The discourse of gastronomy beginning in the nineteenth century was proud of both culture and civilization. It recognized the charms and even the necessity of the local, the indigenous and the traditional. It knew that the love of food began at the family table and the fields, pastures and streams where the food from the family meal originated. But the discourse of gastronomy also imagined that civilization could transform the contingencies of local experience into the necessities of a universal science, whose principles could be universally obeyed. 'Gastronomy is the reasoned comprehension of everything connected to the life of man', we will recall Brillat-Savarin as having stated.[21] The idea of the great systematizers of cuisine in nineteenth- and twentieth-century France was that the principles of good food were scientifically verifiable, down to the chemical compounds in the bread dough and the nerve receptors in the mouth, and that 'civilization' allowed for both the discovery of these principles and their dissemination, even at the expense of overriding local traditions and cultural prejudices. This idea still persists in the practice of 'molecular cuisine', not to mention the curricula of professional cooking schools around the world. And though we may have reason to doubt the claims to universality that the science of traditional gastronomy or the new molecular cuisine might put forward (since after all, no science can tell us that the gastronomic heights of the French or the Spanish avant garde are actually *preferable* to the common food of Italy or China, only how and why they are *different*), we can still see the need to have such a space of negotiation among competing claims to pleasure as civilization, gastronomy and hunger represent. We need culture, but culture is always in the plural; there are always cultures. And civilization and the practices connected with it, from gastronomy to biochemistry, from tolerance to freedom, are required to arbitrate among cultures and their competing claims.

How the dialectic between the forces of culture and the forces of civilization get played out in the rhetoric of food today is plain as day, but also complicated. Take the important case of Slow Food. The movement dedicates itself to the preservation of indigenous foodways. But the Slow Food association operates according to the principles of a non-governmental organization (NGO) within the context of what social scientists refer to as 'civil society' (that level of professionalized social intervention that thrives between individual communities and macro political associations). In its rhetoric, therefore, Slow Food finds itself in the paradoxical position of promoting the local, and promoting it universally, with 'over one hundred thousand members in one hundred thirty-two countries'. Attempting to bring 'systemic change to communities around the world . . . through projects that involve both producers and consumers', it actually exemplifies not a return to the primordial condition of original culture, but rather all the qualities that have been conventionally associated with the benevolent effects of the spread of civilization and progress, going back at least to the *Pax Romana* – even while it does so for the sake of preserving pre-imperial, local traditions. It will bring 'systemic change' to community, in the name of community. It will lead the fight against 'the disappearance of local food traditions' by establishing channels of communication and negotiation between 'producers and consumers' around the globe, collaborating in the space of international commerce.[22] Thus, at one and the same time, the rhetoric of the movement proposes an accommodation between culture and civilization and a struggle for the preservation of the one against the other, in the name of the one against the other, culture *against* civilization, and civilization *against* culture. And it has the movement proposing to do so in favour of a process of accommodation that many of us around the world will find useful, admirable and uncontroversial.

How this same dialectic may be applied to the problem of the restaurant today should be no less clear, although in this case it may be better to shift the emphasis from what is local about the restaurant to what is cosmopolitan about it. For what is a restaurant? Again and again we find a connection to local tradition in any restaurant that is worthy of the name. But again and again, as well, we find that the restaurant is a site of novelty and autonomy, operated in the transactional space of a post-traditional civility. There had been an aristocratic tradition, from before the day when the first restaurant opened, that a fish dish should be eaten after a dish of soup; but there had never been a waiter telling a paying customer that he had to have the soup course first and the fish course second, and taking pride in his momentary social ascendance. Again and again we find that the restaurant involves the institutionalization of a formularity, a new form of continually renewable, improvisational ceremony, where what is essential is on the one hand what is old, and on the other what is continually new – and where in any case one has to pay for both the old and the new.

It is high or low, dear or cheap, in or out, now or then, here or there, multiple or singular, formal or casual, themed or unthemed, unique or common, familiar or strange, any restaurant – or, more likely, it is somewhere between the extremes of these axes of meaning. As soon as the restaurant becomes a part of the physics of everyday life, it enters into the parameters of the world of modern consumption and the axes of meaning and desire that constitute it, and so it develops forms and behaviours and allocates agents to accommodate meaning and desire: mirrors and tablecloths, art works and memorabilia, menus and order taking, waiters and busboys. The restaurant at once articulates a body of meanings and desires and provides a system for accommodating them. It is *sui generis*, it would appear. We are encouraged to find our needs in a space that already articulates needs in advance of us, and articulates them in its own way. But the restaurant is also a function of the social order of which it is a part – in that sense it is not *sui generis* at all – and it answers to needs that already press against the members of the social order.

In fact, the restaurant answers to a plurality of needs, not all of which agree with one another, and it answers to them in a plurality of ways. It answers to a need for differentiation, and the pursuit of social status (we *have* these needs; there is no getting away from it); and it answers to the need to find pleasure and sustenance in the public realm without regard to class distinction and social status (for we have *those* needs too). It answers to the demand for fashion and fashionableness, ruled by the principle of novelty for its own sake; and it answers to the need for routine dependability, governed by the principle of regularity, of habit and custom. (We have both these sets of needs, inevitably, too.) It answers to the need for ceremonial formality, for a heightening of the drama of the everyday; and it answers to the need for friendly informality, for the casual reassurance of belonging as one is, unadorned and un-heightened, in the theatre of the everyday. It answers to the need of thematization – the reassurance of living according to an *idea*, or the fiction of an idea – and it answers to the need of the opposite of thematization, living without an idea, or without the fiction of one: taking things as they come. As we have seen on several occasions, the restaurant answers to needs for uniqueness and needs for commonality, to needs for familiarity and to needs for strangeness, to needs to experience locality and the *heimlich* and needs to experience dislocation, the exotic, the *unheimlich*. *I go there . . . because . . . that restaurant* provides *that* set of answers to my many needs. And I am hoping the answers are momentarily correct, relative to the situation in which I find myself, and which has brought me there.

As I have suggested from the outset, from a philosophic point of view we probably need to have those needs, though not in a simple and unambiguous way. We already have them, in any case, regardless of our philosophic positions. So far as we are members of our postmodern and hypermodern civilization, we must participate in a system of needs that includes demands for class distinction, fashion and so forth, as well for pathways of compensation and counteraction, for coping mechanisms, for negotiations, for re-socialization. Though we may imagine a classless society, or a fashion-free society, we do not live in it, we cannot live in it, and few of us are even capable of *wanting* to live in it. We live where we live. And the restaurant is a part of it. The restaurant is a place where we cope and re-socialize ourselves, given our system of consumption and production and the lives we inevitably lead. So we *need* the restaurant in this sense. Sometimes our need for a restaurant is purely circumstantial. We need to eat and there we are. But usually that need comes along with another: we need to participate in the world around us, we need to experience ourselves and our appetites in a social context, we need to express ourselves and find ourselves expressed in keeping with something which we *are not* and yet which we also *are* – ourselves outside of ourselves, in a social world which we can never entirely appropriate, but which we can never dispense with either.

The question is, living in the society that we do, experiencing the needs we are required to experience, what are we going to do about it? Are we going to allow ourselves to need the needs we have, and use the appropriate means for coping with them? Are we going to find gratification in the experience of satisfying our needs as we do, and our need to have those needs? Are we going to find justification in doing so?

Yes and no, would be my answer to the main philosophic question, in the end. Restaurants provide a *cultural* solution to the problem of the need to eat in a society of eaters. But restaurants also provide a *civil* solution to the same problem. And the two solutions can never be compatible today. You can no more get your *culture* plain in a restaurant today than you can get your *civility* plain, and you can no more get either than you can violate the Sartrean principle, which says that, as a human being, you cannot *be* what you *are*. You can only *play* at it. Restaurants involve a certain kind of risk. And that is why the restaurant for the rest of us, and the need to need it, must also entail a degree of resistance.

Resistance, then. In a restaurant, resistance is something that we generally undertake in the spirit of play. And I don't mean by it, resistance *against* the restaurant. What I mean is resistance against the forces that would undermine the experience. For if the form of play that restaurant-going entails is summoned into existence by the advent of modernity and the invention of man the consumer, it is also threatened with annihilation by the advent of hypermodernity and the accession of Her Majesty the Consumer. It is not just 'culture' that is at risk today. Civilization is at risk as well, under pressures of what is sometimes called 'de-civilization'.[23] That is, the kind of civility that the institution of a restaurant for the rest of us will require, enable and encourage is in danger.

On the side of the restaurateur and restaurant workers, the restaurant for the rest of us poses an inspiring but paradoxical challenge. It is this: let us operate a *business* that is conducted in the spirit of *art* and *hospitality*. Let us participate in the global economy, let us engage in commerce for the sake of making a profit, let us be ruthless in our efficiency, but let us be *generous* too, let us be generous, that is, of *ourselves*. And let us do all this knowing that our goals can never be entirely achieved. Let us do all this knowing that we will always fall short of ourselves *in reality*, and hence *in our work*, so that we can only really succeed in our *play*.

On the side of the rest of us, we consumers, we representatives of *homo restauranticus*, there is also a challenge to be met. Let us be consumers without consumerism. Let us be customers in the spirit not of absolute sovereigns but of fellow citizens. Let us remember that no matter how much money we are able to pay, we can never *deserve* the generosity that a restaurant and its workers may show to us. Though the food and the service may be worth a certain amount of money, and though in the end the money must change hands, and the money is what in fact *earns* us the privilege of being catered to by the restaurant staff, if the food and service is good it is given to us as a gift, and we do not deserve it.

Actually, neither challenge seems all that difficult. To the extent that the restaurant appeals to what is human in ourselves – on the one hand the need to produce and give, on the other the need to receive and consume, and in both respects the need to socialize – nothing should be easier. However, we know that it is not the case that meeting these challenges is easy. It is difficult, even in an era of de-repression, of a worldwide embrace of hedonism for the sake of hedonism, to get people interested in the aesthetics of everyday life – interested in the way that William Morris was talking about, involved with the aesthetics of life in a spirit of curiosity, application, creativity and joy. Among the hundreds of happy restaurant-goers in urban England surveyed by sociologists Warde and Martens in a study in the year 2000, none of them – at least so far as the surveyors were able to tell – took an interest in food as art, or in the restaurant as theatre. It was enough to 'have a good laugh', as they put: to enjoy the company of their friends and family. The respondents were able to react to 'meal events' critically – I liked *this*, I didn't like *that*, I thought *this* place was worth the money and *that* place not – but they were never able to express likes and dislikes in view of a theoretical understanding of food and restaurant-going. They were not apparently aware (although this lack of awareness may be a product of how the interviewers went about the job of checking people's awareness) that good food involves a body of knowledge, or that the business of the restaurant involves an art of life. They could only respond as consumers, with likes and dislikes, more or less well articulated and justified.[24]

Culture was part of the problem. These English provincials had not been raised in a culture where the rudiments of good food and the conviviality of the table were allowed to be part of the meaning of life, and the rules and forms attached to them were understood to be non-negotiable. They had been raised to be picky; they had not been raised to be wise. But the economic realities of civilization were a part of the problem too. The corporate world that dominates the English economy dominates the restaurant business as well, and it has fashioned the very street life of England (not to mention the rest of the West) into a network of traps set to ensnare the purchasing power of *homo sucker*. At the very high end of English life, and in the images promoted by the media, an 'art world' of haute cuisine is encouraged; it is even essential to the workings of the economy, and the enthronement, among select consumers – for this too seems to be necessary to the operation of a certain class formation – of magisterial narcissism. But for the rest of us the economy encourages massive, unthinking and unartful consumption, at the hands of labourers alienated from what they do. The respondents to the sociological survey do not seem to have been very demanding. They had been taught not to expect very much. That is, they had not been taught to expect very much of anything or anybody but themselves. So there was a common decency among them. But the decency came at a price. For from the world itself, as far as they were concerned, from the corner of the objective nature of the social world that food and service inhabit, that is, they demanded very little, and did not even know that there was something more that could be demanded.

There has to be a focus on the food itself, to be sure. Although much that is written about the restaurant focuses on process rather than the products, on the people involved rather than the things they eat, these things have to be the primary interest for any restaurant for the rest of us. The restaurant experience begins with the ministrations of a *cuisine*, a system for making objects of nature into products of culture; it is thereby a system for making food 'work'. Well, we have to respect this work. We have to admire it when it is well accomplished. If the restaurant for the rest of us is not about the excellence of the food – product of nature, of culture and of civilization too – then it is not about anything. This is the real 'it' – the *work* in the *thing*, and our *commitment* to the *gift* of the *thing*, and the joy it provides.

Yet we know that it is precisely from the work of food in this sense that the consumer society is designed to distract us. Instead of culture, we are urged to participate in the simulacra of culture. Instead of civility, we are urged either to elevate ourselves into the condition of majestic consumers or else simply to 'have a good laugh', take what is given and be done with it.[25] Instead of participating in culture and expressing civility, in other words, instead of taking a serious interest in the thing in front of us and the work that has provided it for us, we are encouraged merely to propagate the production of consumption. We chase after things to consume, but we have trouble chasing after the values of the things we consume. We run after IT, but we don't stop long enough to 'take an interest' in 'it'. We pursue more and more of IT, and we keep on lovin' it too, but we are not allowed, and do not allow ourselves, to take the measure of our material world, to come to really know it, take care for it, and in knowing and caring for it really to enjoy ourselves.

To resist the pressure of the logic of corporate capitalism and the consumerism it requires – to resist it, as the restaurant for the rest of us will enable us to do, in the spirit of *play* – may well require concerted *social* effort. Against the machine, the restaurant for the rest of us may require machines of its own. Slow Food or similar organizations may be among those machines; and there may have to be others as well, from the tacit, unorganized support of local communities for indigenous commerce to the intervention of national governments. Le Zouave in Collioure was the work of a creative and dedicated couple; but it was also the work of the town and the region and the nation in which it was able to thrive. And everybody knows this. We may be able to imagine an isolated painter with a minimal set of tools – a palette, a brush, a canvas and paint – to produce, in the privacy of a lonely cell, an excellent painting. But we cannot imagine the restaurant chef to act so alone. The tools of the trade are more complex; the ingredients of the trade are more complex; the economics are more complex. It takes a society to produce a restaurant meal, even if it also takes an autonomous culinary artist to produce a good one. And it takes a society willing and knowing enough to eat, appreciate and patronize a good restaurant.

But what is to be done? Not being an expert in public policy, and being ill suited for political organizing, I cannot say I have any particularly sound or original ideas about the way forward in the public sphere. Not being a restaurateur (though once, right before the bust of 2008, which dried up my sources of capital, I was making plans to become one), I do not have any practical advice for the way forward in commerce. I can only say that public policy and restaurateurs have to get into the act, and to get into it both defensively and offensively. Defensively they have to get into the act because the system of material life that prevails in the developed world pulls in two equally objectionable directions: elitism and majestic consumerism for the few, and McDonaldization for the many. Offensively they have to get into the act because without collective effort, whether at the local, national or even international level, nothing will get done; the enemies of the restaurant for the rest of us will win. As American journalist Michael Pollan has repeatedly argued, the agricultural policies of the developed world, from finance to technological organization, from subsidies to national infrastructure, have for years enforced a hegemony of junk, providing cheap food instead of good food, and cheap restaurants (we may add) instead of good ones. There are exceptions, yes, though more in some parts of the world than in others. There are thousands of exceptions, at every price range, at every sort of junction between the here and there, the now and the then. But that is because there are networks and nexuses of resistance. Against the empire of turbo-capitalism, with its trans-national corporations and the cheapening of all aspects of production and consumption, there is no political revolution.[26] But occasionally there is a good restaurant for the rest of us.

And what about 'us', then? And what about our need to need this artificial paradise? Let us recall, first of all, what the thing itself is all about. The restaurant for the rest of us is all about *art and hospitality* – even if it's also all about pleasure and sociality and profitable commercial transactions. It's all about *the food* – even if food is never a simple thing, being mediated by cuisines and things done to cuisines in the name of culture, civilization and de-civilization. It's all about *gratitude* – even if the gratitude must be expressed by an exchange of money. It's all about *the situation*, the here and now, the there and then – even if I can entertain the illusion that restaurants and what they offer really belong to a generalized space of judgement, where 'the best' and 'the worst' hold sway, and I can turn to critics and bloggers for advice. It's all about *happiness*, really – even if all our moral authorities tell us that happiness is never to be found in mere consumption, or the mere pleasures it affords, and we know that the 'perfect moment' is a sham. It's all about *play*, about not being what you are – even if there should ever hover over our culinary endeavours the threat of bad faith, of inauthenticity, of an over-emphasis on that which is aesthetic in place of that which is ethical, or on that which is convenient or conventional in the place of that which is free.

Hard stuff, perhaps. But there we are. We have a need to need this, and a need to be dutiful toward it. And in the end I can only respond to the challenge to the rest of us by saying what the Handmaid was told in the Margaret Atwood novel, when she was trying to figure out how to cope with her imprisonment.[27] I have already quoted what she was told, but I will quote it again. The Handmaid was imprisoned in a household that was trying to exploit her. In a distant dystopian future, an ageing barren couple was trying to use her for her body. They wanted her fertility. They wanted the Handmaid to give them a child. In other words, the couple wanted the Handmaid's body to be productive, but they wanted it to be productive without (on the Handmaid's part) either possession or enjoyment.[28] For all the echoes of a biblical situation, and for all the novel's dystopian projections into the distant future, the Handmaid, in short, was a modern consumer. How to cope? Well, said a secret message left for the Handmaid by someone who had previously occupied her place, *Don't let the bastards grind you down.*

references

Introduction

1 Honoré de Balzac, *Lost Illusions*, trans. Herbert J. Hunt (Harmondsworth, 2005), pp. 192–3.
2 Slavoj Žižek, *The Sublime Object of Ideology* (London, 1989), p. 82, and 'Surplus-Enjoyment', *Lacanian Ink*, 15 (1999). Žižek's latest thoughts (as of this writing) on the subject of ideology and the practice of capitalism appear in *Living in the End Times* (London, 2010).
3 At http://events.nytimes.com/gst/nycguide.html?detail'restaurants &id'1194811271572. Accessed 25 May 2010.
4 George Ritzer, *The McDonaldization of Society* (Thousand Oaks, CA, 2000) and Ritzer, ed., *McDonaldization: The Reader* (Thousand Oaks, CA, 2002).
5 A. B. De Périgord, *Nouvel almanach des gourmands* (Paris, 1825), pp. 98–9.

one: *Restaurants for the Rest of Us*

1 Calvin Trillin, *American Fried* (New York, 1974).
2 The first three of these are in fact perennial favourites of the *Restaurant Magazine* 'San Pellegrino The World's Best Fifty Restaurants' list, which has been topped in 2010 by a newcomer, the Noma in Copenhagen. The last seems to be an invention of Calvin Trillin's.
3 If a notice I found on the Internet is correct, it has since been sold to another proprietor, and the change 'has not been for the better'. At http://www.cityvox.fr/restaurants_perpignan/le-y mobile.
4 Slavoj Žižek, 'Surplus-Enjoyment', *Lacanian Ink*, 15 (1999).
5 Richard Pillsbury, *From Boarding House To Bistro: The American Restaurant Then and Now* (Boston, MA, 1990); Rebecca Spang,

259

The Invention of the Restaurant: Paris and Modern Gastronomic Culture (Cambridge, MA, 2000).

6 Max Weber, *Theory of Social and Economic Organization* (New York, 1997); George Simmel, 'Fashion', *American Journal of Sociology*, LXII/6 (1957). A modern update of Simmel's basic position, though with allowance for changes from the shift from modernity to postmodernity is Lars Svendsen, *Fashion: A Philosophy*, trans. John Irons (London, 2006). The concept of fashion, however, has not yet been systematically applied to restaurant culture, to my knowledge. Accounts of the history of the restaurant usually allow for the idea of fashionableness, but not for the idea that the history of the restaurant is a fashion history: restaurants are usually understood to have arisen in the modern world as signs of deep structural change within modernity, and not as examples of changeability.

7 'Our famous steaks are seared to perfection at 1800 degrees and topped with fresh butter so they sizzle all the way to your table.' So says the website of the 'world's largest fine dining company', which boasts over 130 locations in North America, including Mexico, Puerto Rico and Huntsville, Alabama. The company also owns Columbus Fish Market, Cameron's Steakhouse, Cameron's Fish House, Mitchell's Steak House and Mitchell's Fish Market.

8 From San Diego Restaurants Dot Com: 'P. F. Chang's China Bistro offers a unique combination of traditional Chinese cuisine and American hospitality in a contemporary bistro setting. Intensely flavoured, highly memorable culinary creations, prepared from the freshest ingredients, including premium herbs and spices imported directly from China.'

9 That is of course the McDonald's in protest of which the Slow Food movement was founded. Apparently it still attracts attention, good and bad, because of its location. See http://joshkramer.wordpress.com/2008/04/26/mcdonalds-at-the-spanish-steps/

10 But despair not, since a second restaurant opened farther inland and Mystic Pizza Frozen Pizza is available in supermarkets throughout the mainland USA.

11 *Stephen Fry in America*, Episode Six, 'Pacific'. Originally aired on BBC Four, 24 January 2009.

two: *Grimod de la Reynière: Eating and Writing*

1 The best account of the phenomenon is Rebecca Spang, *The Invention of the Restaurant* (Cambridge, MA, 2000).

2 The many quarrels historians enter into when discussing the idea of revolution are not necessary to rehearse here. A good sample of some of these debates is to be found in Gary Kates, ed., *The*

French Revolution: Recent Debates and New Controversies
(London, 1998). Although I am intrigued by the revisionist
account championed by François Furet, which shows that in the
event of the Revolution the French people discovered the symbolic
world of 'the political', I am particularly in sympathy with the
position staked by Colin Jones in 'Bourgeois Revolution
Revivified: 1789 and Social Change', in *The French Revolution*,
ed. Kates (pp. 157–91), which insists on the social aspects of the
period. This is because I share with Jones a culturalist perspective,
which sees societies and their politics as material cultures. Also in
this light it is worth consulting David Harvey, *Paris as the Capital
of Modernity* (New York, 2003), pp. 1–22, and, on Grimod and
revolution, Priscilla Parkhurst Ferguson, *Accounting for Taste:
The Triumph of French Cuisine* (Chicago, IL, 2004), pp. 83–96.

3 Grimod de La Reynière, *Écrits gastronomiques*, ed. Jean-Claude
Bonnet (Paris, 1997), p. 77. Critical treatments of Grimod
include the excellent introduction by Bonnet to this volume,
along with the following: Julia Abramson, 'Grimod's Debt to
Mercier and the Emergence of Gastronomic Writing
Reconsidered', EMF, 7 (2001), pp. 141–62; Julia Abramson,
'Legitimacy and Nationalism in the *Almanach des gourmands*
(1803–1812)', *Journal of Early Modern Cultural Studies*, III/2
(2003), pp. 101–35; Priscilla Parkhurst Ferguson, 'A Cultural
Field in the Making: Gastronomy in Nineteenth-Century
France', in *French Food: On the Table, On the Page, and In
French Culture*, ed. Lawrence R. Schehr and Allen S. Weiss (New
York, 2001), pp. 5–50; Michael Garvel, 'Grimod de la Reynière's
Almanach des gourmands: Exploring the Gastronomic New
World of Postrevolutionary France', in *French Food*, ed. Schehr
and Weiss, pp. 51–70.

4 *Écrits gastronomiques*, p. 78.

5 On the socio-cultural revolution of nineteenth-century Paris see
Priscilla Parkhurst Ferguson, *Paris as Revolution: Writing the
Nineteenth-Century City* (Berkeley, CA, 1994); and Christopher
Prendergast, *Paris and the Nineteenth Century* (Oxford, 1992). On
the beginnings of the consumer society in the eighteenth century
(though their focus is on England), see Neil McKendrick, John
Brewer and J. H. Plumb, eds, *The Birth of A Consumer Society:
The Commercialization of Eighteenth-century England*
(Bloomington, IN, 1985).

6 According to Talleyrand, in a famous quote, just the opposite
was the case – and this in spite of the fact that Talleyrand, like
Grimod, was a liberal and a supporter of the Revolution at first.
'He who has not lived in the eighteenth century before the
Revolution does not know the sweetness of life and cannot
imagine what happiness in life can be. That is the century that
had forged all the victorious weapons against that elusive

261

adversary that we call boredom. Love, Poetry, Music, Theatre, Painting, Architecture, the Court, Salons, Parks and Gardens, Gastronomy, Letters, the Arts and Sciences, all combined to bring about the satisfaction of the physical, intellectual and even moral appetites, the refinement of sensuality, of elegance and pleasure. Existence was so well filled that if the seventeenth century was the Great Century of glory, the eighteenth was the century of indigestion.' Charles-Maurice de Talleyrand Périgord, *Mémoires du Prince de Talleyrand: La Confession de Talleyrand* (Paris, 1891), p. 57.

7 On this whole subject, see the essays collected in Marc Jacobs and Peter Scholliers, eds, *Eating Out In Europe: Picnics, Gourmet Dining And Snacks Since The Late Eighteenth Century* (Oxford, 2003).

8 Walter Benjamin, *The Arcades Project*, trans. Howard Eiland and Kevin McLaughlin (Cambridge, MA, 1999), pp. 416–55. 'Our man,' writes Benjamin, 'wants nothing to do with the myriad possibilities offered to sate his appetite' (p. 417) – quite the opposite of Grimod.

9 Giles MacDonogh, *A Palate in Revolution: Grimod de La Reynière and the 'Almanch des Gourmands'* (London, 1987), pp. 22–4. Also see Ned Rival, *Grimod de la Reynière: le gourmand gentilhomme.* (Paris, 1983), pp. 165–9; and Gustave Desnoiresterres, *Grimod de la Reynière et son groupe* (Paris, 1877), pp. 228–36. It was a fact that at the time Grimod worked as a lawyer representing members of the lower classes.

10 In the true spirit of French gastronomic pride, Robert Pitte, in *French Gastronomy: The History and Geography of a Passion*, trans. Jody Golding (New York, 2002), argues that Parisians whether adoptive or native have *always* been gourmands, up and down the social hierarchy, from the washerwoman to the duchess, from the footman to the financier, ever since there was such a thing as Paris. He may be right, though the evidence is incomplete. And Grimod, in any case disagrees, though in terms of a timeworn saying: 'In the last few years an interest in food has grown in Paris, even exploded, to an extent hitherto unknown. Our ancestors only ate in order to live, their descendants seem only to live in order to eat' (*Écrits Gastronomiques*, p. 164).

11 Grimod de la Reynière, *Almanach des gourmands, servant de guide dans les moyens de faire excellente chère*, 8 vols (Paris, 1803–12), vol. II, p. 7.

12 Ibid., vol. II, p. 2

13 David Hume, 'Of the Standard of Taste', in *Selected Essays* (Oxford, 1996), pp. 133–53, at p. 142.

14 A. B. De Périgord [Horace-Napoléon Raisson], *Nouvel almanach des gourmands* (Paris, 1825), pp. 33–4.

15 Colin Campbell, *The Romantic Ethic and the Spirit of Modern Consumerism* (Oxford, 1987), p. 70. I don't agree with the whole

of Campbell's analysis, which depends on a somewhat diffuse notion of the practice of daydreaming, of imagining material satisfactions apart from the satisfactions themselves, but what he says about the 'spirit of modern consumerism' in this context certainly applies well to Grimod and the invention of gastronomy during the Romantic era.

16 Erving Goffman, *Interaction Ritual: Essays in Face-to-face Behavior* (New York, 2003); Randall Collins, *Interaction Ritual Chains* (Princeton, NJ, 2005).
17 *Manuel des Amphitryons*, in *Écrits gastronomiques*, pp. 245–6.
18 *Écrits gastronomiques*, p. 170.
19 Ibid., p. 170.
20 Ibid., pp. 180, 193.
21 *Almanach*, vol. VII, p. 214.
22 Ibid., vol. III, p. 133.
23 Ibid., vol. IV, p. 140.
24 Ibid., vol. V, p. 220.
25 Ibid., vol. V, p. 240.
26 Ibid., vol. V, p. 240.
27 Ibid., vol. VII, p. 214.
28 Ibid., vol. I, p. 34.
29 Ibid., vol. I, p. 194.
30 Ibid., vol. VI, p. 221.
31 Introduction, *Écrits Gastronomiques*, p. 22.
32 The best discussions of the jury are in Desnoiresterres, *Grimod de la Reynière*, pp. 228–36; and Rival, *Grimod de la Reynière*, pp. 165–9.
33 *Almanach*, vol. III, p. vii.
34 Ibid., vol. IV, p. xv.
35 Ibid., vol. IV, p. 138.
36 Ibid., vol. V, p. x.
37 Ibid., vol. VI, pp. 219–20.
38 Ibid., vol. V, pp. 315–16.
39 Ibid., vol. VII, p. 18.
40 Ibid., vol. VII, p. 202.
41 Ibid., vol. VIII, p. xi.

three: *Nausea*

1 Jean-Paul Sartre, *Nausea*, trans. Lloyd Alexander (New York, 1964), p. 6.
2 The main passage the rest of this chapter refers to is found on pages 103–24 of this English translation. It is also to be found in the original French, Jean-Paul Sartre, *La nausée* (Paris, 1938), pp. 151–78. I shall be quoting from the English translation, but occasionally referring to the original French; in the latter cases my

quotes are marked with an asterisk. In my discussion of *Nausea* and Sartre's attitude toward food I have been aided by a number of works in the vast secondary literature devoted to Sartre. Above all, I must cite Catharine Savage Brosman, 'Les Nourritures sartriennes', in *Littérature et gastronomie*, ed. Ronald W. Tobin (Paris, 1985), pp. 229–63. Everything I write here has been influenced by that article. I am also indebted to Anthony Manser, *Sartre: A Philosophic Study* (Westport, CT, 1966); Rhiannon Goldthorpe, *La Nausée* (London, 1991); Richard Kamber, 'Sartre's Nauseas', in *mln*, XCVIII/5 (1983), pp. 1279–85; Jerome Neu, 'Divided Minds: Sartre's "Bad Faith" Critique of Freud,' *Review of Metaphysics*, XLII/1 (1988), pp. 79–101; the essays in *The Cambridge Companion to Sartre*, ed. Christina Howells (Cambridge, 1992) and *Sartre's Nausea: Text, Context, Intertext*, ed. Alistair Rolls and Elizabeth Rechniewski (Amsterdam, 2005); Vincent de Coorebyter, *Sartre avant la phénoménologie: Autour de 'La nausea' et de la 'Légende de la vérité'* (Brussels, 2005); and David Sherman, *Sartre and Adorno: The Dialectics of Subjectivity* (Albany, NY, 2007). On homophobia in *Nausea* see Lawrence R. Schehr, 'Sartre's Autodidacticism', in *Sartre's Nausea*, ed. Rolls and Rechniewski, pp. 31–51.

3 This is a point especially emphasized by Brosman in 'Les Nourritures sartriennes', going to the heart of what Brosman calls Sartre's 'anti-gastronomy', as well as in Michel Onfray, *Les Ventres des Philosophes* (Paris, 1989), pp. 133–46, which especially emphasizes Sartre's aversion to (slimy) crustaceans.

4 Jean-Paul Sartre, *Being and Nothingness*, trans. Hazel E. Barnes (Abingdon, 2003). 'Bad faith' is discussed at length on pp. 70–94.

5 Erving Goffman, *The Presentation of the Self in Everyday Life* (London, 1990), esp. pp. 109–40.

6 At http://en.wikipedia.org/wiki/Farce. Accessed 22 November 2009. There was actually a farce performed about gastronomy early on, published as Eugène Scribe et Brulay, *Le Gastronome sans argent. Vaudeville en un acte* (Paris, 1821). It is all about, as the title says, a 'gastronome without money', a parasite who fools his way into a receiving a free meal.

7 He did, however, publish the notebooks he produced on the subject in the late 1940s, translated into English as Jean Paul-Sartre, *Notebooks for an Ethics*, trans. David Pellauer (Chicago, IL, 1992).

8 *Being and Nothingness*, p. 646.

9 This is especially important in the first volume, published in English as Jean-Paul Sartre, *The Age of Reason*, trans. Eric Sutton (London, 1947).

10 *Being and Nothingness*, p. 82.

11 Ibid., p. 93.

12 Ibid., p. 82.

13 Said the former call girl known as Belle du Jour to a television

interviewer, 'Like very many other jobs, you do turn on an aspect of your personality. It isn't that Belle wasn't me – Belle is the more confident part of me. Belle isn't the part of me that when someone opens the door is thinking, "do I look all right?" Belle has to walk in and feel she looks alright . . . Confidence is required. I'm not glamorising it, so much as saying you do have to believe something about yourself is untouchable by this. By whatever work you do, whatever happens to you and whatever you go through in your life; that you are who you are and not what you are, that's what's important.' Caroline Davies, *Guardian*, Thursday, 26 November 2009. Alison Owings, *Hey, Waitress!: The USA From the Other Side of the Tray* (Berkeley, CA, 2002), provides many poignant examples of how this works for the American waitress today. On the one hand, the server has to put herself into her role with enthusiasm, *as herself*. On the other hand, the waitress always has another life, and is perfectly capable of seeing her role as a server as merely a role she plays. Moreover, the server has to put herself into her role for the sake of extrinsic rewards, above all pride in what she is doing and money; but in America waitressing is a very low-status job, and the pay is bad. As of this writing, a majority of waitresses in America have little job security and little if any health insurance. Yet, says one of the women Owings interviews (p. 195), 'I come out with the humour of all these places. The thing is, everyone was playing a part. I couldn't believe these people were *serious*: the role of customer, the role of waiter. I'd think you've got to be reading *scripts*.'

14 *Being and Nothingness*, pp. 82–3.
15 To this point too, especially with regard to a social distinctiveness expressing a relation of the dominating to the dominated, the view is similar to Pierre Bourdieu in *Distinction: A Social Critique of the Judgement of Taste*, trans. Richard Nice (Cambridge, MA, 1987).
16 Eric H. Du Plessis, 'Sartre, Existentialism and Panic Attacks', *Linacre Quarterly*, LIX/2 (1992), pp. 63–8; Carole Haynes-Curtis, 'Sartre and the Drug Connection', *Philosophy*, 70 (1995) pp. 87–106; Thomas Smith, 'On Sartre and the Drug Connection: A Response to Haynes-Curtis', *Philosophy*, LXX/274 (1995), pp. 590-93.
17 *Being and Nothingness*, p. 53.
18 Ibid., p. 362.
19 Michel Serres, *The Five Senses: A Philosophy of Mingled Bodies*, trans. Margaret Sankey and Peter Cowley (London, 2008). But Serres completely resists the Cartesianism that rules Sartre's concept of auto-sensation.
20 Luce Irigaray, *This Sex Which is Not One*, trans. Catherine Porter and Carolyn Burke (Ithaca, NY, 1985).
21 *Being and Nothingness*, p. 630.

22 Ibid., pp. 630–31.
23 Ibid., p.635. As Michel Onfray puts it, for Sartre 'taste is a road of access to subjectivity'. *Ventres*, p. 144.
24 'The American Sublime', in *Collected Poems of Wallace Stevens* (New York, 1990).
25 *Being and Nothingness*, p. 635.
26 George Ritzer, *The McDonaldization of Society* (Thousand Oaks, CA, 2000).
27 *Notebooks*, p. 4.
28 Ibid., p. 5. A recent discussion of authenticity in early Sartre by Ronald E. Santoni, *Bad Faith, Good Faith and Authenticity in Sartre's Early Philosophy* (Philadelphia, PA, 1995) seems unconvincing to me, failing to come to terms with Sartre's nihilism and anti-conformism.
29 See Simone de Beauvoir, *Adieux: A Farewell to Sartre*, trans. Patrick O'Brien (Harmondsworth, 1984), especially pp. 331–4; Robert Pitte, *French Gastronomy: The History and Geography of a Passion* (New York, 2002), p. 56; Onfray, *Ventres*, p. 133.

four: *Her Majesty the Consumer*

1 Sigmund Freud, 'On Narcissism: An Introduction', in *The Standard Edition of the Complete Psychological Works of Sigmund Freud*, trans. James Strachey (London, 1957), vol. XIV, p. 91.
2 A partial version of this 1930s visualization of Le Havre is found in Marcel Carné's film *Le quai des brumes* (1937), DVD 2007.
3 Jean Baudrillard, *Simulacra and Simulation*, trans. Sheila Faria Glaser (Ann Arbor, MI, 1994). The restaurant in Le Havre is not, for all that, a 'simulacra' in Baudrillard's sense, for the latter is an 'imitation without an original', whereas the Le Bistrot des Halles has a number of original models, and does nothing to undermine the models it is following. But it is certainly a 'simulation' with ironic distance from the thing it simulates.
4 Marc Augé, *Non-places: Introduction to an Anthropology of Supermodernity*, trans. John Howe (London, 1995). A typical 'non-place' would be an airport lounge – in an airport just about anywhere in the developed world. A simulation-restaurant like Bistrot des Halles is only partially a 'non-place', for the food (despite the Lyonnais dressing) is largely typical of Normandy, and there is in any case a long tradition in France, going back to the founding of the famed Trois Frères Provençaux in Paris, a favourite of Grimod's, of restaurateurs from one region of France bringing their cuisine to another region. It is perhaps more accurate to think of the Bistrot des Halles as a *thematized* restaurant, the juxtaposition of regional styles of food and presentation being its theme.

5 Naguib Mahfouz, *Midaq Alley*, trans. Trevor Le Gassick (London, 1975), p. 46.

6 Victor Lebow, 'The Nature of Postwar Retail Competition', *Journal of Marketing*, IX/I (1954), p. 7.

7 Jean Baudrillard, *The Consumer Society: Myths and Structures* [1970], trans. Chris Turner (London, 1998). I follow Baudrillard's early analysis throughout this book, but his early thought underwent important
modifications to which my thought is also (though less closely) attached, as in, for example, *For a Critique of the Political Economy of the Sign*, trans. Charles Levin (New York, 1981).

8 See Diane Jacob, *Will Write for Food* (New York, 2005) and Louise Purwin Zobel, *Travel Writer's Handbook: How to Write, and Sell, Your Own Travel Experiences* (Chicago, 2002).

9 Freud first brings out the connection between the two phenomena, narcissism and exhibitionism, in an essay written about the same time as 'On Narcissism', 'Instincts and the Vicissitudes', also in volume XIV of *The Complete Psychological Works*, especially pp. 129–33.

10 Most famously, in Christopher Lasch, *The Culture of Narcissism: American Life in an Age of Diminishing Expectations* (New York, 1978), the point of whose protest against the de-politicization and commodification of everyday life is missed in an otherwise interesting review of the history of the idea, Imogen Tyler, 'From "The Me Decade" to "The Me Millennium": The Cultural History of Narcissism', *International Journal of Cultural Studies*, X/3 (2007), pp. 343–63. A view of consumption as narcissism already hovers in Veblen's *Theory of the Leisure Class*, and finds specific articulation in Baudrillard, *The Consumer Society*, p. 95, where Baudrillard argues two related points: a) that consumer society as a whole is narcissistic (society is in love with itself and only itself) and operates narcissistically; b) that individual consumers reflect this narcissism as a whole within their own individual, narcissistic consumption. Thus, 'the narcissism of the individual in consumer society *is not an enjoyment of singularity; it is a refraction of collective features*' (emphasis in the original). The idea finds recent development in Zygmunt Bauman's notion of 'subjectivity fetishism' in Zygmunt Bauman, *Consuming Life* (Cambridge, 2009), pp. 14–20. But perhaps the most classic statement is found in Richard Sennett, *The Fall of Public Man* [1977] (London, 1984): 'In modern social life adults must act narcissistically to act in accordance with society's norms. For that reality is so structured that order and stability and reward appear only to the extent that people who work and act within its structures treat social situations as mirrors of self, and are deflected from examining them as forms which have a non-personality meaning' (pp. 326–7).

11 The most profound reflection on these matters that I know of, outside of Marx, is Shakespeare's *Merchant of Venice* (1597).

12 José Ortega y Gasset, *The Revolt of the Masses* [1932] (New York, 1994).

13 See Fernand Lotte, 'Balzac et la table dans *La Comédie humaine*', *L'Année Balzacienne* (1962); and of course, Émile Zola, *The Kill*, trans. Brian Nelson (Oxford, 2004), pp. 123–35.

14 Of special interest here, take a look at 'Ten Things You Should Know About Food Bloggers': http://www.notquitenigella.com/2009/07/13/10-things-you-should-know-about-food-bloggers

15 M.F.K. Fisher, *The Art of Eating* (Hoboken, NJ, 2004), p. 401.

16 Francesco Colonna, *Hypnerotomachia Poliphili: The Strife of Love in a Dream*, trans. Joscelyn Godwin (New York, 1999), pp. 106–7. Earlier cited in Robert Appelbaum, *Aguecheek's Beef, Belch's Hiccup, and Other Gastronomic Interjections: Literature, Culture and Food Among the Early Moderns* (Chicago, 2006), pp. 151–54.

17 The story is beautifully recounted in Joan Reardon, *Poet of the Appetites: The Lives and Loves of M.F.K. Fisher* (New York, 2005).

18 A. J. Liebling, *Between Meals: An Appetite for Paris* (New York, 1986); Calvin Tomkins, *Living Well Is the Best Revenge* (New York, 1971); Elizabeth David, *An Omelette and a Glass of Wine* (Guilford, CT, 1997); Peter Mayle, *Bon Appétit! Travels through France with Knife, Fork, and Corkscrew* (London, 2001).

19 M.F.K. Fisher, *Not Now But Now* [1947] (London, 1984).

20 David Kamp, *The United States of Arugula: How We Became a Gourmet Nation* (New York, 2006).

21 The story of the wilderness of American cuisine is best told in John L. Hess and Karen Hess, *The Taste of America* (Champaign, IL, 2000).

22 See Simon Wright, *Tough Cookies: Tales of Obsession, Toil and Tenacity from Britain's Culinary Heavyweights* (London, 2005).

23 Ruth Reichl, *Tender at the Bone* (New York, 1998), p. x. The fictionalization is less evident in what is perhaps the best of the three memoirs, *Comfort Me With Apples* (New York, 2001), which is more confessional. The third book, *Garlic and Sapphires: The Secret Life of a Food Critic* (New York, 2005), is intellectually the most interesting of the three, taking disguise, desire and journalism as its theme. In an appendix Reichl writes, 'I have to admit that with this book I have taken many liberties that do not follow journalistic principles . . .' (p. 332).

24 On Michelin critics, see Pascal Rémy, *L'inspecteur se met à table* (Paris, 2004) and Jean-François Mesplède, *Trois étoiles au Michelin: Une histoire de la haute gastronomie française et européenne* (Paris, 2004). On the New York Times, see Mimi Sheraton, *Eating My Words: An Appetite for Life* (New York, 2004).

25 In France the equivalent is the still highly active yet always invisible

François Simon, critic for the *Figaro* and author of the blog 'Simon Says': http://francoissimon.typepad.fr/

26 Report from the Meals-on-Wheels website, www.mealcall.org/faq.htm#What%20is%20Meal-On-Wheels: 'What is included with a meal? This varies from day to day and program to program. An example of a cold meal might be a sandwich, a piece of fruit (or juice) and one or two side dishes. An example of a hot meal might be a serving of meat, a vegetable, and a roll or biscuit. A piece of dessert could also be included . . . Look for an adequate meal but not huge quantities. Light eaters might possibly have enough leftovers for a snack or a second meal, but this should not necessarily be expected . . . Neither should you expect meals that are expensive, take tons of time to prepare, or must be served and consumed within minutes of preparation. Where meals are delivered, it can take awhile between the time the meals are picked up from the prep location and when they are delivered. This means that certain foods are not good candidates for being included in a meal,'

27 Gael Greene, *Insatiable Me: Tales of a Life of Delicious Excess* (New York, 2006), p. 308.

28 Reichl, *Comfort Me With Apples*, pp. 6–7.

29 Ibid., p. 18.

30 Reichl, *Garlic*, pp. 226–29

31 Ibid., p. 47.

32 Ibid., pp. 52–3.

33 Ibid., p. 33.

five: *Dining Out in Paris and London*

1 George Orwell, *Down and Out in Paris and London* (London, 2001).

2 'Most people who love Paris love it because the first time they came they ate something better than they had ever eaten before, and kept coming back to eat it again.' Adam Gopnik, *Paris to the Moon* (New York, 2001), p. 147.

3 Says a London restaurateur recently to the press: 'When I started in this business ten years ago we were just coming out of that phase where people said the UK is the most appalling food place on the planet and there were any decent restaurants anywhere . . . And now I think London is the most exciting, vibrant capital in the world for food.' Jamie Barber to anonymous reporter in 'Social Democracy', *Restaurant*, January 2010, p. 21.

4 They all seem to be owned by Cameron Mitchell Restaurants, from Ocean Prime to Molly Woo's Asian Bistro. The chain was founded in Columbus in 1993.

5 For Melbourne: Joanne Finkelstein, *Dining Out: A Sociology of*

Modern Manners (Cambridge, 1989). For Preston: Alan Warde and Lydia Martens, *Eating Out: Social Differentiation, Consumption and Pleasure* (Cambridge, 2000).

6 Rachel Cooke, 'I could have opened a safe little brasserie like the Ivy', *The Observer*, 9 November 2003.

7 See J.A.G. Roberts, *China to Chinatown* (London, 2002).

8 Although I didn't know it, I had been anticipated in this, in Margarethe Kusenbach, 'Street Phenomenology: The Go-Along as Ethnographic Research Tool', *Ethnography*, 4 (2003), pp. 455–85.

9 On the latter, see Kevin Jackson and Richard Heeps, *Fast: Feasting on the Streets of London* (London, 2006).

10 Pascal Rémy, *L'inspecteur se met à table* (Paris, 2004); Jean-François Mesplède, *Trois étoiles au Michelin: Une histoire de la haute gastronomie française et européene* (Paris, 2004); François Simon, *Pique assiette: La fin d'une gastronomie française* (Paris, 2008).

11 Lady Morgan, *France*, 4th edn (London, 1818), pp. 132–5.

12 William Playfair, *France As It Is, Not Lady Morgan's France*, 2 vols (London, 1819), vol. I, pp. 261–2.

13 Francis W. Blagdon, *Paris as It Was and as It Is; Or A Sketch of the French Capital*, 2 vols (London, 1803), vol. II, pp. 440–55.

14 Abraham Hayward, in *The Art of Dining: Or, Gastronomy and Gastronomers* (London, 1852), pp. 33–4.

15 A. J. Liebling, *Between Meals: An Appetite for Paris* (New York, 1986), p. 124; Elizabeth David, *An Omelette and a Glass of Wine* (Guilford, CT, 1997), p. 66; Gopnik, *Paris to the Moon*, pp. 148–9; Michael Steinberger, *Au Revoir to All That: The Rise and Fall of French Cuisine* (London, 2009), p. 11.

16 Charles Baudelaire, *The Flowers of Evil*, trans. William Aggeler (Fresno, CA, 1954).

17 Roland Barthes, 'Pour une psycho-sociologies de l'alimentation contemporaine', in *L'histoire de l'alimentation*, ed. J.-J. Hérmardiquer (Paris, 1970), p. 313. Translated and quoted in Dana Strand, 'Film, Food, and "La Françité": From *le pain quotidien* to McDo', in *French Food: On the Table, On the Page, and in French Culture*, ed. Lawrence R. Schehr and Allen S. Weiss (New York, 2001), p. 204.

18 'Jason Burke in Paris', *The Observer*, Sunday, 25 February 2007.

19 Orwell, *Down and Out*, p. 216.

six: *The Production of Production: Novelists and Cooks*

1 The outstanding treatment of these issues is Michael Pollan, *Omnivore's Dilemma: A Natural History of Four Meals* (New York, 2007).

2 George Ritzer, *The McDonaldization of Society* (Thousand

Oaks, CA, 2000). With regard to the de-personalization of service in a McDonaldized institution, it should nevertheless be observed that depersonalization is itself culturally variable. Yunxiang Yang thus reports that in Beijing McDonald's itself is prized by locals for the friendliness, courteousness and efficiency of the service. Yunxiang Yang, 'Consuming McDonald's in Beijing', in *The Cultural Politics of Food and Eating: A Reader*, ed. James L. Watson and Melissa Caldwell (Malden, MA, 2005).

3   Anthony Bourdain, *Kitchen Confidential: Adventures in the Culinary Underbelly* (London, 2001), p. 303.

4   Jeffrey Steingarten, 'Kitchen Confidential: Why are the Foodies Fuming?', at www.slate.com/id/2000186/entry/1005738/.

5   Gary Alan Fine, *Kitchens: The Culture of Restaurant Work* (Berkeley, CA, 1996). One of Fine's field notes (p. 120) captures a good part of the spirit of the kitchen. 'Paul, the head chef, pretends to chop my arm off with a large meat saw. Later Phil, the owner, throws an empty soft drink can at Paul's back. Paul then briefly locks Phil in the cooler.'

6   Bill Buford, *Heat: An Amateur's Adventures as Kitchen Slave, Line Cook, Pasta-Maker and Apprentice to a Butcher in Tuscany* (London, 2006).

7   Louis Marin, *Utopics: Spatial Play*, trans. Robert A. Vollrath (Atlantic Highlands, NJ, 1984).

8   Karl Marx and Frederick Engels, 'The German Ideology', in Marx and Engels, *Collected Works*, vol. v (New York, 1976), p. 47. For a discussion of Marx's seemingly whimsical notion, in ways which also illuminate Morris's thought, see William James Booth, 'Gone Fishing: Making Sense of Marx's Concept of Communism', *Political Theory*, XVII/2 (1989).

9   William Morris, *News from Nowhere* (Oxford, 2003), p. 12.

10 Ibid., p. 13.

11 Ibid., pp. 86–7.

12 Ibid., pp. 51–2.

13 Ibid., p. 79.

14 Buford, *Heat*, p. 279.

15 Morris, *News from Nowhere*, pp. 80–81.

16 Ibid., p. 52.

17 Ibid., p. 152.

18 Ibid., p. 180.

19 Priscilla Parkhurst Ferguson, *Accounting for Taste: The Triumph of French Cuisine* (Chicago, IL, 2004), pp. 187–201.

20 Isak Dinesen, 'Babette's Feast', in *Anecdotes of Destiny* [1958] (London, 2001), p. 65.

21 Of course, as has been noted several times in the French press, it was highly unlikely for a woman to be the head chef of a luxurious Parisian restaurant in the mid-nineteenth century; none is known to the historical record.

22 Interesting and informative in this regard is Michael J. Shapiro, 'Political Economy and Mimetic Desire: A Postmodernist Reading of "Babette's Feast"', *History of European Ideas*, XIII/3 (1992).

23 Dinesen, 'Babette's Feast', p. 67.

24 Ibid., p. 68.

25 Judith Thurman, *Isak Dinesen: The Life of Karen Blixen* (Harmonsdworth, 1982), pp. 376–7.

26 Dinesen, 'Babette's Feast', p. 60.

27 Thurman, *Isak Dinesen*, esp. pp. 422–4.

28 Isak Dinesen, 'Tempests', in *Anecdotes of Destiny*, pp. 145–6. Interesting readings of the story about the pearl fisher, 'The Diver', and about 'Tempests' are included in Lynn R. Wilkinson, 'Hannah Arendt on Isak Dinesen: Between Storytelling and Theory', *Comparative Literature*, LVI/1 (2004).

29 I owe this point originally to Deane Curtin, 'Food/Body/Person', in *Cooking, Eating, Thinking: Transformative Philosophies of Food*, ed. D. Curtin and L. Hedke (Indianapolis, IN, 1992). The main reference to Plato is the *Gorgias*, which has some pretty nasty things to say about Pericles and the Acropolis too. Hannah Arendt, *The Human Condition* (Chicago, IL, 1999), provides an extensive model of the notions of labour, work and action, where activities like cookery are given a very subordinate place, their being outside, for Arendt, the realm of 'freedom'.

30 Dinesen, 'Babette's Feast', p. 67.

31 Ibid., p. 68.

32 On this, see especially Marcel Mauss, *The Gift: The Form and Reason for Exchange in Archaic Societies*, trans. W. D. Halls (London, 1990). Jean Baudrillard applies Mauss's theory with surprising effect to modern society in *Symbolic Exchange and Death*, trans. Ian Hamilton Grant (London, 1993).

33 Anne Tyler, *Dinner at the Homesick Restaurant* (London, 1992), p. 121.

34 On the American scene, see Richard Pillsbury, *From Boarding House To Bistro: The American Restaurant Then And Now* (Boston, MA, 1990) and William Grimes, *Appetite City: A Culinary History of New York* (New York, 2009).

35 Tyler, *Dinner*, p. 129, p. 132.

36 Ibid., p. 123.

37 Ibid., p. 123, p. 141.

38 Ibid., p. 126.

39 Ibid., p. 141.

40 For a perceptive psychoanalytic reading of the family romance here, see Joseph B. Wagner, '"The Absent Presence" in *Dinner at the Homesick Restaurant*', in *The Fiction of Anne Tyler*, ed. C. Ralph Stephens (Jackson, MI, 1990).

41 Derek Pardue, 'Familiarity, Ambience and Intentionality: An

Investigation into Casual Dining Restaurants in Central Illinois', in *The Restaurants Book: Ethnographies of Where We Eat*, ed. David Beriss and David Sutton (Oxford, 2007), pp. 65–78. Other contributions to this volume also take up this theme.

42 Tyler, *Dinner*, p. 139.
43 Ibid., p. 140.
44 Ibid., p. 257.
45 Joseph Wechsberg, *Blue Trout and Black Truffles: The Peregrinations of an Epicure* (Chicago, 1985), pp. 271, 263.
46 Perceptive reviews, in alphabetical order by author, include William Grimes, 'Londonstan', *New York Times*, 6 August 2009; Stephanie Merritt, 'Check into the Imperial Hotel at your peril', *The Observer*,
3 May 2009; Sukhdev Sandu, 'Sukhdev Sandhu finds nothing cooking in Monica Ali's *In the Kitchen*', *Daily Telegraph*, 30 April 2009; Christopher Tayler, 'Christopher Tayler samples Monica Ali's cook's tale', *The Guardian*, 18 April 2009.
47 See Simon Wright, *Tough Cookies: Tales of Obsession, Toil and Tenacity from Britain's Culinary Heavyweights* (London, 2005), especially pp. 147–88.
48 Brian Appleyard, 'Brick Lane's reluctant queen of outrage', *Times*, 18 November 2007.
49 Another (non-American, non-Jewish) novelist to whom Ali is obviously indebted is J. M. Coetzee, who also writes stories of this type. Some of the plot and imagery of *In the Kitchen* – particularly, the adoption by a representative of an empire (Gabriel's 'Imperial Hotel') of a wounded subservient woman, whose feet the man washes as a form of both atonement and sexual play – seems to be adopted from *Waiting for the Barbarians* (London, 1980).
50 Mary Douglas, *Purity and Danger: An Analysis of Concepts of Pollution and Taboo* (London, 1991).
51 Monica Ali, *In the Kitchen* (London, 2009), p. 28.
52 Ibid., p. 20.
53 Ibid., p. 8.
54 Ibid., p. 11.
55 Ibid., p. 30.
56 Ibid., p. 75.
57 Ibid., pp. 148–50.

seven: *Culture, Civilization and Resistance*

1 See Gary Alan Fine, *Kitchens: The Culture of Restaurant Work* (Berkeley, CA, 1998), p. 134 and *passim*. Fine writes before recent developments that have made this 'food world' a more international affair, more beholden to the cult of celebrity. The pathways of

apprenticeship in this new food world are discussed at length in Bill Buford, *Heat: An Amateur's Adventures as Kitchen Slave, Line Cook, Pasta-Maker and Apprentice to a Butcher in Tuscany* (London, 2006). For a general discussion, see Howard S. Becker, *Art Worlds*, revd edn (Berkeley, CA, 2008).

2 'General Advice: Restaurants in Yemen', at www.virtualtourist.com/travel/Middle_East/Yemen/Restaurants-Yemen-BR-1.html

3 On the reality of the modern British diet, see Joanna Blythman, *Bad Food Britain: How a Nation Ruined Its Appetite* (London, 2006).

4 Of course, there will be exceptions, especially in America, I think: chain restaurants that local operators and workers have appropriated as if they were their own. Although the food may remain the same as any other example of the same chain, the spirit of community and hospitality may shine through.

5 Marcel Mauss, 'Les techniques du corps', *Journal de Psychologie*, XXXII (1936).

6 For some of the media reports on the difference between French and British eating habits of the young, see www.healthy-kid-recipes.com/frencheating.html.

7 Massimo Montanari, *Food Is Culture*, trans. Albert Sonnenfeld (New York, 2004), pp. 139–40.

8 Douglas Harper, *The Italian Way: Food and Social Life* (Chicago, IL, 2010).

9 See Carlo Petrini, *Slow Food: The Case for Taste*, trans. William McCuaig (New York, 2004); and Carlo Petrini and Gigi Padovani, *Slow Food Revolution: A New Culture for Eating and Living* (New York, 2006). And see below, note 15.

10 'Italy bans kebabs and foreign food from cities', *Times*, 31 January 2009; Rachel Donadio, 'A Walled City in Tuscany Clings to Its Ancient Menu', *New York Times*, 12 March 2009.

11 *France 2009* (2009), p. 283.

12 Alice Waters, *The Chez Panisse Menu Cookbook* (New York, 1982), p. x. And see David Kamp, *The United States of Arugula: How We Became a Gourmet Nation* (New York, 2006), pp. 231–66.

13 At www.tobycarvery.co.uk.

14 See Kwame Anthony Appiah, *Cosmopolitanism* (London, 2006), and Jacques Derrida, *On Cosmopolitanism and Forgiveness*, trans. Mark Dooley and Michael Hughes (London and New York, 2001).

15 I discuss Rousseau along with Immanuel Kant and the philosophical distaste for civilization in *Aguecheek's Beef, Belch's Hiccup, and Other Gastronomic Interjections: Literature, Culture and Food Among the Early Moderns* (Chicago, 2006), pp. 287–306, as well as in the article from which some of the material in this chapter has been adapted, Robert Appelbaum,

'The Civility of Eating', in *Food and Morality*, ed. Susan Friedland (Totnes, 2008), pp. 29–38. Both works also address the question of the 'civilizing process' as discussed in Norbert Elias, *The Civilizing Process*, trans. Edmund Jephcott (Oxford, 1994).

16 César Beccaria, *On Crimes and Punishments and Other Writings*, ed. Richard Bellamy, trans. Richard Davies, Virginia Cox and Richard Bellamy (Cambridge, 1995), p. 141.

17 Jean-Marc Ferry, *De la civilisation: civilité, légalité, publicité* (Paris, 2001), p. 21. Also see Hélène Merlin-Kajman, 'Civilité: une certain modalité du vivre-ensemble', in *Civilization in French and Francophone Literature*, French Literature Series, 33, ed. Buford Norman and James Day (Amsterdam and New York, 2006), pp. 205–19.

18 Ibid., p. 58.

19 John Hannigan, *Fantasy City: Pleasure and Profit in the Postmodern Metropolis* (London, 1998). Hannigan offers a scathing appraisal of the phenomenon he aptly identifies. I am myself trying to take a somewhat sunnier view of things.

20 Ernest Hemingway, *The Sun Also Rises* [1926] (New York, 2003), p. 237.

21 See above, n. 19.

22 At www.slowfood.org.uk/Cms/Page/home.

23 Stephen Mennell, 'L'Envers de la medaille: les processes de décivilisation,' in *Norbert Elias: La politique et l'histoire*, ed. Alain Garrigou and Bernard Lacroix (Paris, 1997), pp. 213–36. Also see Merlin-Kajman, 'Civilité', pp. 205–19.

24 Alan Warde and Lydia Martens, *Eating Out: Social Differentiation, Consumption and Pleasure* (Cambridge, 2000).

25 My notion of civility, it will be noticed, has nothing to do with the 'civility' promoted in Joanne Finkelstein, *Dining Out: A Sociology of Modern Manners* (Cambridge, 1989), where social intercourse in a commercial setting is confused with deliberation on policy and philosophical discussion in the public sphere, and social hierarchy of any kind can never really exist. It's a fanciful utopian idea, the 'civility' that Finkelstein thinks should be a condition of all social life, and it has little relevance to the real world of eating and drinking.

26 See Michael Hardt and Antonio Negri, *Empire* (Cambridge, MA, 2000).

27 Margaret Atwood, *The Handmaid's Tale* (London, 1993).

28 There might be 'surplus enjoyment' for the Handmaid, a surplus that comes from renunciation imposed from without, but not enjoyment in and of itself.

select bibliography

Abramson, Julia, 'Legitimacy and Nationalism in the *Almanach des gourmands* (1803–1812)', *Journal of Early Modern Cultural Studies*, III/2 (2003)
——, 'Grimod's Debt to Mercier and the Emergence of Gastronomic Writing Reconsidered', EMF, 7 (2001)
Appelbaum, Robert, 'The Civility of Eating', in *Food and Morality*, ed. Susan Friedland (Devon, 2008)
——, *Aguecheek's Beef, Belch's Hiccup, and Other Gastronomic Interjections: Literature, Culture and Food Among the Early Moderns* (Chicago, IL, 2006)
Appiah, Kwame Anthony, *Cosmopolitanism* (London, 2006)
Arendt, Hannah, *The Human Condition*, revised 2nd edn (Chicago, IL, 1999)
Atwood, Margaret, *The Handmaid's Tale* (London, 1993)
Augé, Marc, *Non-places: Introduction to an Anthropology of Supermodernity*, trans. John Howe (London, 1995)
Balzac, Honoré de, *Lost Illusions*, trans. Herbert J. Hunt (Harmondsworth, 2005)
Barthes, Roland, 'Pour une psycho-sociologies de l'alimentation con-temporaine', in *L'histoire de l'alimentation*, ed. J.-J. Hérmardiquer (Paris, 1970)
Baudelaire, Charles, *The Flowers of Evil*, trans. William Aggeler (Fresno, CA, 1954)
Baudrillard, Jean, *The Consumer Society: Myths and Structures* [1970], trans. Chris Turner (London, 1998)
——, *For a Critique of the Political Economy of the Sign*, trans. Charles Levin (New York, 1981)
——, *Simulacra and Simulation*, trans. Sheila Faria Glaser (Ann Arbor, MI, 1994)
——, *Symbolic Exchange and Death*, trans. Ian Hamilton Grant (London, 1993)
Bauman, Zygmunt, *The Art of Life* (Cambridge, 2008)
——, *Consuming Life* (Cambridge, 2009)

Beardsworth, Alan, and Teresa Keil, *Sociology on the Menu: An Invitation to the Study of Food and Society* (London and New York, 1997)

Beauvoir, Simone de, *Adieux: A Farewell to Sartre*, trans. Patrick O'Brien (Harmondsworth, 1984)

Beccaria, César, *On Crimes and Punishments and Other Writings*, ed. Richard Bellamy, trans. Richard Davies, Virginia Cox and Richard Bellamy (Cambridge, 1995)

Becker, Howard S., *Art Worlds*, Revised Edition (Berkeley, CA, 2008)

Bell, David, 'Fragments for a New Urban Culinary Geography', *Journal for the Study of Food and Society*, VI/1 (2002)

Bell, David, and Gill Valentine, *Consuming Geographies: We Are Where We Eat* (London, 1997)

Benjamin, Walter, *The Arcades Project*, trans. Howard Eiland and Kevin McLaughlin (Cambridge, MA, 1999)

Beriss, David, and David Sutton, eds, *The Restaurants Book: Ethnographies of Where We Eat* (Oxford, 2007)

Blagdon Francis, *Paris as It Is and Was; Or A Sketch of the French Capital*, 2 vols (London, 1803)

Blythman, Joanna, *Bad Food Britain: How a Nation Ruined Its Appetite* (London, 2006)

Booth, William James 'Gone Fishing: Making Sense of Marx's Concept of Communism', *Political Theory*, XVII/2 (1989)

Bourdain, Anthony, *Kitchen Confidential: Adventures in the Culinary Underbelly* (London, 2001)

Bourdieu, Pierre, *Distinction: A Social Critique of the Judgement of Taste*, trans. Richard Nice (Cambridge, MA, 1987)

Buford, Bill, *Heat: An Amateur's Adventures as Kitchen Slave, Line Cook, Pasta-Maker and Apprentice to a Butcher in Tuscany* (London, 2006)

Burnett, John, *England Eats Out: A Social History of Eating Out in England from 1830 to the Present* (Edinburgh, 2004)

Campbell, Colin, *The Romantic Ethic and the Spirit of Modern Consumerism* (Oxford, 1987)

Certeau, Michel de, *The Practice of Everyday Life*, trans. Steven Rendall (Berkeley, CA, 1984)

——, Luce Girard and Pierre Mayol, *The Practice of Everyday Life: Volume Two, Living and Cooking*, trans. T. J. Tomasik (Minneapolis, 1998)

Colonna, Francesco, *Hypnerotomachia Poliphili: The Strife of Love in a Dream*, trans. Joscelyn Godwin (New York, 1999)

Colquhoun, Kate, *Taste: The Story of Britain Through Its Cooking* (London, 2007)

Cooke, Rachel, 'I could have opened a safe little brasserie like the Ivy', *Observer* (November 9, 2003)

Coorebyter, Vincent de, *Sartre avant la phénoménologie: Autour de 'La nausée' et de la 'Légende de la vérité'* (Brussels, 2005)

Curtin, D., and L. Hedke, *Cooking, Eating, Thinking: Transformative Philosophies of Food* (Indianapolis, IN, 1992)

David, Elizabeth, *An Omelette and a Glass of Wine* (Guilford, CT, 1997)

Derrida, Jacques, *On Cosmopolitanism and Forgiveness*, trans. Mark Dooley and Michael Hughes (London and New York, 2001)

Desnoiresterres, Gustave, *Grimod de la Reynière et son groupe* (Paris, 1877)

Dinesen, Isak, *Anecdotes of Destiny* [1958] (London, 2001)

Douglas, Mary, 'Deciphering a Meal', in *Implicit Meanings* (London, 1977)

——, *Purity and Danger: An Analysis of Concepts of Pollution and Taboo* (London, 1991)

Driver, Christopher, *The British at Table 1940–1980* (London, 1983)

Elias, Norbert, *The Civilizing Process*, trans. Edmund Jephcott (Oxford, 1994)

Ferguson, Priscilla Parkhurst, *Accounting for Taste: The Triumph of French Cuisine* (Chicago, IL, 2004)

——, 'A Cultural Field in the Making: Gastronomy in Nineteenth-Century France', in *French Food: On the Table, On the Page, and In French Culture*, ed. Lawrence R. Schehr and Allen S. Weiss (New York, 2001)

——, *Paris as Revolution: Writing the Nineteenth-Century City* (Berkeley, CA, 1994)

Ferry, Jean-Marc, *De la civilisation: civilité, légalité, publicité* (Paris, 2001)

Fine, Gary Alan, *Kitchens: The Culture of Restaurant Work* (Berkeley, CA, 1998)

Finkelstein, Joanne, *Dining Out: A Sociology of Modern Manners* (Cambridge, 1989)

Fisher, M.F.K., *The Art of Eating* (Hoboken, NJ, 2004)

——, *Not Now But Now* [1947] (London, 1984)

Freud, Sigmund, 'On Narcissism: An Introduction', in *The Standard Edition of the Complete Psychological Works of Sigmund Freud*, trans. James Strachey (London, 1957), vol. XIV

——, 'Instincts and the Vicissitudes', in *Complete Psychological Works*, vol. XIV

Garvel, Michael, 'Grimod de la Reynière's *Almanach des gourmands*: Exploring the Gastronomic New World of Postrevolutionary France', in *French Food* (New York, 2001)

Goffman, Erving, *Frame Analysis: An Essay in the Organization of Experience* (Boston, MA, 1986)

——, *The Presentation of Self in Everyday Life* (London, 1990)

Goldthorpe, Rhiannon, *La Nausée* (London, 1991)

Goody, Jack, *Cooking, Cuisine and Class: A Study in Comparative Sociology* (Cambridge, 1982)

Gopnik, Adam, *Paris to the Moon* (New York, 2001)

279

Grimod de la Reynière, *Almanach des gourmands, servant de guide dans les moyens de faire excellente chère*, 8 vols (Paris, 1803–12)

——, *Écrits gastronomiques*, ed. Jean-Claude Bonnet (Paris, 1997)

Gvion-Rosenberg, Liora, Review of *Dining Out*, in *The American Journal of Sociology*, XCVI/3 (1990)

Hannerz, Ulf, 'Cosmopolitans and Locals in World Culture', in *Global Culture: Nationalism Globalization, and Modernity*, ed. M. Featherstone (London, 1990)

Hannigan, John, *Fantasy City: Pleasure and Profit in the Postmodern Metropolis* (London, 1998)

Harper, Douglas, *The Italian Way: Food and Social Life* (Chicago, IL, 2010)

Harvey, David, *Paris as the Capital of Modernity* (London, 2003)

Hayward, Abraham, *The Art of Dining: Or, Gastronomy and Gastronomers* (London, 1852)

Hemingway, Ernest, *The Sun Also Rises* [1926] (New York, 2003)

Hess, John L., and Karen Hess, *The Taste of America* (Champaign, IL, 2000)

Howells, Christina, ed., *The Cambridge Companion to Sartre* (Cambridge, 1992)

Hume, David, 'Of the Standard of Taste', in *Selected Essays*, ed. Stephen Copley and Andrew Edgar (Oxford, 1996)

Irigaray, Luce, *This Sex Which is Not One*, trans. Catherine Porter and Carolyn Burke (Ithaca, NY, 1985)

Jackson, Kevin, and Richard Heeps, *Fast: Feasting on the Streets of London* (London, 2006)

Jacob, Diane, *Will Write for Food* (New York, 2005)

Jacobs, Marc, and Peter Scholliers, eds, *Eating Out In Europe: Picnics, Gourmet Dining And Snacks Since The Late Eighteenth Century* (Oxford, 2003)

Jones, Martin, *Feast: Why Humans Share Food* (Oxford, 2007)

Kamber, Richard, 'Sartre's Nauseas', in *MLN*, XCVIII/5 (1983)

Kamp, David, *The United States of Arugula: How We Became a Gourmet Nation* (New York, 2006)

Kates, Gary, ed., *The French Revolution: Recent Debates and New Controversies* (London, 1998)

Kaufman, Jean-Claude, *The Meaning of Cooking* (Cambridge, 2010)

Lahire, Bernard, 'From the Habitus to an Individual Heritage of Dispositions. Towards a Sociology at the Level of the Individual', *Poetics*, 31 (2003)

Lasch, Christopher, *The Culture of Narcissism: American Life in an Age of Diminishing Expectations* (New York, 1978)

Lebow, Victor, 'The Nature of Postwar Retail Competition', *Journal of Marketing*, IX/1 (1954)

Liebling, A. J., *Between Meals: An Appetite for Paris* (New York, 1986)

Lotte, Fernand, 'Balzac et la table dans *La Comédie humaine*',

L'Année Balzacienne (1962)

MacDonogh, Giles, *A Palate in Revolution: Grimod de La Reynière and the 'Almanach des Gourmands'* (London, 1987)

McKendrick, Neil, John Brewer and J. H. Plumb, eds, *The Birth of A Consumer Society: The Commercialization of Eighteenth-century England* (Bloomington, IN, 1985)

Mahfouz, Naguib, *Midaq Alley*, trans. Trevor Le Gassick (London, 1975)

Manser, Anthony, *Sartre: A Philosophic Study* (Westport, CT, 1966)

Marin, Louis, *Utopics: Spatial Play*, trans. Robert A. Vollrath (Atlantic Highlands, NJ, 1984)

Marx, Karl, and Frederick Engels, 'The German Ideology', in Karl Marx and Frederick Engels, *Collected Works*, vol. V (New York, 1976)

Mauss, Marcel, *The Gift: The Form and Reason for Exchange in Archaic Societies*, trans. W. D. Halls (London, 1990)

——, 'Les techniques du corps', *Journal de Psychologie*, XXXII (1936)

Mayle, Peter, *Bon Appétit! Travels through France with Knife, Fork, and Corkscrew* (London, 2001)

Mennell, Stephen, *All Manners of Food: Eating and Taste in England and France from the Middle Ages to the Present* (Oxford, 1983)

——, 'L'Envers de la medaille: les processus de décivilisation,' in *Norbert Elias: La politique et l'histoire*, ed. Alain Garrigou and Bernard Lacroix (Paris, 1997)

Merlin-Kajman, Hélène, 'Civilité: une certain modalité du vivre-ensemble', in *Civilization in French and Francophone Literature*, French Literature Series, 33, ed. Buford Norman and James Day (Amsterdam and New York, 2006)

Mesplède, Jean-François, *Trois étoiles au Michelin: Une histoire de la haute gastronomie française et européene* (Paris, 2004)

Montanari, Massimo, *Food Is Culture*, trans. Albert Sonnenfeld (New York, 2004)

Morgan, Lady, *France*, 4th edn (London, 1818)

Morris, William, *News from Nowhere* (Oxford, 2003)

Neu, Jerome, 'Divided Minds: Sartre's "Bad Faith" Critique of Freud', *Review of Metaphysics*, XLII/1 (1988)

Onfray, Michel, *Les Ventres des Philosophes* (Paris, 1989)

Ortega y Gasset, José, *The Revolt of the Masses* [1932] (New York, 1994)

Owings, Alison, *Hey, Waitress!: The USA From the Other Side of the Tray* (Berkeley, CA, 2002)

Panayi, Panikos, *Spicing Up Britain: The Multicultural History of British Food* (London, 2008)

Pardue, Derek, 'Familiarity, Ambience and Intentionality: An Investigation into Casual Dining Restaurants in Central Illinois', in *The Restaurant's Book: Ethnographies of Where We Eat*, ed.

David Beriss and David Sutton (Oxford, 2007)

Périgord. A. B. De [Horace-Napoléon Raisson], *Nouvel almanach des gourmands* (Paris, 1825)

Petrini, Carlo, *Slow Food: The Case for Taste*, trans. William McCuaig (New York, 2004)

——, and Gigi Padovani, *Slow Food Revolution: A New Culture for Eating and Living* (New York, 2006)

Phillips, Cath, ed., *Time Out London: Eating and Drinking 2007* (London, 2007)

Pillsbury, Richard, *From Boarding House To Bistro: The American Restaurant Then And Now* (Boston, MA, 1990)

Pitte, Robert, *French Gastronomy: The History and Geography of a Passion*, trans. Jody Golding (New York, 2002)

Playfair, William, *France As It Is, Not Lady Morgan's France*, 2 vols (London, 1819)

Prendergast, Christopher, *Paris and the Nineteenth Century* (Oxford, 1992)

Raynor, Jay, 'All Taste and No Waste', *Observer Food Monthly* (March 2007)

Reardon, Joan, *Poet of the Appetites: The Lives and Loves of M.F.K. Fisher* (New York, 2005)

Reichl, Ruth, *Comfort Me With Apples* (New York, 2001)

——, *Garlic and Sapphires: The Secret Life of a Food Critic* (New York, 2005)

——, *Tender at the Bone* (New York, 1998)

Rémy, Pascal, *L'inspecteur se met à table* (Paris, 2004)

Ritzer, George, *The McDonaldization of Society* (Thousand Oaks, CA, 2000)

——, ed. *McDonaldization: The Reader* (Thousand Oaks, CA, 2002)

Rival, Ned, *Grimod de la Reynière: le gourmand gentilhomme* (Paris, 1983)

Roberts, J.A.G., *China to Chinatown: Chinese Food in the West* (London, 2003)

Rolls, Alistair, and Elizabeth Rechniewski, eds, *Sartre's Nausea: Text, Context, Intertext* (Amsterdam, 2005)

Santoni, Ronald E., *Bad Faith, Good Faith and Authenticity in Sartre's Early Philosophy* (Philadelphia, PA, 1995)

Sartre, Jean-Paul, *The Age of Reason*, trans. Eric Sutton (London, 1947)

——, *Being and Nothingness*, trans. Hazel E. Barnes (Abingdon, 2003)

——, *Nausea*, trans. Lloyd Alexander (New York, 1964)

——, *La nausée* (Paris, 1938)

——, *Notebooks for an Ethics*, trans. David Pellauer (Chicago, IL, 1992)

Scribe et Brulay, Eugène, *Le Gastronome sans argent. Vaudeville en un acte* (Paris, 1821)

Sennett, Richard, The *Fall of Public Man* [1977] (London, 1984)

Serres, Michel, *The Five Senses: A Philosophy of Mingled Bodies*, trans. Margaret Sankey and Peter Cowley (London, 2008)

Shapiro, Michael J., 'Political Economy and Mimetic Desire: A Postmodernist Reading of "Babette's Feast"', *History of European Ideas*, XIII/3 (1992)

Sheraton, Mimi, *Eating My Words: An Appetite for Life* (New York, 2004)

Sherman, David, *Sartre and Adorno: The Dialectics of Subjectivity* (Albany, NY, 2007)

Simmel, George, 'Fashion', *American Journal of Sociology*, LXII/6 (1957)

Simon, François, *Pique assiette: La fin d'une gastronomie française* (Paris, 2008)

Spang, Rebecca, *The Invention of the Restaurant: Paris and Modern Gastronomic Culture* (Cambridge, MA, 2000)

Steinberger, Michael, *Au Revoir to All That: The Rise and Fall of French Cuisine* (London, 2009)

Steingarten, Jeffrey, 'Kitchen Confidential: Why are the Foodies Fuming?', at www.slate.com/id/2000186/entry/1005738/

Stephens, C. Ralph, ed., *The Fiction of Anne Tyler* (Jackson, MI, 1990)

Strand, Dana, 'Film, Food, and "La Françité": From *le pain quotidien* to McDo', in *French Food* (New York, 2001)

Svendsen, Lars, *Fashion: A Philosophy* (London, 2006)

Talleyrand Périgord, Charles Maurice de, *Mémoires du Prince de Talleyrand: La Confession de Talleyrand* (Paris, 1891)

Thurman, Judith, *Isak Dinesen: The Life of Karen Blixen* (Harmondsworth, 1982)

Tomkins, Calvin, *Living Well Is the Best Revenge* (New York, 1971)

Tyler, Anne, *Dinner at the Homesick Restaurant* (London, 1992)

Tyler, Imogen, 'From "The Me Decade" to "The Me Millennium": The Cultural History of Narcissism', *International Journal of Cultural Studies*, X/3 (2007)

Urry, John, *The Tourist Gaze*, 2nd edn (London, 2002)

Veblen, Thorsten, *The Theory of the Leisure Class* [1899] (New York, 1994)

Warde, Alan, and Lydia Martens, *Eating Out: Social Differentiation, Consumption and Pleasure* (Cambridge, 2000)

——, 'Urban Pleasure?: On the Meaning of Eating Out in a Northern City', in *Food, Health and Identity*, ed. Pat Caplan (London, 1997)

Waters, Alice, *The Chez Panisse Menu Cookbook* (New York, 1982)

Wechsberg, Joseph, *Blue Trout and Black Truffles: The Peregrinations of an Epicure* (Chicago, IL, 1985)

Wilkinson, Lynn R., 'Hannah Arendt on Isak Dinesen: Between Storytelling and Theory', *Comparative Literature*, LVI/1 (2004)

Wood, Roy C., 'Dining Out on Sociological Neglect', *British Food Journal*, XCVI/10 (1994)

Wright, Simon, *Tough Cookies: Tales of Obsession, Toil and Tenacity from Britain's Culinary Heavyweights* (London, 2005)

Yang, Yunxiang 'Consuming McDonald's in Beijing', in *The Cultural Politics of Food and Eating: A Reader*, ed. James L. Watson and Melissa Caldwell (Malden, MA, 2005)

Žižek, Slavoj, *Living in the End Times* (London, 2010)

——, *The Sublime Object of Ideology* (London, 1989)

——, 'Surplus-Enjoyment', *Lacanian Ink*, 15 (1999)

Zola, Émile, *The Kill*, trans. Brian Nelson (Oxford, 2004)

acknowledgements

Funding for this project was provided by the Arts and Humanities Research Council, to which I am deeply grateful. Some seed money and additional research funds were also provided by the Faculty of Arts and Social Sciences of the University of Lancaster.

Most of the bookish research for this volume was carried out with the assistance of my home library at Lancaster and on-site at several rare book rooms, namely the British Library, The Brotherton Library of Leeds University; the Wellcome Collection; and University College London. My thanks to the helpful staff in each, beginning with the Interlending people at Lancaster.

The non-bookish research began well before I had conceived of this work. My thanks to everyone who has eaten with me over the years, and my thanks especially to everyone who has fed me.